SELVES AND OTHER TEXTS

SELVES AND OTHER TEXTS

THE CASE FOR CULTURAL REALISM

JOSEPH MARGOLIS

THE PENNSYLVANIA STATE UNIVERSITY PRESS

UNIVERSITY PARK, PENNSYLVANIA

LIBRARY OF CONGRESS CATALOGING-IN-PUBLICATION DATA

Margolis, Joseph, 1924–
    Selves and other texts : the case for cultural realism / Joseph Margolis.
        p.   cm.
    Includes bibliographical references and index.
    ISBN 0-271-02150-0 (alk. paper)
    1. Aesthetics. 2. Art—Philosophy. 3. Analysis (Philosophy)
    4. Culture—Philosophy 5. Self (Philosophy) I. Title.

    BH39 .M3942 2001
    111'.85—dc21

                                                        2001021462

It is the policy of The Pennsylvania State University Press to use acid-free paper
for the first printing of all clothbound books. Publications on uncoated stock
satisfy the minimum requirements of American National Standard for Information
Sciences—Permanence of Paper for Printed Library Materials, ANSI Z39.48–1992.

for Coco

AT THE START OF THE NEW MILLENNIUM

CONTENTS

ACKNOWLEDGMENTS

The chapters based on previously published papers have been considerably altered. The original papers include the following: Chapter 1, "The Eclipse and Recovery of Analytic Aesthetics," in Richard Shusterman (ed.), *Analytic Aesthetics* (Basil Blackwell, 1989), pp. 161–89; Chapter 2, "Farewell to Danto and Goodman," *British Journal of Aesthetics* 38 (1998), pp. 353–74; Chapter 3, "The Endless Future of Art," in Arto Haapala, Jerrold Levinson, and Veikko Rantala (eds.), *The End of Art and Beyond: Essays after Danto* (Humanities Press, 1997), pp. 2–26; Chapter 5, "The Deviant Ontology of Artworks," in Noël Carroll (ed.), *Theories of Art Today* (University of Wisconsin Press, 2000), pp. 109–29; Chapter 6, "Selves and Other Texts," *Annual American Catholic Philosophical Quarterly Proceedings* 62 (1998), pp. 1–29. The original paper on which Chapter 4 is based, "The Metaphysics of Interpretation," was first presented in a symposium: "Interpretation in Art and Texts and History," at the World Congress of Philosophy, Boston, Massachusetts, summer 1998.

PREFACE

In a letter drawn from his correspondence with Ludwig Ficker, which Stephen Toulmin cites in *Wittgenstein's Vienna* (Allan Janik, coauthor, Simon & Schuster, 1973), Wittgenstein says that the *Tractatus* "consists of two parts: the one presented here plus all that I have *not* written. And *it is precisely this second part that is the important one*" (p. 192). In that sense, what is not said—because it cannot be said—decisively colors what *is* said in the "first part": the second part is there as well!

It gradually dawned on me, in putting *Selves and Other Texts* in finished form, that, in a rather different but not altogether unrelated sense, I have tried to formulate what is not normally said in analytic English-language philosophy about the nature of cultural life *and* the profound bearing of cultural life on the standard problems of analytic philosophy. I don't happen to share Wittgenstein's conviction that ethical and aesthetic and transcendental matters, and whatever (as he says) "is higher" and concerns the meaning of life, cannot be "said" in a language suited to the conditions of factual discourse, but only "shown." It hardly matters. I have taken a small liberty for the sake of a potentially very large effect. For I believe that what Wittgenstein says here he says because he finds himself constrained by the terms of discourse of the *Tractatus* itself. But when he writes in the very different spirit of *Philosophical Investigations*, he *could* have written about his "higher" matters in the same language that articulated what is presented. Where he demurs, it cannot be for the original reason.

I have tried to escape the same bonds that constrain the *Tractatus*. I have written a heterodox account of the world of human culture; chiefly about human selves and artworks, with some asides on history and language—a defense, in effect, of what I call *cultural realism*. The idea, of course, was to explicate the sense in which the realism of human culture is radically different from that of physical nature, without proposing any discontinuity between the two or any extravagant dualisms to account for their distinction. As far as I know, that is a largely neglected issue in English-language philosophy, apart from the important but fragmentary and noticeably limited work of the classic pragmatists. I would be pleased to think that the account that follows was, indeed, a convincing extension and an up-to-date restatement of the principal pragmatist themes that originally gained strength from the same post-Kantian resources—chiefly Hegel's and the tradition Hegel inspired—that may, however unbidden, have reached as far as Wittgenstein's *Investigations*. These are the same philosophical resources that first addressed the conceptual connection between physical nature and human culture in a sustained way. They provide the best clue for an adequate philosophy of art. Beyond that, I believe, the proper analysis of art and culture is essential for a needed correction of the most fashionable tendencies of recent analytic accounts of physical nature and reality at large.

In the twentieth century, English-language philosophy eliminated almost completely all the signs of the need to bring inquiry to bear on that most important enabling connection—the relationship between nature and culture. It may be possible, now, to enlarge the resources of analytic philosophy beyond the academically enforced strictures that have drummed out, as dubious or unsatisfactory, all the *sine qua nons* on which the excellent philosophical work of earlier ages had depended. Now, bridging the end of the twentieth century and the start of the twenty-first, the recovery is palpably impossible to effect directly by working solely with the master themes and doctrines of Anglo-American analysis in epistemology, in the philosophy of mind, in the philosophy of the physical sciences, and even in the philosophy of language.

The natural way to proceed will be to thread our way through the philosophy of art and the philosophy of history: that is, to examine the arts and history with pointed care. What the analytic philosophy of art required, of course, was a full-fledged recovery of the entire range of continental European philosophy that had been effectively split off from the "analytic" branch of philosophy at the very start of the twentieth century. The split effected by the joint efforts of Bertrand Russell and G. E. Moore was continued, at mid-century, by W. V. Quine and Donald Davidson.

That enormous effort succeeded beyond anyone's wildest dreams, and we are the impoverished beneficiaries of it. The task that now confronts English-language philosophy is, it seems to me, how to recover, without yielding anything against the genuine rigor of analytic philosophy, the richer themes that first begin to take impressive form with the post-Kantians; those, especially, that concern the ontic and epistemic issues posed by the cultural world. There's a lacuna there of about two hundred years.

It's in this sense, as I say, that I have tried to *say* what has not been spoken of in the most admired and influential work of the analytic tradition. I happen to have labored through most of my mature research under the distinct disadvantage of admiring both "analytic" and "continental" work in about equal measures, in spite of the fact that, as my philosophical style betrays, I am myself "analytically" inclined in spirit. But I think it *is* possible—in fact, I think it is necessary—to translate the philosophical achievements of the continental tradition that have been grievously ignored, in the local idiom of the analysts. Otherwise, it will take a very long time for analytic philosophy to catch up, now that the canonical doctrines, pretty well known to informed readers on "both sides," have lost their magic touch. I have tried to make a beginning here, and in doing so have tried to show how the best puzzles of epistemology, the philosophy of mind, and the other disciplines favored in the analytic world could be productively recovered *via* the seemingly marginal questions raised in the philosophy of art and history and culture.

I hope this attempt at recovery may also explain the motivation for the pointed way in which, in the first part of what follows, I press a number of the leading analytic voices in the philosophy of art. By *speaking* of what is missing in their accounts, I have found it possible to recover what has not been *said*—but colors whatever is said—about how the puzzles posed by the arts, history, and culture bear on the whole of modern philosophy. I offer that recovery also as a gloss on the meaning of Wittgenstein's extreme pronouncement.

I take the occasion as well to thank Ruth Brooks for her customary care in putting my manuscripts in legible form; and Sandy Thatcher of Penn State Press, for simply "being there."

J. M.
Philadelphia
September 2000

PREAMBLE

Contemporary cosmology speculates in a precisely calibrated way about how the whole of our known universe may have evolved from some so-called "singularity," a grand explosion of sorts—the Big Bang— about the origin of which, in turn, it makes no sense to speculate, since to do so would violate the conditions of the first speculation. That is a perfectly splendid piece of conceptual economy, which, rightly understood, seals off the retreat of the notorious infinite-regress argument that armies of honest toilers have cracked their heads on for ages. But it leaves in its place an ineluctable puzzle and conjecture that produces its own antinomy, a benign antinomy if I understand the matter aright, but a paradox nevertheless that bleeds back into the thesis of the Big Bang. It goes like this: There must have been many emergent transformations of the *materia* of the Big Bang, many intervening transitional forms that may no longer exist, that made all the later developments possible, which, according to our best arguments, account for whatever we now acknowledge to be the actual reality of our existent world. And yet of course the entire conjecture is the exclusive labor of human investigators whose own gifts must, according to the thesis, have emerged from the same Bang; but that means that the Origin (in the new sense that eclipses an entire fleet of honorable theologies) is, in some sense, an artifact of a late but indispensable development itself imagined to have been yielded, whether contingently or necessarily, by the generative processes of the first.

I say that this is a benign antinomy, because one line of argument traces the order of what is real, and another, in the opposite direction, the order of what is known or is intelligible. That their respective priorities favor one over the other *in turn* is a kind of optical illusion (of the mind) that depends on assuming that it makes sense to disjoin in principle the analysis of reality and the analysis of knowledge. But that cannot be true. For, if, seen *that* way, the antinomy is indeed an antinomy that must be resolved—but cannot be—then *that* part of the organizing conjecture must be false! It means, I should add, that if causal explanation is ultimately—if it has realist pretensions—reductive or generative in accord with the supposed time-line of the Big Bang, then causal explanation is conceptually inadequate wherever the reduction of the cultural world fails.

I am, I confess, a partisan of the antinomy and also of the solution suggested: there is no manageable disjunction between our theories of reality and our theories of thought and knowledge. The division is the deepest error of the whole line of speculation, at once philosophical and scientific, that can be traced in the modern world from René Descartes's still towering eminence to our own time, as well as through the whole of Western cosmology from the presocratics on. If so, then the speculation about the Big Bang is a blip in a larger story. It is a stubborn blip, however, that refuses to ignore the reality and strategic importance of that emergent continuum in which the paradigm of knowledge—the exclusive human ability to report, to describe, to explain the way the world is and the conditions under which we know it to be so—is itself open to objective analysis. I conjecture that *that* ability is *sui generis,* an emergent local singularity, a kind of black hole (if you please) produced by the original singularity, that we know no way of abandoning or replacing and that (within the terms of the antinomy) governs (in a cognitive sense) whatever we say about the world "independent" of that artificing influence.

If you find this line of reasoning plausible, then I suggest the emergent world in which our cognizing competence takes form (and whatever that makes possible or indeed generates) *is quite real,* as real as the physical world from which it "must" have evolved. In fact, if that is so, then physical cosmology must provide a place, among its own *denotata,* for the emergent entities and phenomena that make science itself possible. Since, on my conjecture, that presupposes and entails the achievement of a language of the human sort (though I have nothing against the creatures of alien worlds), the analysis of (human) *culture* must be an essential part of (physical) cosmology! Yet you will hardly find that fact admitted in the most refined disputes of the most advanced cosmologists.

That is the precise precondition of the account that follows. I have long believed that the world of the great arts—of literature and music and painting and theatre, and the movies of course—have *emerged* from the physical and biological world in some *sui generis* way, a way that is quite different from that in which life forms emerged from the inanimate world or, indeed, the various ways in which the complex structures of the known physical world emerged from whatever we conjecture were the forms "physical reality" took in the first millimillimilli . . . seconds following the originating Singularity. By "emergent," I mean *either* whatever we take to be real that derives somehow from the resources of the Big Bang, but that we cannot explain in terms of categories restricted to one or another of any of the intervening phases of the Bang (most interestingly, its purely "physicalist" phases), *or* that we can satisfactorily explain by reference to some close "lower level" of emergence that we cannot explain in turn in the same way. I see no reason to suppose that these alternatives exclude one another in the same world; and, of course, the antinomy supports our tolerance.

In short, the reflexively assigned competence of human beings to *know* and *think* and *act* in that way that depends paradigmatically on the mastery of language is an artifact of the life of societies possessing a distinctive, a *cultural*, structure that "must" have been facilitated by small incremental biological changes that, at the point of some suitably late development (and only there and then discerned), permitted the retrospective pronouncement that that was so! Human beings, I would say, are "second-natured"—"enlanguaged" and "encultured"—artifacts of that same process: in a word, *selves*. Seen thus, the arts, the sciences, and history are what such selves characteristically "utter" (say, make, create, do). As it happens, those utterings prove so stable that they permit an objective analysis of their own properties and what their interventions disclose about the "independent" world: that is, disclose to hybrid creatures like ourselves, to whom they are inextricably tethered. Call that thesis *cultural realism,* without prejudice to whatever its study may reveal.

What follows is my speculation about what it does disclose, beginning with the "uttered" arts and ending with "uttered" selves. I am amazed to find again and again how extraordinarily different the cultural world is from the canonical picture of the physical world. And yet, if that is so, then, on the argument sketched, the physicalist picture must be false or wildly incomplete or distorted. Language and culture remain inexplicably emergent, empirically (but not conceptually), relative to the physical world from which they "must" have emerged.

It is conceivable that the cultural world is an illusion of some huge kind: not in the sense that it is a fiction, but that its apparent structure (the structure of history and language and art and knowledge) can actually be replaced in a realist sense by structures that have no descriptive or explanatory need for the familiar features the cultural world is said to manifest. There's no point in protesting the possibility. But there is also no compelling argument to suit that finding: although, to be sure, if it held, the *emergence* of the cultural world would prove a conceptual mistake.

If, however, we cannot overcome the late "singularity" caught by what I have termed a benign antinomy, then the realist standing of the physical world itself implicates the reality (hence, the realist standing) of the cultural world. This may strike you as a heady speculation, but what it signifies is no more than the conceptual inseparability of our analysis of physical nature and our analysis of ourselves. More than that, I view the linkage as unavoidable and, still more pointedly, as the master theme of post-Kantian philosophy, which we are forever in danger of forgetting. It is the abiding intuition of my entire inquiry. In a word, I postulate the reality of the cultural world and all it contains—human selves (ourselves) and what they utter—in postulating my antinomy as a reasonable corollary of the Big Bang; and I propose to account for the antinomy's being entirely benign by offering an argument in favor of cultural realism. In that way, I hope to outflank the well-known inability of physicalism to provide for the description and explanation of cultural (and mental) phenomena, without urging any conceptual extravagances that would violate the spirit of the best work of the physical sciences. But that, of course, is an ulterior objective of the account that follows; it does not play a role in the running argument.

In what follows I offer an argument for cultural realism. That argument gathers force from a mosaic of specialized disputes, but there must be endless ways to reach the same conclusion.

PART ONE

1

THE ECLIPSE AND RECOVERY OF ANALYTIC AESTHETICS

If we ask ourselves to explain the eclipse of analytic
aesthetics, the short answer is this: time has overrun all
its entrenched positions. I speak with some authority as
a partial victim at least, spared (if that is the term) by
running before the flood. Nevertheless, to admit this
much is hardly to judge what has been gained and lost
and not quite to say where the high ground will eventually reappear.

The best way to catch the change is to note its
effects on acknowledged exemplars; and the best
economy is to link these effects jointly to the principal
themes of analytic philosophies of art and analytic philosophy in general—for they should be the same. They
are indeed the same, and with only negligible exception
the essential themes may be drawn from the work of
relatively influential members of the "analytic" community of philosophers of art. I select four specimens
and four themes: Monroe Beardsley, Nelson Goodman,
Arthur Danto, and Joseph Margolis (myself); and, but
not coordinately, empiricism, extensionalism and nominalism, physicalism, and (what already in an alien
idiom is termed) presence (or, perhaps, foundationalism or cognitive privilege). All of this will need to be
explained of course. But by the economy intended,
what has happened to these four theorists effectively

marks what has happened to analytic aesthetics over a period of somewhat more than one (the last) generation. Each has made telltale adjustments, whether primarily in aesthetics or in philosophy in general, that signify (not always intentionally) accommodations favoring theses substantially subverting whatever may be fairly taken to belong to the analytic canon.

There is no explicit canon of course, but there can be little doubt that "analysts" have always been strongly disposed to subscribe to one. Also, each of the four theorists mentioned has proceeded in a way that suggests an entirely natural enlargement and shift in their respective views: so that although analytic aesthetics has been effectively subverted, the changes favored in the views of each hardly justify a straightline application of that finding to each of them. In fact, with the exception of Beardsley, the theorists in question have clearly evolved as frank and vigorous opponents of certain themes distinctly favored in the analytic camp. It needs to be said, also, that if we do not concede within analytic aesthetics a penchant for the canonical, there would be little point in speaking of its eclipse. Since this cannot fail to be a quarrelsome matter, there is bound to be a touch of fiction about the manner of reporting adopted here.

Two caveats need to be mentioned. For one, both the substantive themes indicated and the disciplined manner of working that the analysts favor have come under severe fire—precisely because they are so intimately related. For another, the recovery of something not very distant from the canon is promisingly joined with options linked to the critique of the original themes. The truth is that the original analytic themes and the assured "method" of analysis were always contested within the practice of analytic philosophy—and within analytic aesthetics. So the admission of the eclipse of analysis is already part of its anticipated recovery.

These are cryptic remarks no doubt. But they may explode the fiction that we are facing the imminent collapse of a monolithic philosophical program because of essential mistakes that ineliminably define the dogmas of the entire movement. (Perhaps, some might suppose, something matching the collapse of logical positivism.) There are no such dogmas. In fact, *none* of the themes attributed to the canon were ever permitted to run uncontested; and no one can rightly claim to formulate *the* canonical method of analysis. Certain themes and methods have dominated the movement; their distinct pretensions were regularly punctured by the best and most powerful practitioners of that movement; but then, of course, those same practitioners went blithely on with their own favored projects—against their own instruction.

To lose sight of the fact is to exaggerate the meaning of the "eclipse." To insist too casually on its "recovery" is to miss the extent of the transformation required. To yield up the executive standing of extensionalism, nominalism, and physicalism, the unity of science, and privilege is, quite simply, to recover forbidden (or at least officially opposed or discouraged) conceptual fruit. And yet, the effective subversive strategies are all traceable, in an admittedly thin way, to the central work of Anglo-American analytic philosophy. Their recovery—and the recovery of analysis—signifies the need for a frank rapprochement between Anglo-American and continental European philosophical currents. For it is clearly among the latter that such themes as the historicist, the hermeneutic, the preformational, the structuralist and poststructuralist, the deconstructive, the genealogical, the praxical have been consistently and productively favored; and it is only by quite openly accommodating those themes (and the varieties of conceptual strategy that addressing them must subtend) that analytic philosophy and analytic aesthetics *can* be recovered at all.

The truth is, the analytic tradition has tended to impoverish itself by a kind of increasing neglect of the leading themes of cultural life—*a fortiori,* the leading themes that inform the world of the arts. It has also neglected the subterranean possibilities of its own best work. The irony remains that, with regard to the *pre*-analytic period, both in philosophy in general and in the philosophy of art, the themes of intentionality, historical tradition, preformative history, discontinuity and incommensurability, the impossibility of conceptual closure, the symbiosis of the individual and the societal, the denial of cognitive transparency, the critique of critique, the emergence of human culture, the priority of practices, interpretive indeterminacy and consensual tolerance, and a thousand related themes had already been in place and had already been most vigorously dissected. The hegemony of the analytic has, quite unpardonably, done as much as it could to dismiss the full complexity of these matters in its zeal to install its own executive vision. And many, notably our specimen theorists, who by their own interest should have been alert enough to have resisted that tendency, have often been coopted by it and, on occasion, have been quite pleased to lead compliant troops over the philosophical cliff.

So the point of the recovery is clear. The "analytic" represents a measure of discipline that, at least saliently, at least with regard to the work of the formal and physical sciences (and whatever may fairly be associated with such work within the study of language, history, practice, art, and psychology), clearly succeeded in displacing what was perceived to be the incompetence, confusion, informality, and sheer error of pre-analytic philosophy. In aesthetics, the chief villain was idealism.[1] But it *was* (and still is) unpardonable to have impoverished the field of analysis as unconscionably and as carelessly as the vanguard of analytic philosophy was prepared to do—and did do. Now, the matter haunts its progeny, and, now, many of that progeny are simply too fixed in their own prejudices to reopen the case.

I

The most general picture of the span of analytic philosophy of the entire century—certainly of the last twenty-five years—is reasonably fixed by the conceptual linkage between W. V. Quine's well-known theory of indeterminacy of translation and Richard Rorty's notorious recommendation that "epistemology-centered philosophy" is (or ought to be) at an end.[2] This is not to say that either Quine or Rorty has pursued his own theme in the most perspicuous or most irresistible way. Actually, neither has—which complicates the tale to be told. It is rather to say that what is most tenable in the accounts of each symbiotically entails that of the other, and that, at their peril, analytic philosophers of art have (until recently) tended to ignore the implied lesson. The "eclipse" of analytic aesthetics may fairly be said to depend on ignoring that lesson; its "recovery" depends on accommodating it. The irony is that, both in general philosophy and in aesthetics, the incompleteness of Quine's and Rorty's arguments—their frank prejudices and disinclination to explore the options they themselves have very nearly prepared—promises to enrich both analytic philosophy and analytic aesthetics in ways that could not be easily foreseen from their own exertions.

Quine is essentially a holist, a pragmatist who rejects all forms of

1. See, for instance, William Elton, ed., *Aesthetics and Language* (Oxford: Basil Blackwell, 1954); and Joseph Margolis, ed., *Philosophy Looks at the Arts* (New York: Charles Scribner's Sons, 1962).

2. Richard Rorty, *Philosophy and the Mirror of Nature* (Princeton: Princeton University Press, 1979), 390.

cognitive privilege and treats distributed claims as functioning only within the space of the preformative parsings of societally entrenched "analytical hypotheses"—hypotheses that are themselves reflexively specified only by way of more attenuated such "hypotheses."[3] From this and Quine's profound demonstration that there is no principled disjunction between analytic and synthetic truths, between distinctions of meaning and distinctions of fact,[4] the indeterminacy thesis ineluctably follows: "There can be no doubt [Quine affirms] that rival systems of analytical hypotheses can fit the totality of speech behavior to perfection, and can fit the totality of dispositions to speech behavior as well, and still specify mutually incompatible translations of countless sentences insusceptible of independent control."[5] The trouble is that Quine never satisfactorily explained how "sentence," "behavior," and "fit" between sentence and behavior could be managed or reconciled with his own severe theory; or, what might be the *non*behavioral evidence of "incompatible translations" fitting behavior "to perfection"; or, what "truth" might mean under such circumstances; or, indeed, what constraints within holism itself might reasonably be proposed to facilitate the comparative assessment of rival analytical hypotheses. Quine never tells us whether "the totality of speech behavior" falls within or outside of our "analytical hypotheses."

On all of these matters Quine is disappointingly silent—even though it is plain that he favors physicalism, favors the rejection of intentionality, favors extensionalism, behaviorism, and a general empiricist bent congenially but loosely committed to something like the unity of science program. The bearing of Quine's work on aesthetics rests with the double theme: (*a*) that analytic aestheticians (influenced by the tendencies Quine has spawned and nourished) have themselves tended to favor physicalist, extensionalist, and behaviorist strategies with respect to puzzles about art and criticism; and (*b*) that those strategies have proved to be peculiarly vulnerable in aesthetics because they were never satisfactorily secured in analytic philosophy in general and because they hobbled the chances of formulating any adequate analytic philosophy of art. Holism, in Quine's account, could easily (but was never intended to) be a bridge to cognate

3. W. V. Quine, *Word and Object* (Cambridge: MIT Press, 1960), 15–16.
4. W. V. Quine, "Two Dogmas of Empiricism," *From a Logical Point of View* (Cambridge: Harvard University Press, 1953).
5. Quine, *Word and Object*, 72.

continental themes—the hermeneutic circle for instance; and the indeterminacy of translation might have been generalized (though that was hardly Quine's intention) to range over the whole of natural-language discourse. Still, at this late date, both doctrines suggest an enlargement of analytic resources that have only rarely been pursued.

Rorty is more radical about the radical import of having taken Quine's lesson (and Wilfrid Sellars's lesson) to heart—even against the "failure" of those two worthies (on Rorty's reading) to understand that the traditional philosophy of the West is at an end as a direct result of their own labors:

> To drop the notion of the philosopher as knowing something about knowing which nobody else knows so well would [Rorty offers] be to drop the notion that his voice always has an overriding claim on the attention of the other participants in the conversation [of mankind]. It would also be to drop the notion that there is something called "philosophical method" or "philosophical technique" or "the philosophical point of view" which enables the professional philosopher, *ex officio*, to have interesting views about, say, the respectability of psychoanalysis, the legitimacy of certain dubious laws, the resolution of moral dilemmas, the "soundness" of schools of historiography or literary criticism, and the like. . . . I do not know whether we are in fact at the end of an era. . . . Perhaps a new form of systematic philosophy will be found which has nothing whatever to do with epistemology but which nevertheless makes normal philosophical inquiry possible.[6]

Quine does not offer an explicit or satisfactory account of how we proceed with the distributive claims of any disciplined inquiry *within* his own holism; and Rorty does not satisfactorily explain what is entailed *in* his favoring the work of the sciences or other inquiries within that same constraint. Quine does not concede that *his* extreme holism disqualifies philosophy in the least; Rorty argues that it does but never shows us why. Quine never really uses his holism in an operative way, though he claims its advantage; and Rorty never really abandons epistemology and metaphysics, though he assures us that he has. And we, caught between these two lines of argument, insist on saving whatever may be saved of the

---

6. Rorty, *Philosophy and the Mirror of Nature*, 392–94.

empirical sciences and other first-order inquiries we believe deserve an inning. But we too need to explain what we have salvaged in salvaging that.

Quine simply disallows programs of analysis that go against the elimination of intentionality, for instance, as in his well-known attack on Brentano: "In the strictest scientific spirit we can [he says] report all the behavior, verbal and otherwise, that may underlie our imputations of propositional attitudes, and we may go on to speculate as we please upon the causes and effects of this behavior, but so long as we do not switch muses, the essentially dramatic idiom of propositional attitudes will find no place."[7] But if anything is clear about the theory of art, it is that we cannot make sense of the structure of artworks, their cultural status, their history, the detection and interpretation of their properties without featuring intentionality. Analytic aestheticians either have actually tried to restrict themselves to a deintentionalized idiom (Monroe Beardsley, for instance) or have been drawn in a distinctly divided way toward and against physicalism, toward and against an idiom congenial to the unity-of-science idiom (Arthur Danto, for instance). Quine's influence is unmistakable here.

Once we see matters this way, the radical incompleteness of Quine's program and the radical arbitrariness of Rorty's stare us in the face. Their joined claims—that is, the claims for which they are now regularly made the totemic bearers (holism with respect to the analytic penchant for rejecting transcendental arguments, for naturalizing epistemology, for promoting physicalism and extensionalism [Quine]; and holism with respect to repudiating the viability of all epistemology and metaphysics, despite favoring, in first-order discourse, an inherited physicalism and extensionalism [Rorty])—signify what is popularly perceived as the "eclipse" of analytic philosophy (a fortiori, the eclipse of analytic aesthetics). On the other hand, the perception of the incompleteness and arbitrariness of their respective programs signifies the beginning of the best program for the "recovery" of analytic philosophy (and, of course, of analytic aesthetics). Rorty's claim—hardly restricted to analytic aesthetics—is that "epistemology-centered philosophy," philosophy in the Western tradition, analytic philosophy as it has been canonically practiced, is now doomed. On the Rortyan line, Quine's program of analysis is best reinterpreted as a

---

7. Quine, *Word and Object*, 219.

contribution to a supposedly radically different model of philosophy, the model of the "*conversation* [of mankind] as the ultimate context within which knowledge is to be understood."[8]

But what does that mean? Certainly, it means that *any* inquiry—scientific, philosophical, critical, interpretive, historical—must: (i) give up the pretense of the transparency of reality with respect to human cognition; (ii) admit the preformative and pluralized historical contingency of the conditions of understanding under which the members of any society make inquiry; (iii) concede the impossibility of drawing from the holist conditions under which we dwell in the world, and survive as a species, any direct, distributed consequences affecting the truth of particular claims made within the space of those conditions; (iv) recognize that our critical speculations about the enabling conditions under which the strongest sciences prosper are themselves subject to the same tacit preconditions as all other inquiries; and (v) acknowledge that philosophical work cannot be apodictic, cannot be known to be universally binding, synthetic *a priori,* or formulated for all conceivable conditions. To accept constraints (i)–(v) is to embrace what is convincing and common to Quine's and Rorty's views all right—to embrace what is common to pragmatism and analytic philosophy and a good deal of continental philosophy. *But it is not tantamount to disallowing an "epistemology-centered philosophy" at all*—as Rorty's mentors (including Quine, Sellars, and Davidson) have either implicitly grasped or at least never denied.[9]

To embrace (i)–(v) is, effectively, to disallow what has disapprovingly been called the philosophy of "presence."[10] But it is not—certainly it need not be—to disallow philosophy *tout court,* to disallow epistemology, metaphysics, legitimative argument in particular. It is only to insist that philosophy must henceforth confine itself within the terms of (i)–(v) or within the terms of other corollary constraints of the same sort. Quine nowhere supposes it is impossible to do so, and Rorty nowhere shows that it *is* actually impossible. The recovery of analytic philosophy, *a fortiori* the recovery of analytic aesthetics, follows apace: merely proceed as before, or

8. Rorty, *Philosophy and the Mirror of Nature,* 389.

9. See, further, Joseph Margolis, *Pragmatism without Foundations; Reconciling Realism and Relativism* (Oxford: Basil Blackwell, 1986).

10. See Richard Rorty, "Overcoming the Tradition: Heidegger and Dewey," *Consequences of Pragmatism: Essays 1972–1980* (Minneapolis: University of Minnesota Press, 1982). For an up-to-date assessment of Rorty's general approach, see Joseph Margolis, "Richard Rorty: Philosophy by Other Means," *Metaphilosophy* 31 (2000).

proceed as would now be congenial to how one proceeded before, under the "new" constraints. I should take advantage, here, of having offered the tally just given, to say that, by "preformation," I mean specifically the historically preexisting conditions of cultural formation by which the members of *Homo sapiens* acquire their first language and home culture and thereby come to function as selves. The idea threads its way through the European tradition that includes Hegel, Marx, Nietzsche, Dilthey, Heidegger, Gadamer, and Foucault. It helps to explain the inseparability of the ontology of selves and of artworks, since artworks will prove to be what only selves can "utter."

II

Turn, now, to our exemplars. I am not concerned here to render a full and reasoned account of each of our four specimen figures. My interest lies rather in gauging the viability of analytic aesthetics in the face of certain philosophical challenges that appear to threaten its continued effectiveness—coming mainly from continental European sources and condensing in what (it may be hoped) we now see to be the pointless extravagance of Rorty's dismissal of analytic epistemology and metaphysics.

There can be little doubt that Monroe Beardsley is, of the four, the most devoted objectivist. This is the entire point of Beardsley's most widely discussed book, *The Possibility of Criticism*—which is committed to the rejection of intentionalism in criticism and relativism in interpretation; and committed to the affirmation of the stable objective presence of literary artworks (and artworks in general), on the admission of which depends the very "possibility" (in the Kantian sense) of a discipline of critical reading that could be said to function as a fair analogue of the characteristic work of the empirical sciences.[11]

Beardsley never wavered in these commitments, though it is true that his candor and inventiveness led him, first, to admit "we can never establish . . . decisively [what is] 'in' or 'out' [of a given literary work]";[12] and, second, to incorporate into his analysis of a poem a speech-act model that installed the strong intentionalism of speech acts themselves, although

---

11. See Monroe C. Beardsley, *The Possibility of Criticism* (Detroit: Wayne State University Press, 1980).
   12. Ibid., 36.

Beardsley clearly hoped that the device of illocutionary acts would ultimately be dropped from his account.[13]

"If there were no principles involved in criticism," says Beardsley, "I do
not see how it could be kept from collapsing into something purely intuitive and impressionistic."[14] Apart from the questionable use of the phrase
"purely intuitive and impressionistic," this quote admirably fixes the sense
in which Beardsley was a straightforward naturalist or objectivist;[15] it
marks the point of his quarrels with E. D. Hirsch (about author's intentions) and Joseph Margolis (about relativism in interpretation). The latter
theorists, of course, may also be said to have exhibited a similar sort of
objectivism, even if they disagreed with Beardsley's line of argument.[16]

The essential challenge to a strong analogy between artworks and
physical phenomena construed as *objects* suitably stable and determinate
for the purposes of description, interpretation, criticism, and explanation
(wherever and in whatever way pertinent for the disciplines in question)
rests largely with the bearing of the puzzles of intertextuality on the
determinate identity and intentional structure of artworks. *If* artworks
cannot be fixed as referents for continuing critical discourse stable enough
that their reidentification entails that their internal structure (their "nature" as distinct from their "number") remains relatively fixed and finitely
bounded through the very process of critical interpretation, then Beardsley's project must fail and the extension, to criticism, of something like the
unity-of-science model is doomed.

The theme of intertextuality (or holism), perhaps most floridly flaunted
by Roland Barthes in the notorious manifesto, "Every text, being itself the
intertext of another text, belongs to the intertextual,"[17] has by this time
largely undermined any simple objectivism of Beardsley's sort in the prac-

13. Ibid., 14; and "Testability of an Interpretation," in *The Possibility of Criticism*.
14. Beardsley, *The Possibility of Criticism*, 14.
15. See Richard J. Bernstein, *Beyond Objectivism and Relativism: Science, Hermeneutics,
and Praxis* (Philadelphia: University of Pennsylvania Press, 1983).
16. See E. D. Hirsch, Jr., *Validity in Interpretation* (New Haven: Yale University Press,
1967); and Joseph Margolis, *The Language of Art and Art Criticism: Analytic Questions in
Aesthetics* (Detroit: Wayne State University Press, 1965). The latter volume was considerably
reworked and enlarged as *Art and Philosophy: Conceptual Issues in Aesthetics* (Atlantic
Highlands, N.J.: Humanities Press, 1980), though it exhibits much the same orientation. I
mention these texts to give some sense, in passing, of how my views have evolved.
17. Roland Barthes, "From Work to Text," trans. Josué V. Harari, in *Textual Strategies*,
ed. Josué V. Harari (Ithaca: Cornell University Press, 1979), 77.

tice of literary criticism. Whatever may be the ultimate fate of Yale deconstructive views (notably, Harold Bloom's) or reader-response theories (notably, Wolfgang Iser's) or of such maverick theorists as Stanley Fish, it is precisely the intentionality and historicized existence of artworks, both opposed by Beardsley, that have forced a radical revision in the conception of the methodology of criticism.[18]

In any case, although Beardsley pursued, particularly toward the end of his life, all the principal currents of European and continentally-inspired aesthetics, he never saw the need to modify the strong objectivism he favored, an objectivism that clearly approached (however informally) the extensionalist severities of Quine's program and of programs associated with the unity of science.[19] Nevertheless, as has already been implicitly noted, Quine's notion of "analytical hypotheses" is itself a thin pragmatist counterpart to continental themes of preformation (and holism)—the key philosophical themes that eventually yielded increasingly radical notions of intertextuality.[20]

We must be clear that the limitation of Beardsley's form of analytic aesthetics is a dual one: it is partly the consequence of an excessively optimistic empiricism in the face of intentional, historical, interpretive, productive complexities that have taxed the ingenuity of his New Critical orientation beyond its apparent resources; and it is partly the consequence, *via* those complexities, of his never having come to terms with the preformational, intransparent, conceptually discontinuous, incommensurable features of discourse about art and culture (and, by extension, about science itself), or, indeed, the familiar puzzles about the determinacy of the

18. For an early overview of mine regarding these and similar currents, see Joseph Margolis, "What Is a Literary Text?" in *At the Boundaries: Proceedings of the Northeastern University Center for Literary Studies, Vol. 1, 1983*, ed. Herbert L. Sussman (Boston: Northeastern University Press, 1984). The account needs to be compared with my *Interpretation, Radical But Not Unruly: The New Puzzle of the Arts and History* (Berkeley and Los Angeles: University of California Press, 1995) to appreciate how my "analytic" account has evolved.

19. I should add that Beardsley read Roland Barthes's *S/Z* as a straightforward objectivist semiotics of literature (a form of structuralism in short) and failed completely to appreciate the subversively deconstructive intent of Barthes's essay. That is, where he was able to assimilate the poststructuralist literature, Beardsley regularly read it as something like a continuation of New Criticism—which indeed it superficially resembles. Otherwise, just as Derrida serves as a straightforward (!) deconstructionist (*Of Grammatology*), Beardsley serves as a straightforward and uncompromising New Critic.

20. For a sense of the most uncompromising analytic reading of holism, see Jerry Fodor and Ernest Lepore, *Holism: A Shopper's Guide* (Oxford: Basil Blackwell, 1992).

ontological structure of artworks. Analytic aesthetics (like analytic philosophy) can no longer pursue such simplifications if it is to survive. That texts and artworks are *not* suitably similar to physical objects, that their intentional structure obliges us to reflect on what it means to affirm or deny that artworks *have* determinate or completely determinate structures, is certainly the single most important theoretical issue confronting all philosophies of art at the present time as well as the practice of history and criticism.

The bare question makes no sense in terms of Beardsley's framework—or, indeed, in terms of any first-order work drawn from Quine's orientation. The pivotal issue is the one already identified, namely, that *every* form of truth-bearing discourse must accommodate the constative functions of reference and predication; that no such discourse can be committed for that reason alone to a form of cognitive privilege; and that no holism (of sense or experience or intentional structure or reason) makes any sense if it does not provide for determinate truth-claims in the inquiries we wish to pursue—whether in physics or literary criticism. The upshot is that Beardsley's philosophical pursuit of *objectivity* is *not* a disabling weakness of his "analytic" aesthetics: it is only his particular way of securing it that is indefensible (inspired by empiricism and the unity of science and opposed to the holism of meanings and cultural preformation). He solves the holism and determinacy issues by a kind of reductive feat that he nowhere earns.

In many ways, Goodman's aesthetics, particularly when qualified along the lines of his *Ways of Worldmaking* and *Of Mind and Other Matters,*[21] appears to bridge the divide between the two sorts of inquiry Beardsley scants. But Goodman hardly has that in mind. As with Beardsley, questions need to be raised about Goodman's substantive views regarding the arts as well as about the general philosophical orientation of his most recent publications. The truth is, there is no clear way of reconciling the peculiar fixities—bordering on essentialism—of *Languages of Art* with the so-called "irrealism" of *Ways of Worldmaking.*[22] Those fixities are in fact particularly doubtful on internal grounds.

The most noticeable oddity about Goodman's general philosophy, which remains pretty constant from *The Structure of Appearance* and

---

21. See Nelson Goodman, *Ways of Worldmaking* (Indianapolis: Hackett, 1978); and *Of Mind and Other Matters* (Cambridge: Harvard University Press, 1984).
22. See Goodman, *Ways of Worldmaking,* x.

Fact, Fiction, and Forecast to the latest books (despite the incompatibility between the visions of the two pairs), is that Goodman's entire effort is centered on epistemological puzzles although he never actually engages those puzzles in explicitly epistemological terms. For instance, he raises the question of the viability of nominalism,[23] but then he treats the matter in purely formal terms, without the least attention to biological or cultural constraints that should rightly bear on the effective, spontaneous use of discriminated resemblances or general terms in natural-language contexts, and he converts the nominalist issue into an exclusively logical matter regarding the (ontological) eliminability of nonindividual entities.[24] Again, he poses the seemingly methodological question of valid "projectibles" within the context of induction,[25] but he nowhere pursues it in cognitive terms. That theory depends inescapably on an account of "entrenchment"—which is clearly an epistemological matter and, equally clearly, nowhere discussed in Goodman.[26]

Furthermore, although the notion of entrenchment reappears in Goodman's later writings (in fact, in the context of his aesthetics),[27] Goodman's handling of it is utterly irreconcilable with the notion developed in *Fact, Fiction, and Forecast*: it remains completely undeveloped in epistemological terms now so urgently required by his own irrealism (that is, by the proliferation of plural, "made," actual worlds), and it is clearly at odds with the strong essentializing tendencies of *Languages of Art*. The matter is complicated, but it bears in a decisive way on the structure of Goodman's aesthetics.

An instructive clue may be gained by reminding ourselves of the stern once-and-for-all application of the (intended) testing of would-be projectibles in a world that seemed (once) to be so orderly that Goodman's new riddle of induction seemed almost to capture the methodology of the sciences. Entrenchment seemed so promising that Goodman could afford to announce:

23. See, for instance, Nelson Goodman, "Seven Strictures on Similarity," in *Experience & Theory*, ed. Lawrence Foster and J. W. Swanson (Amherst: University of Massachusetts Press, 1970).

24. See Nelson Goodman, *The Structure of Appearance*, 2d ed. (Indianapolis: Bobbs-Merrill, 1966), chap. 2.

25. See Nelson Goodman, "Prospects for a Theory of Projection," in *Fact, Fiction, and Forecast*, 2d ed. (Indianapolis: Bobbs-Merrill, 1965).

26. Goodman, *Fact, Fiction, and Forecast*, 94–99.

27. See Goodman, *Of Mind and Other Matters*, 32–33.

The obvious first step in our weeding-out process in determining (true) projectibility is to eliminate all projected hypotheses that have been violated. Such hypotheses, as already remarked, can no longer be projected, and are thus henceforth unprojectible. On similar grounds, all hypotheses having no remaining unexamined instances are likewise to be ruled out. However, neither the violated nor the exhausted hypotheses are thereby denied to have been projectible at an earlier time.[28]

Of course, all of this was meant by Goodman to be read in terms of "the passing of the possible": "Possible processes and possible entities vanish. . . . All possible worlds lie within the actual one."[29]

All of this is now forgotten, swept away, or reduced to an utter shambles inasmuch as (pertinently for his theory of art) Goodman now affirms:

Irrealism does not hold that everything or even anything is irreal, but sees the world melting into versions and versions making worlds, finds ontology evenescent, and inquires into what makes a version right and a world well-built. . . . How, then, are we to accommodate conflicting truths without sacrificing the difference between truth and falsity? Perhaps by treating these versions as true in different worlds. Versions not applying in the same world no longer conflict; contradiction is avoided by segregation. A true version is true in some worlds, a false version in none. Thus the multiple worlds of conflicting true versions are actual worlds, not the merely possible worlds or nonworlds of false versions. So if there is any actual world, there are many. For there are conflicting true versions, and they cannot be true in the same world.[30]

There is, however, no explanation in Goodman of how to individuate worlds or world-versions, or what it means to say that something is true in one (actual) world but not in another (and yet not false), or what it means to say that what is false is false in all actual worlds (despite the fact that

28. Goodman, *Fact, Fiction, and Forecast,* 83.
29. Ibid., 57.
30. Goodman, *Of Mind and Other Matters,* 29, 31.

what is true in one world may be in "conflict" with what is true in another), or what it means to say that *we* can sort such different worlds, or indeed what the logical relationship is between "true" and "false." All of this amounts to a complete abandonment of the epistemological questions of entrenchment.

My own gloss on what Goodman "must" have meant by his "made" worlds is that he realized (correctly) that (in both the arts and sciences) we must accommodate some form of relativism (in my own idiom, "incongruent" judgments: judgments that, on a bivalent logic, but not on a relativistic "logic," would yield incompatible or contrary judgments—which we do not wish to treat bivalently, that is, disjunctively). Since that would, in any ordinary way, require yielding ground against certain canonical constraints, bivalence and extensionalism in particular, Goodman preferred the strenuous option of finding some analogue of "possible worlds"—his made and continually remade actual worlds—ample enough to admit a relativism of "worlds" while, at the same time, saving his canonical commitments.

Goodman has found a way of *suggesting* that he is accommodating anti-analytic attacks on objectivism in the most ramified way. But it is extremely difficult to find any such accommodation, and it is frankly difficult to make the case that his theory remains coherent in this regard;[31] *and,* whatever its motivation, it is quite impossible to draw out of it—or reconcile with it—the salient claims of *Languages of Art.* The essential point is this: Goodman's irrealism and apparent historicizing of the construction of plural worlds (in *Ways of Worldmaking*) are *never* intended to make any concessions in the direction of radically intentionalizing the world of art (or the world of science for that matter); it is simply a device for avoiding palpable infelicities in a Quinean-like unitary world (which he eschews) governed (as he sees matters) by a nominalist and extensionalist canon. Goodman uses the device of plural actual worlds in order to make nominalism and extensionalism succeed *in the domain of art and culture.* This is why it is important to note that Goodman fails to address the (apparently) *historicized* puzzle of entrenching projectibles in epistemic terms. If he had, he would not have been able to avoid the problems of textuality or of intentionality or of the limits of nominalistic models.

31. See Hilary Putnam, "Reflections on Goodman's *Ways of Worldmaking,*" *Philosophical Papers,* vol. 3 (Cambridge: Cambridge University Press, 1983).

There can be little doubt that *Languages of Art* is written in a straightforwardly objectivist spirit. There is nothing in it that manifests the slightest qualm along phenomenological or deconstructive or genealogical lines—that is, concerns about preformational forces standardly admitted, say, in hermenuetic or phenomenological or other pertinent continental sources. On the contrary, apart from the extremely important development of a semiotic idiom for the handling of philosophical issues about the arts—which certainly can and ought to be redeemed by an analytic aesthetics—Goodman is peculiarly intransigent about the *nature* and *properties* of the arts, a matter that might seem at odds both with his nominalism and his (later, or at least more explicit) irrealism. Two doctrines are of particular importance. In one, he contrasts in a strongly disjunctive way what he calls allographic and autographic arts.[32] That is, he not only introduces the formal distinction, he surveys the arts and finds that music and literature are (it seems, essentially) allographic; that is, individuated and identified by purely extensional or notational means.

The ulterior reason for the distinction may escape our notice: it is simply meant to bring discourse about the arts into a satisfactory alignment with an extensionalist model. The autographic arts are ones in which "even the most exact duplication of an original does not thereby count as genuine."[33] So intentional complexities are disallowed by ensuring uniqueness of reference. And the allographic arts are ones in which all apparent discrepancies, variations, differences (as of performance in music and printing or etching) may be tolerated (and discounted) as far as numerical identity and individuation are concerned, provided only that the individuating marks preserved satisfy completely extensional scores or notations. Goodman struggles manfully with the notational informalities of the history of music; but he never quite comes to terms with its profoundly historical and intentional nature. He is ultimately driven to the obviously unnecessary (even intolerable) conclusion:

> The innocent-seeming principle that performances differing by just one note are instances of the same work risks the consequence—in view of the transitivity of identity—that all performances whatso-

32. See Nelson Goodman, *Languages of Art* (Indianapolis: Bobbs-Merrill, 1968), 113–22.

33. Ibid., 113.

ever are of the same work. If we allow the least deviation, all assurance of work-preservation and score-preservation is lost; for by a series of one-note errors of omission, addition, and modification, we can go all the way from Beethoven's *Fifth Symphony* to *Three Blind Mice*.[34]

If Goodman had but found "ontology evanescent" enough, he might have allowed intentional informalities to flower, or at any rate cognitive fixities to go more informal. For example, if one concedes that the numerical identity of a dance (as in reidentifying one and the same dance in different performances) is a function of its *stylistic* features, and if its stylistic features are profoundly intentionalized, historicized, *incapable* of being captured by any strict extensionalized notation, then it may well be that all so-called allographic arts are ineluctably autographic—and, in being autographic, irreconcilable with the severe nominalism and extensionalism Goodman means to favor.[35] The truth is, Goodman nowhere actually analyzes the stylistic *properties* of artworks (with regard to their intentional complexity)—or the predicates purporting, in a logically relaxed way, to designate such properties; he never goes beyond merely insisting that any and all such properties *are* capable of being extensionally regimented. Clearly, the collapse of that claim would place Goodman's sort of analytic aesthetics in serious jeopardy. Symptomatically, Goodman nowhere discusses the logic of interpretation in the arts. But you may glimpse in this maneuver a possible clue to Goodman's notion of a plurality of "made" worlds. If so, then its defect augurs the defeat of the more general "irrealism."

The other large issue that Goodman addresses—tied to the present one because there is, in Goodman's work, no actual discussion of the structure of artworks—concerns the notion of exemplification. It concerns the nature of artistic expression and so borders once again on the complexities of intentionality. Goodman's key is given by the following: "Expression [in a work] is not, of course, mere possession [by the work, of the putatively expressive property]. Apart from the fact that the possession involved in

34. Ibid., 186–87.

35. See Joseph Margolis, "The Autographic Nature of the Dance," in *Illuminating Dance: Philosophical Explorations*, ed. Maxine Sheets-Johnstone (London and Toronto: Associated University Presses, 1984); and Goodman, "The Status of Style," in *Ways of Worldmaking*. See also Chapter 2 below.

expression is metaphorical, neither literal nor metaphorical possession constitutes symbolization at all. . . . [But] an object that is literally or metaphorically denoted by a predicate or the corresponding property, may be said to exemplify that predicate or property. Not all exemplification is expression, but all expression is exemplification."[36] Once again, the essential point remains that Goodman treats expression (semiotically) as metaphorical, *because* to treat the expressive property *of* an artwork as "literally" possessed by it would entail serious complications *for any extensional treatment of art*—hence, for the autographic/allographic distinction as well. Nevertheless, Goodman nowhere justifies the *metaphorical* ascription[37]: he literally *has* no ontology of art; and he nowhere provides a suitable clue about how philosophical inquiries regarding the arts should proceed. He has no genuine analytic aesthetics.

That is, Goodman practices a variety of analytic aesthetics, but he nowhere entertains questions about the nature of philosophical strategies in the large. As a result, it is impossible to gain from Goodman's work a clear idea of how analytic aesthetics should meet the challenge of anti-analytic currents; although it remains both true and provocative that Goodman's notion of worldmaking has been seen—for instance by the phenomenologically and hermeneutically-minded French philosopher, Paul Ricoeur—as promising a new view of "fiction" (Ricoeur is thinking of Goodman's symbol systems: quite another matter), as a sort of "productive imagination" by which we "make and remake reality" in ways that would obviously defeat any straightforwardly objectivist stance.[38] But whether Goodman would, or could, accept Ricoeur's adventurous suggestion is difficult to say. In fact, the essential irony is just that *Ricoeur* favors Goodman's view of worldmaking because he, Ricoeur, sees this as a powerful concession in the direction of historically preformative forces that lay a proper foundation for the admission and treatment of the intentional or hermeneutic features of artworks; whereas Goodman's motivation is to extricate a strongly antihermeneutic (that is, a formal semiotic) conception of artworks *for* his own favored extensionalism. Also, Ricoeur openly

36. Goodman, "The Status of Style," 52.
37. See Margolis, *Art and Philosophy*, 12–14.
38. Paul Ricoeur, "The Narrative Function," in *Hermeneutics and the Human Sciences*, ed. and trans. John B. Thompson (Cambridge: Cambridge University Press, 1982), particularly 292–93.

favors a form of idealism, whereas Goodman means to avoid canonical idealisms. There could not be a more curious marriage of ideas.

III

Of our four specimen analysts, Arthur Danto affords the most detailed sense of adjusting a theory of art to the actual phases of the history of contemporary art—chiefly painting. He is particularly attentive to modernist, postmodernist, and especially conceptual art. For that reason, he is sensibly disinclined to specify any essentialist definition of art. For instance, he is suitably brief regarding George Dickie's institutional conception of art,[39] and he ultimately dismisses Goodman's thesis of expression as metaphorical exemplification with the following rather nice piece of tact: "It would be unfortunate to conclude that expressive predicates are never literally true of works of art."[40] He is also noticeably hospitable to Hegelian and broadly phenomenological currents. Nevertheless, it is quite clear that his general philosophical orientation is uneasily—and unsatisfactorily—divided between his appreciation of the complexities of cultural phenomena, particularly historicity and intentionality, and his residual commitment to a relatively inflexible physicalism and extensionalism. In fact, in his discussion of the issue of expression, which in the context of the rhetoric of art occupies his principal attention, Danto actually concludes: "The philosophical point [of the discussion of some of Cézanne's paintings and other artworks] is that the concept of expression can be reduced to the concept of metaphor, when the *way* in which something is represented is taken in connection with the subject represented."[41] By this device, Danto recovers what Goodman does not quite accommodate—but in an ingenious way that preserves his ulterior convergence with Goodman's extensionalism and tendency toward physicalism.

This is a large and rather complicated matter, not easily grasped or conceded. My intention here, remember, is to draw the thread of analytic aesthetics from a number of its principal champions in order to weigh the

39. Arthur C. Danto, *The Transfiguration of the Commonplace* (Cambridge: Harvard University Press, 1981), 92–95.
40. Danto, *Transfiguration*, 189–97, particularly 192.
41. Ibid., 197.

prospects for its continuing along the same lines. Let it therefore be said of Danto's work (in the philosophy of art) that its fatal weakness lies with his failure to have resolved the analysis of what he himself had memorably identified as "the 'is' of artistic identification."[42] The point to grasp is that Danto's difficulty with the "is" of artistic identification (not, of course, a difficulty Danto feels) is both the mate of similar difficulties that surface in all of his philosophical work—in his theory of history and in his theory of action, for instance[43]—and a clue to his essential philosophical strategy.

But, it needs to be said, most readers of Danto do not sense the conceptual strain in his aesthetics because they do not take seriously enough the bearing of the "is" of artistic identification on *all* of his perceptive discussions of artworks. That is, *most* readers accept Danto's straightforward account of the complexities of art without attempting to reconcile his critical and appreciative remarks with his fundamental philosophical orientation. It is not that Danto embraces the empiricism, physicalism, nominalism, extensionalism, unity-of-science orientation so characteristic of the analytic tradition: it is rather that his theory is fatally encumbered by the traces of such affiliations; he is divided in his heart about the adequacy of those doctrines and their disciplined application to the world of action, history, art, language, and culture, *and* he fails (by reason of that divided allegiance) ever to resolve the puzzle of the "is" of artistic identification.

The objective of Danto's entire strategy (going well beyond aesthetics) is to marry two disparate projects: one, the articulation of an idiom ample enough for the entire span of cultural life—notably, art, history, action, knowledge; the other, adherence to an underlying ontology, more or less faithful to the inspiration of the unity of science program and of a strong physicalism. *That* is what the "is" of artistic identification is all about, and that explains why Danto takes such pains to distinguish it from the "is" of (numerical) identity.

If, however, *what* is *constituted* by the first "is" *is* real as such, then the

---

42. The notion first appeared, unanalyzed, in Arthur Danto, "The Artworld," reprinted in *Philosophy Looks at the Arts*, 3d ed. (Philadelphia: Temple University Press, 1987).

43. See Joseph Margolis, "Ontology Down and Out in Art and Science," *Journal of Aesthetics and Art Criticism* 46 (1998); and in T. Anderberg, T. Nilstun, and I. Persson, eds., *Aesthetic Diction* (Lund: Studentlitteratur, 1998). The relevant texts include: Arthur C. Danto, *Narration and Knowledge* (New York: Columbia University Press, 1985)—the enlarged second edition of Danto's *Analytical Philosophy of History* (1964); and *Analytical Philosophy of Action* (Cambridge: Cambridge University Press, 1973).

second "is" *would* ineluctably apply to *it*. So the trick is that Danto manages to hold that artworks are "constituted" as artworks by the "is" of artistic identification all right, but that *that same constitution does not yield an entity or real phenomenon about which it may be said that it is both real (in the ontological sense) and self-identical as such*. What is true of "it" is held at arm's length from what is real, kept from capturing the actual properties of "mere" physical phenomena (not quite the equivalent of what Danto calls "mere real things").[44] But the motivation for that maneuver is still not very distant from Sartre's insistence that art is "unreal," that is, superior to what is "merely" real.[45]

All this comes out reasonably clearly in Danto's relatively recent objection to Susan Sontag's view of interpretation. Here is what he says:

> Hers [that is, Sontag's objections regarding the nature of interpretation] is against a notion of interpretation which makes the artwork as an explanandum—as a symptom, for example. My theory of interpretation is instead constitutive, for an object is an artwork *at all* only in relation to an interpretation. We may bring this out in a somewhat logical way. Interpretation in my sense is transfigurative. It transforms objects into works of art, and depends upon the "is" of artistic identification. Her interpretations, which are explanatory, use instead the "is" of ordinary identity. Her despised interpreters see works as signs, symptoms, expressions of ulterior or subjacent realities, states of which are what the artwork "really" refers to, and which requires the interpreter to be master of one or another kind of code: psychoanalytical, culturographic, semiotical, or whatever. In effect, her interpreters address the work in the spirit of science. . . . Mine is a theory which is not in the spirit of science but of philosophy. If interpretations are what constitute works, there are no works without them and works are misconstituted when interpretation is wrong. And knowing the artist's interpretation is in effect identifying what he or she has made. The interpretation is not something outside the work: work and inter-

---

44. See Danto, "Works of Art and Mere Real Things," in *Transfiguration*.

45. See Jean-Paul Sartre, *The Psychology of Imagination*, trans., reprinted (Secaucus, N.J.: Citadel Press, n.d.); see also Arthur C. Danto, *Jean-Paul Sartre* (New York: Viking, 1975), chap. 1.

pretation arise together in aesthetic consciousness. As interpretation
is inseparable from work, it is inseparable from the artist if it is the
artist's work.[46]

Now, the transfigurative "is" is meant to accommodate absolutely everything of interest that may be said about artworks, but it collects all of that
only *in a relational way.* That is, it is initially the artist's intention *with
respect to* a merely physical object (or, in a more relaxed provisional sense,
with respect to a "mere real thing" that may even happen to be an
artifact—a snow shovel or bottlerack, for instance); and it is subsequently,
therefore, the viewer's (or aesthetic percipient's) recovery of *that* (or something like that) *constituting relationship* (the interpretation) that permits
the viewer to "see" it *as* an artwork: "To see something as art requires
something the eye cannot de[s]cry—an atmosphere of artistic theory, a
knowledge of the history of art: an artworld."[47] The trick is that Danto
does not believe that physical objects are relationally linked to our perceptual abilities in a way that is analogous (however different) to the relational connection between artworks and our ability to "descry" artworks.
This is, I concede, a very large question; but I see no reason to deny that
if realist standing can be accorded "mere real things," it can be accorded
artworks as well. The two continue to be very different in "nature,"
nevertheless.

This suggests the reason Danto is so comfortable in declaring (as we
have seen) that "the concept of expression *can* be reduced to the concept
of metaphor," after having dismissed Goodman's version of a related thesis. *Danto* has a better way of holding on to all the complexity of art,
while reaching for the same extensional and physicalist model Goodman is
more explicitly attracted to. But it cannot be enough *if,* as seems plain,
human persons themselves, the paradigms of culturally complex entities,
are *not* similarly reducible (by the "is" of identity) to mere physical bodies.[48] After all, if persons were thus reduced, then there would be no

46. Danto, *The Philosophical Disenfranchisement of Art* (New York: Columbia University Press, 1986), 44–45.

47. Danto, "The Artworld," 162.

48. See, further, Joseph Margolis, "Constraints on the Metaphysics of Culture," *Review
of Metaphysics* 39 (1986). Here and throughout this chapter, I try to convey a sense of a
number of early transitional pieces through which I first began to reconcile analytic and
continental treatments of the metaphysics and epistemology of the cultural world.

independent entities capable of *relating* to other physical objects, by suitable interpretation or theory, in such a way that those "objects" would be imaginatively "transfigured" (but *not* ontically transformed) into artworks (or human actions or historical events or speech). Otherwise, Danto would merely be the stock figure of a reductive physicalism (would hold that artworks just are—by the "is" of identity—physical objects), whereas (in truth) he means to be a *non*reductive physicalist.[49] In fact, Danto's account provides no objective basis for valid interpretation (that he wishes to support). Interpretive objectivity would require a suitable realism, but the rhetoric of "transfiguration" precludes realism.

Danto is never sufficiently clear, ultimately, about the relationship between the intentionally complex language of human culture and the language of physicalism—which is what the true physicalist (whether reductive or nonreductive) cannot permit to remain inexplicit. That is why his account fails. More than that, his endeavor fixes the plain sense in which, for all his considerable ingenuity and perceptiveness, his version of analytic aesthetics remains essentially bound to the objectivism that we noted at the start in Beardsley's very much simpler aesthetics.

Nevertheless, it would be churlish not to admit the finesse of Danto's sustained discussion of the historical and intentional complexities of art. What Danto manages to show thereby—against his own intentions—is that, by a logically small adjustment, fatal to the older strains of analytic aesthetics, these exemplary observations could revive the analytic orientation by embracing just the kind of complication the older strains disallow. Danto is too well informed to disallow them; but he is also too loyal to those older strains to work out an explicit ontology fitted to the kind of critical remarks he himself regularly favors. Hence, he never skimps on the critic's role; but then he also never addresses the obvious theoretical pressure that that role imposes on a realism essentially committed to the constraints of physicalism. He has, in fact, never bridged the gulf.

IV

The fourth of our specimens, Joseph Margolis (myself, of course, if I dare speak in the third person), is the only one of the four to have attempted

---

49. For an ingenious version of nonreductive physicalism, see John F. Post, *The Faces of Experience* (Ithaca: Cornell University Press, 1987). See also Joseph Margolis, *Texts Without Reference* (Oxford: Basil Blackwell, 1989), chap. 6.

systematically to reconcile the strategies of analytic philosophy with the principal currents of anti-analytic philosophy—chiefly, with those that appear in Husserl, Heidegger, Gadamer, Derrida, and Foucault, that is, with phenomenological and hermeneutic and poststructuralist currents. Margolis's general argument insists that, first of all (as already remarked), there is no way to avoid the constative function of discourse; and, second, that all such discourse (whether first-order or second-order, whether intended to be descriptive of the world or intended to be legitimative with respect to what purports to be descriptive—there being no way to disengage the one from the other) must submit to some form of critique, that is, some way of attending to the preformative (culturally holist) conditions under which constative discourse functions as such.[50]

This has the effect of "phenomenologizing" naturalistic discourse or of "naturalizing" phenomenological or deconstructive or genealogical discourse; for the absence of the first leaves the naturalistic vision blind, and the absence of the second leaves the phenomenological and the deconstructive pointless and empty. The point is that second-order *critique* is entirely "internalist"—preformed but not privileged—and viable as such, that is, restricted in the same way any first-order inquiry (science or literary criticism) would be. In short, despite being second-order and legitimative, critique utterly eschews cognitive privilege.[51] There's the point at which analytic and continental philosophies must converge: the matter has nothing (necessarily) to do with avoiding holism or intentionality.

It is a very pretty and uncomplicated consequence that the postmodernist conception of philosophy—preeminently, Rorty's—simply fails at a stroke, that is, fails in the sense that there are no professional practices of cognitive inquiry that can escape the need for legitimative reflection, even if (or precisely because) the "loyalty" we may manifest with respect to such practices "no longer needs an ahistorical backup."[52] Rorty's point is that the metaphysical, transparent, cognitively privileged, essentialist, correspondentist, mirrored, objectivist, transcendental, presenced, logocentric idiom of Kant and Descartes is neither necessary nor defensible. Fine. He

50. See Margolis, *Pragmatism Without Foundations*, chap. 8; and *Texts without Reference*, Pt. I.

51. On "internalist" strategies, see Margolis, *Pragmatism without Foundations*, chap. 11.

52. Richard Rorty, "Postmodernist Bourgeois Liberalism," *Journal of Philosophy* 80 (1983); reprinted in *Hermeneutics and Praxis*, ed. Robert Hollinger (Notre Dame: Notre Dame University Press, 1985): the material quoted appears on 216 (in Hollinger's edition).

offers two options: one, a historicized and naturalistic but *not* philosophical or epistemological source of reasons and arguments for the practices in question (which he judges to be a version of a naturalized Hegelian line); the other (that of the "postmodernist bourgeois liberal," also "Hegelian"), which simply abandons at a stroke the entire need *for* a justification of practices—contenting itself with the notion that: "On a Quinean view, rational behavior is just adaptive behavior of a sort which roughly parallels the behavior, in similar circumstances of the other members of some relevant community."[53]

But this is simply intellectual bankruptcy. For one thing, we cannot eliminate (Rorty does not wish to eliminate) constative discourse. And for a second, the *practice*—any practice, the practice of any community of inquirers—must have a rationale *regarding how to go on to new cases not included in the paradigms learned in learning the original language or practice.* Therein lies the essential disability of Goodman's nominalism and of every nominalism construed in a cognitively pertinent sense; and therein also lies the defect and defeat of the postmodernist maneuver. For the problem is not merely one of how to go on extending the scope of complex predicates in new circumstances but also one of how to go on giving rational or critical redirection to any sustained and disciplined inquiry. The first is the *pons* of nominalism; the second, of postmodernism.

If analytic aesthetics is to survive—if analytic philosophy or any philosophy is to survive, if any rational inquiry is to survive—then: (1) it must be possible to bridge the difference between naturalism and the "more" continental currents (phenomenology, deconstruction, genealogy, hermeneutics, historicism, and the like) that are hospitable to the complexities of holism and intentionality and the profound difference between the physical and the cultural; and (2) it must be possible to provide for second-order legitimative discourse that does not fail in the "Kantian" manner Rorty is at such pains to dismantle. Margolis's entire philosophical effort is committed to working out the conceptual conditions for satisfying (1) and (2), with attention particularly to the metaphysics and epistemology of culture and art. This is at least a viable proposal regarding a *new* program and orientation for analytic aesthetics—again, of course, considered here only in the spirit of tracing the prospects of analytic aesthetics. It would put into question all the older doctrines of objectivism, physicalism, nomi-

53. Rorty, "Postmodernist Bourgeois Liberalism," 217.

nalism, extensionalism, and unity of science constraints; and it would embrace, at least as pertinent options, historicism, intentionality, preformation, intertextuality, relativism, cultural emergence, nonreductive materialism, critique, incommensurabilism, legitimation. The vista is large enough.

Through a marvel of innuendo but not argument, Rorty declares and insinuates at one and the same time: "Analytic philosophy *cannot,* I suspect, be written without one or the other of these two distinctions": that is, the two "Kantian" distinctions said to be repudiated by Quine and Wilfrid Sellars respectively, namely, the "necessary-contingent" distinction and the "given-interpretation" distinction.[54] The juxtaposition of the italicized "cannot" and the coy "I suspect" permits Rorty to play the enormously pleasant game of agreeing with all his critics for the sake of the ongoing "conversation" while at the same time cutting philosophy (and science and criticism) off at the knees. So he adds, catching up the point of what we took note of before: "Behaviorism claims that if you understand the rules of a language-game, you understand *all* that there is to understand about why moves in that language-game are made. (All, that is, save for the extra understanding you get when you engage in various research programs which nobody would call epistemological—into, for example, the history of the language, the structure of the brain, the evolution of the species, and the political or cultural ambiance of the players.)"[55]

But that is just what one does *not* understand, unless one understands the rationale, the legitimative rationale, the second-order moves in accord with which we recommend—dialectically, historically, contingently, without foundations—how to go on rationally.[56] If we give up the "Kantian" position, which we must, then we need second-order legitimative discourse more than ever—not less—because we need the best rational guess about what the conditions of inquiry and truth-claims are by which to guide ourselves in extending our practice. That's what philosophy is all about;

54. Richard Rorty, "Epistemological Behaviorism and the De-Transcendentalization of Analytic Philosophy," *Neue Hefte für Philosophie* 9 (1978); reprinted in *Hermeneutics and Praxis,* 95–96. Rorty professes to follow Lyotard, of course, in characterizing his own view as postmodern. See Jean-François Lyotard, *The Postmodern Condition: A Report on Knowledge,* trans. Geoff Bennington and Brian Massumi (Minneapolis: University of Minnesota Press, 1984).

55. Rorty, "Epistemological Behaviorism and the De-Transcendentalization of Analytic Philosophy," 98; italics added.

56. See Margolis, *Pragmatism Without Foundations,* chap. 11.

and that no one has ever convincingly shown to be disposable. To be sure, "rational" (like "true" and "false") also *has* a history, which complicates philosophy enormously. But it complicates philosophy, it does not rule it out. Even Foucault rather wistfully acknowledges the point in reviewing the threatening incoherence of his own poststructuralist efforts.[57] There *cannot* be a recovery of analytic aesthetics, now faced with its own stalemate, without a "rational" second-order redirection of its energies. Rorty's is simply a counsel of despair or irresponsibility. The solution must go in the direction of constructivism and historicism—but that would be enough.

Margolis, then, has deliberately sought to reconcile what the objectivist and naturalistic idioms have correctly perceived—namely, that constative discourse is ineliminable and that first-order and second-order (legitimative) discourse are inseparable—with the best elements of non-naturalistic (but not necessarily non-"analytic") philosophy; while at the same time he abandons the objectionable "logocentric" or privileged discourse that "continentally"-minded thinkers have rightly perceived to be entrenched in most of analytic philosophy. Thus, the famous "subject/object" relationship that theorists like Husserl (and Heidegger and Derrida) so much inveigh against cannot be eliminated but, *once* placed in an appropriate preformational or critical context (*without,* then, reclaiming privilege on its own), the relationship affords a perfectly adequate and viable (and necessary) basis for recovering epistemological and metaphysical inquiry—in aesthetics as elsewhere. There you have the clue to what must be preserved regarding cultural preformation (or a holism of meanings) and the operative separation of cognizing subjects and cognized objects in any truth-bearing discourse.

It is true that Margolis has come to this rapprochement somewhat later than his characteristic accounts of the ontology of artworks, of the logic of interpretation, and of relativistic judgments in general.[58] The result is that there is a distinct vestigial objectivism in these early discussions that

57. See, for instance, Michel Foucault, "Questions of Method: An Interview with Michel Foucault," trans. Alan Bass, in *Ideology and Consciousness,* VIII (1981); reprinted in Kenneth Baynes et al., eds., *After Philosophy: End or Transformation* (Cambridge: MIT Press, 1987).

58. See, for instance, Margolis, *Art and Philosophy;* see also Joseph Margolis, *Culture and Cultural Entities* (Dordrecht: D. Reidel, 1984), chap. 1.

needed to be exorcised (and eventually was).[59] This is as it may be, a matter entirely local to Margolis's own efforts. They are of little consequence in the present context. In his more recent work, Margolis explores the threat of ontic indeterminacy, the historicized openness, the lack of essential fixity that artworks exhibit. The fact remains that the analysis of the nature of art and culture, of description and interpretation, of texts, of histories, of reference, of judgment, of relativistic and nonrelativistic truth-values is entirely congenial to both the rapprochement sketched and the continuance of analytic aesthetics.

In fact, Margolis's themes have characteristically been hospitable to the full recovery of intentional phenomena, the irreducibility of culture to nature, the inadequacy of both reductive and nonreductive physicalisms, the admission of emergence, the replacement of the unity of science program, the abandonment of a comprehensive extensionalism, the acknowledgement of the complexities of historicism, the advocacy of something other than ontic determinacy, the acknowledgement of conceptual incommensurabilities, of divergent pluralisms, of relativistic values, the rejection of closed systems, the insistence on the inseparability of the psychological and the societal at the human level, the denial of the disjunction between realism and idealism, and the endorsement of constructivist concessions regarding selves and world. These are all themes peculiarly favorably attuned to phenomenologizing naturalism and naturalizing phenomenology—meaning by that to accommodate all forms of critique (say, the Marxist as well as the Nietzschean) that seriously address the question of the pursuit of first- and second-order inquiry under contingently preformational conditions that, at the level of both first- and second-order discourse, we cannot fathom in a privileged way.

Margolis is particularly known for his defense of the coherence and pertinence—in aesthetics and in general—of relativism and historicism. [60] But these doctrines are themselves called into play and legitimated by a deeper discussion of the metaphysical and epistemological differences between physical nature and human culture.[61] Here, the simple novelty of

59. See, for instance, Margolis, *Interpretation Radical But Not Unruly* (Berkeley and Los Angeles: University of California Press, 1995).

60. See, for instance, Joseph Margolis, *The Truth about Relativism* (Oxford: Basil Blackwell, 1991); and *The Flux of History and the Flux of Science* (Berkeley and Los Angeles: University of California Press, 1993).

61. See Joseph Margolis, *Historied Thought, Constructed World: A Conceptual Primer*

Margolis's approach rests with attempting to work out the conceptual requirements of a realism that spans *selves* (uniquely enlanguaged, "second-natured" human agents) and their Intentional *utterances* (intrinsically interpretable artworks, histories, deeds, speech acts), reconciled (as emergent) with whatever is required by any realism restricted to mere physical nature. His is one of a very few such efforts tendered within the practice of analytic philosophy—not wedded to the canonical forms of physicalism or extensionalism or naturalism. Margolis's governing intuition is that cultural entities are as real as physical entities but possess inherently distinctive structures—"Intentional," or culturally significative, intrinsically interpretable structures—that mere physical entities simply lack. This is the essential pivot of his challenge to the models of art offered by Beardsley, Goodman, and Danto alike.

The solution he offers requires the admission: (i) that the cultural world has emerged in a *sui generis* way from the physical and biological world (probably by way of small changes that first made the evolution of natural language possible); (ii) that the phenomena of the cultural world can be analyzed only "Intentionally" (say, in terms of their representational, expressive, linguistic, semiotic, symbolic, rhetorical, stylistic, historical, institutional, traditional, rule-like properties); and (iii) that the realist standing of cultural entities entails their being indissolubly *embodied* in actual physical and biological entities (with respect to which they are emergent *sui generis*), and entails as well their properties being indissolubly *incarnate* in actual physical and biological properties (with respect to which they are interpretively specified). The characteristic objectivity of interpretive criticism in the arts and history depends, in much the same sense in which discourse in the natural sciences depends, on the conceptual match (or "adequation") between *denotatum* and attributes.

Margolis offers a two-step strategy in support of his general constructivism (constructive realism), of his contrast between physical and cultural entities, and of his advocacy of relativism and historicism. By the first, he argues that all truth-bearing or constative discourse relies on referential and predicative resources but adds that success in these regards cannot rest on evidentiary or criterial grounds in any cognitively determinate way. Success never counts as *savoir* (the exercise of an adequate cognitive

---

for the Turn of the Millennium (Berkeley and Los Angeles: University of California Press, 1995).

faculty) but only as *savoir-faire* (practical conjecture and matched action consensually tolerated as adequate). Thus, for example, reference (to individual *denotata,* whether stones or sculptures) cannot be gained by any predicative means (agreeing with Leibniz and against Quine[62]), and haecceity cannot be discerned in any cognitively determinate way at all (as Duns Scotus seems to have conceded).

Again, we are forced to admit that, if (as is obviously true) we have no inkling of how to access Platonic Forms or natural essences epistemically, success in predicative matters cannot be anything but consensual without their thereby being criterial; that is, predicative success cannot but accord (in an entirely informal way) with the collective tolerance of our predicative practices and interests.[63] Furthermore, there is reason to suppose that the pattern of such tolerance diverges among societies and changes over time, within any society, in accord with the drift of local history. If you grant that much, then every viable realism must be a constructivism and, in principle, relativistic and historicist considerations are bound to affect our sense of objectivity everywhere.

If you grant the point, you have in fact exposed the arbitrariness of Rorty's objection to philosophy. For, although it is true (as Rorty insists) that the philosopher has no privileged source of knowledge by which to take precedence over first-order inquiry (Kantian transcendental resources, for instance), it remains true (against Rorty's objection) that the second-order questions philosophy raises are both needed and answerable. My own claim is that they are answered by reviewing the conditions of "know-how" rather than of (a privileged source of) "knowledge." The best attempts at such a review belong, as I see it, to the Hegelian tradition construed so broadly that figures like Dewey and Wittgenstein may count among its number. (That means, of course, discounting whatever Kantian vestiges cling to Hegel's own thought.)

The second step of the argument holds that the referential or denotative determinacy of cultural entities is on a par with that of physical objects but that the nature or predicative determinacy of cultural entities need not be (for that reason alone) determinate in the same sense in which physical

62. See H. G. Alexander, ed., *The Leibniz-Clarke Correspondence* (Manchester: Manchester University Press, 1956); and Quine, *Word and Object,* §§37–38.
63. I take this to be the master theme of Ludwig Wittgenstein, *Philosophical Investigations,* trans. G. E. M. Anscombe (New York: Macmillan, 1953).

objects are said to be. The reason is simply that cultural entities possess, and physical objects lack, Intentional properties. Thus, for instance, if a physical object is (said to be) red, we normally suppose that *that* red (determinate in being a particular red, but determinable in being open to further determination as this or that particular red) can always be thought to be more determinate without supposing that there is any infimate red in any particular instance.

By contrast, in making a particular interpretation "more determinate" (say, in interpreting *Hamlet*), we cannot convincingly claim that the "increased" determinacy of what is interpretively predicated will be more determinate in the same "linear" sense in which, say, red might be. No. The situations are altogether different. We are forced to admit: (*a*) that objectivity takes a constructivist form everywhere; but (*b*), in the physical world, it is largely limited by the inherent informalities of reference and predication; and (*c*) the Intentional attributes or predicables of the cultural world are determinable but not determinate in the sense in which physical attributes are said to be. Once you grant this much, it becomes impossible to deny that a relativistic and a historicist treatment of objectivity cannot be disallowed *a priori* (if it can be made internally consistent and coherent), wherever, at the very least, Intentional properties are being addressed.

Add, to this, two further qualifications and you have the nerve of Margolis's argument: first, that history is cognitively blind, so that historicism is invoked only retrospectively, from whatever cognitive vantage we suppose we occupy, in accord with which the norms and exemplars of predicative similarity may be expected to change under historical forces; and second, that we are free to choose our "logic," our range of truth-values or truth-like values, relative to whatever domain of inquiry we pursue, so that, where Intentional properties are at stake (but possibly also elsewhere, for other reasons), we may favor a set of many-valued values over a strict bivalence (though the two may be used, with care, in tandem)—where, that is, we wish to support contending interpretations ("incongruent" judgments, as Margolis says) that, on a bivalent logic but not now, would count as contraries or contradictories or incompatibles.

It would take us too far afield to attempt to strengthen any of these proposals.[64] The point here is only to show that the option is entirely

---

64. See Joseph Margolis, *What, After All, Is a Work of Art? Lectures in the Philosophy of Art* (University Park: The Pennsylvania State University Press, 1999), chap. 2.

coherent and workable; opposed to the salient accounts in analytic aesthetics but compatible with analytic rigor; and hospitable to hermeneutic, poststructuralist, and related continental currents that abandon all necessities *de re* and *de cogitatione* and yield in the direction of holism, constructivism, relativism, and historicism.

In short, to return to the original premise: analytic philosophy—and analytic aesthetics in particular—cannot be expected to prosper without recovering (at least selectively) the questions raised here, within the subtler space of an inquiry that avoids the older forms of cognitive privilege and foundationalism, or without resisting altogether the siren attraction of a know-nothing postmodernism. But there is reason to think the imminent future will transform these implied recommendations into a prophecy— and a fulfillment.

In any case, the best prospects of analytic aesthetics depend on two adjustments: (i) the pursuit of all the themes just mentioned, which go entirely counter to the canonical tendencies of analytic philosophy but are not at all incompatible with its native discipline; and (ii) the ability to steer a middle course between the older tendency toward ahistorical privilege and the newest tendency to disallow, within historicized conditions, suitably adjusted versions of philosophy's legitimate legitimative concern.

2

PERCEIVING ARTWORKS: FAREWELL TO DANTO AND GOODMAN

There's a closet scandal that's been brewing in the philosophy of art for a good many years, noticed in passing by nearly everyone reasonably well informed, but only rarely mentioned explicitly and almost never closely analyzed. The matter should be examined with some care, however; for one thing, it goes to the heart of the theories of two of the best-known and most influential contemporary philosophers of art and, for a second, it bears very pointedly on certain themes regarding cultural realism and historicity that are now gaining considerable attention in ways that were never strongly featured when the texts embodying the "scandal" mentioned first appeared.

That's not terribly long ago, as it happens, a fact that suggests an accelerating interest in lines of objection (to the claims in question) that would not have commanded (in fact, did not command) sufficient interest when they were first bruited. But, now, various themes of social constructionism, cultural realism, historicity, the role of intentionality in cultural matters, the possible inadequacy of the usual forms of materialism and of theories of formal semiotics to account for the complexities of art, texts, language, histories, and human existence itself have gained a great deal of respect in their own right. They lead us back, ineluctably, to slighted puzzles—like the pair I have alluded to—that should never have been shrugged off in the first place.

I remind you of them, because, on review, it turns out that the weaknesses I have in mind do indeed open on to a truly large and important terrain of theory, itself neglected in recent work in the philosophy of art, which, rightly construed (in the company of the intended exposé), bids fair to reorient our sense of failed and viable theories. Since the story involves the work of two leading discussants—Arthur Danto and Nelson Goodman—the charge cannot fail to be provocative; and, if it can be made to stick in a way that is not contrived, then others active in the field (and drawn to Danto and Goodman) are likely to find themselves obliged to explain the adequacy of their own way of boarding the issues at stake. I hope so.

The claims Danto and Goodman make are very well known, are absolutely central to the defense of their own theories, are impossible to defend on the finding I am about to put forward, are focused on unavoidable questions any reasonable theory of the arts would wish to address, and are quite remarkably placed for assessing the largest philosophical strategies regarding the arts and the whole of the cultural world.

That's a bit of a laundry list. But I hope it will pique your curiosity long enough to stay for the argument. If so, then please excuse the frontal tone I've adopted. I mean it as a form of economy, not discourtesy, since, to be perfectly honest, I have been addressing bits of the "scandal" from the time of the first appearance of Danto's "Artworld" paper and Goodman's account of forgery. I am not primarily interested in an *explication* of the texts of either one, though, of course, there is no way to avoid some exegesis here and there. I am much more interested in what we may rightly suppose are the minimal constraints on what to mean by the *perception* of an artwork, or the sense in which artworks may be admitted to be *real*, or (also) what to make of the conceptual linkage between these two notions.

Put in very broad terms, part of the scandal comes to this: Goodman says that the difference between a real work of art (a painting, say) and a forgery of it will always (eventually) be confirmed by way of a perceptual difference not previously noted. I judge Goodman's claim to be completely arbitrary, not evidentially motivated at all, certainly not necessarily true, very likely false if we constrain sensory perception in a suitably narrow way (as Goodman intends) and if we do not allow, within the boundaries of the "perceptual," talk of the "perception" of Intentional or (in particular) historically "discernible" features inseparable from what remains discernible in the first sense Goodman favors.

By contrast, Danto says there may be no perceptual (sensorily discernible) differences between an artwork and a "mere real thing" or between two quite different artworks; he holds that there are always nondiscernible differences between such paired items, differences that bear on history (particularly, the history of production) and artists' intentions. I find Danto's claim to be either incoherent or paradoxical; it cannot be made to accord with the practices of the artworld Danto favors, or other parts of human culture. And, of course, there is a fundamental opposition between Danto's and Goodman's claims, which needs to be drawn out.

My bottom line is that Danto's and Goodman's theories fail irremediably—for the same underlying reason; and that, to resolve the questions at stake, we require a series of concessions about the constructive realism of artworks (and human selves) and about the perceptual standing of the properties of paintings (viewed as a metonym for the other arts). That goes directly counter to both Danto and Goodman.

What follows, partly as a symptom of the untenability of Danto's and Goodman's theories, is that, against Goodman, a work of art and a forgery of it are impossible to characterize except in terms that cannot be confined to any set of merely material or sensory or semiotic properties; and, against Danto, the mere fact of being an artwork *and* being accessible as such—allowing an "indiscernibility" like that involving *Brillo Box* (or, of course, Duchamp's *Fountain* and its matched urinal "transfigured" in the readymade), or like Danto's well-known set of red squares painted or merely daubed, which Danto sorts, intriguingly, as a set of very different paintings or as pairs of matched art objects and non-art objects—cannot be coherently formulated in Danto's idiom. Well, there you have the unvarnished charges: Goodman's thesis is arbitrary or false; Danto's is incoherent or paradoxical in the extreme.

The proximate consequences are these: Goodman's distinction between autographic and allographic art collapses—all art is autographic (to speak with Goodman but against his theory), and *style* (as a critical concept) cannot be predicatively captured in any purely formal way, any more than a dance can be captured, descriptively, by a dance notation; and Danto's practice as a well-informed art critic turns out, oddly, to be *about* what, on his own theory, does not and cannot actually exist. These are meant to be *reductios*—and they are, if my argument holds. I don't expect you to accept them on my say-so. You will require a brief. Fair enough. But then, if the objections are as fundamental as I suppose, they must be answered. At the very least, the issue is not merely a matter of philosophical "taste," as if to say: you proceed on these assumptions and I, on those. No, I mean to press a *reductio,* to expose the self-defeating features of Goodman's and Danto's theories. If they fail, they fail *sans phrase.*

I

I begin by introducing what Danto has to say against Goodman, which, in effect, rests, inexplicitly, on the central theme of his own theory. In this way, I can, by one and the same stroke, make clear that, in opposing both Danto and Goodman, I agree with much that each claims—though not (by my own lights) with enough to justify what each finally advances as his own theory of art. Danto's summary of what's wrong with Goodman's account of forgery is very good: so good, in fact, that there's no point in inventing another summary for the sake of separate authorship. First, Danto cites the art dealer's worry that opens Goodman's well-known discussion of "authenticity": "The hardheaded question why there is any aesthetic difference between a deceptive forgery and an original work challenges a basic premise on which the very functions of collector, museum, and art historian depend. A philosopher of art caught without an answer to this question is at least as badly off as a curator of paintings caught taking a Van Meegeren for a Vermeer."[1]

I agree. *We* must be as "hardheaded" as Goodman advises. Danto demonstrates very clearly that Goodman is hardly hardheaded enough. But neither is Danto, as far as concerns the implications, for his own theory, of his objection against Goodman. For, if I understand him rightly, then, all things considered, Danto actually eliminates, *as not real,* the very object (the work of art) he invokes in rightly criticizing Goodman's resolution of the forgery question.

Here is what Danto says:

1. Nelson Goodman, *Languages of Art: An Approach to a Theory of Symbols* (Indianapolis: Bobbs-Merrill, 1968), 99. I've included the final line of Goodman's paragraph, which Danto omits.

the entire structure of the examples with which we [Danto himself] have been working cries out for an answer to the inverse of Goodman's question [just cited], whether an unnoticed, and let us even suppose an unnoticeable difference can make an aesthetic difference. To be sure, we are not yet in a position to ponder aesthetic differences, ours being a prior question of the ontological difference between artworks and their nonartistic counterparts, and there is a question whether this difference, which again is unnoticeable so far as examination of the objects is concerned, can make anything like an aesthetic difference.[2]

The "examples" Danto has in mind are, as it happens, the amusing set of "red squares" with which he begins Chapter 1 of *The Transfiguration of the Commonplace* and Borges's well-known little story, "Pierre Menard," with which he begins Chapter 2—from which, in fact, the passage just cited is taken (following a reminder of these same pretty cases). By that maneuver, Danto completely outflanks the forgery issue, bringing Goodman's remark explicitly back to the "ontology" issue. Bear that in mind.

There's much that falls into place with just these bits of citation. For Danto insists on the "priority" of the "ontological" question over Goodman's question and takes note of the separate issue of whether "indiscernible" differences count or contribute to "aesthetic differences." (I shall return to these separate matters a little later: it's the priority of the ontological question that ultimately defeats Danto out of his own mouth.) For the moment, I draw your attention to the obvious fact that *if* what Danto offers holds—in his account of the famous (imaginary) painted red squares (including one that happens to have red paint daubed all over it but is *not* actually *painted*) and the "Pierre Menard"—then Goodman's theory will have been put at mortal risk.[3]

Danto brings the lesson to bear on Goodman's account:

2. Arthur C. Danto, *The Transfiguration of the Commonplace: A Philosophy of Art* (Cambridge: Harvard University Press, 1981), 42.

3. See Danto, *Transfiguration*, 1–3. Danto moves at once to offer more general versions of his thesis, in particular an analogy between artworks and actions (4–6). Notice, too, that in summarizing his own examples, Danto pointedly warns that the paired indiscernibles he has in mind "may have radically distinct ontological affiliations" (4). Just so. We shall have to confront Danto on this precise point.

Goodman [he says] in a curious way rejects one of the conditions of the question, namely the condition of indiscernibility. And it appears to be his view that indiscernibility is only momentary, that sooner or later differences will emerge. . . . There is a great deal to be said for Goodman's analysis. [It's often true that we learn "to make exceedingly fine distinctions . . . we can learn to see things that would have been invisible before."] But that is as much, I think, as can be said finally for Goodman's analysis. The logical point, while it guarantees that if *a* is not identical with *b,* then there must be a property F such that *a* is F and *b* is not F, does not require that F be a perceptual property, and we have had enough practice with indiscernibilia to be able to offer actual instances where the differences are not such as may be registered by the senses. In fact, it is not clear that concepts like "work of art" and "forgery" are translatable into sets of simple perceptual predicates.[4]

If I do not treat this as an absolute *reductio* of Goodman's thesis, it is only because Danto harbors a fatal equivocation on "perceive" and "indiscernible" with regard to his own examples; but what he says here *is,* nevertheless, an absolute *reductio* of Goodman's thesis, *if read in Goodman's terms.* It does *not,* however, vindicate Danto's own examples, *if read in Danto's terms!* There's the difficulty.

It's an interesting fact that Danto does not address Goodman's distinction between autographic and allographic art here. (At least I haven't found it on a casual scanning.) But, *if* the examples hold, then Goodman must be *utterly* mistaken in two linked regards: in one, in the sense that he treats the autographic and the allographic disjunctively; and, in another, in the sense that, *relying* on that disjunction, he claims there can be no forgeries of musical or literary works (in the decisive sense).

Once cases like the red squares and the "Pierre Menard" are conceded, however, then, *contra* Goodman, *every* artwork has (cannot fail to have) an autographic aspect that bears on its standing *as* an artwork and as the artwork it is. (An indiscernible feature, on Danto's account.) Goodman fails to explain (and, on the evidence, cannot explain) just how the generic concept of an artwork can be defined in terms neutral, and hospitable, to the distinction between the autographic and the allographic.

4. Ibid., 42–44.

Even *if* it should be true (though it may be disputed, in music as well as literature) that, *once* we recognize particular literary and musical artworks (however we do that), they may be treated allographically, *that* goes no distance toward disjoining the allographic from the autographic. Even the denial of musical and literary forgery (in Goodman's sense) depends on attenuating the autographic features of the originals. There's the deeper import of Goodman's distinction. But with the collapse of the autographic/allographic disjunction goes Goodman's entire theory of art.

"There is no such thing as a forgery of Gray's elegy," Goodman says.[5] "There are, indeed, compositions fairly purporting to be by Haydn as there are paintings falsely purporting to be by Rembrandt; but of the *London Symphony,* unlike the *Lucretia,* there can be no forgeries."[6] Of course Goodman presupposes that a musical composition depends on a composer's producing an entirely adequate score from which "authentic" performances can always be determined. But he fails to consider music that is not scored at all or is provisionally or interpretively scored (or edited) by different hands, so that there may not be any single set of (allographically) discernible properties that count as the properties of a particular work. In fact, it is very difficult to imagine how a nominalist like Goodman could possibly rest his case on allographically relevent properties. (I shall come back to that.)

In any case, the problem plainly arises among, say, Dürer's etchings (autographic artworks, to be sure); and if it does, then analogues can easily be supplied in musical and literary cases. If so, then the whole point of Goodman's argument about the detection of forgeries by perceptual means fails and Danto's amusing cases (the red squares) draw us on to the inevitable conclusion that what we count *as* artworks depends on how we view the history of their production, including artists' intentions (where, and to whatever extent, available). Once you grant that much, forgery becomes a minor issue and the allographic is seen to depend on prior autographic considerations. (This affects in the deepest way our theory of music scores and dance notations. It's not so much that *some* literary or musical works can't be forged; it's rather that *others* can be.)

The argument is complicated, I must warn you, because precisely what undermines Goodman's thesis is not available in an entirely coherent way to Danto; although it is also true that what Danto has hit on here (the

5. Goodman, *Languages of Art,* 114.

"indiscernibility" issue) *does* indeed confound Goodman's claim. Goodman cannot justify his unsupported thesis: viz., *that* a perceptual difference between real and forged works will eventually be made out; but, for his part, Danto cannot reconcile *that* fact with his own account of perceptual indiscernibility. There's a pretty pass.

The effective argument against Goodman—not Danto's argument—is that artworks *are* autographic, even if, once admitted, questions like that of forgery can (if we choose) be dismissed in music and literature along allographic lines. But in spite of that (if it is conceded), Goodman's more important notions—functioning as an artwork, notationality, style, the distinction of "aesthetic" properties—are themselves all features (against Goodman's claim) of the dependency of the allographic on the autographic. These and other matters—notably, conditions on the objective interpretation of artworks (including music and literature)—are profoundly occupied with intensionally complex intentional considerations. (Call these autographic if you like, though the original disjunction will have lost its purpose.)

I am persuaded that Goodman's insistence on the discernible resolution of the forgery issue is intended to minimize our reliance on autographic (or intentional) difficulties even among the autographic arts; hence, is intended to minimize (or eliminate) the intentional threat to the allographic arts—by way of a completely extensional treatment of perceptual properties that might otherwise have been inten*t*ionally (or inten*s*ionally) troublesome, style for instance. Once artworks are construed autographically (apart from the matter of forgery), once the allographic is seen not to be a co-equal alternative for individuating and identifying artworks, the whole point of Goodman's theory begins to unravel.

You may recall that Goodman explicitly weighs the parallel between performing a piece of music (in various ways) and drawing prints from the same plate ("however much [the prints] may differ in color and amount of ink" and the like), but finally rejects the convergence between the autographic and the allographic.[6] But if he had been familiar with the editing and splicing of music tapes either in the way Glenn Gould has publicly preferred or in the way pop music can now be (and is sometimes) "composed," he might have thought better of the autographic possibilities of forging music. Or of literature. What would Goodman have made of

6. Ibid., 112.

Thomas Chatterton's or Thomas MacPherson's (Ossian) forgeries? At any rate, this certainly shows that Goodman was protecting his theory (at considerable cost) from anticipated difficulties when he remarked that "one notable difference between paintings and music is that the composer's work is done when he has written the score, even though the performances are the end-products, while the painter has to finish the picture."[7] *That* this is or is not so is itself a profoundly autographic question, which Goodman resolves unconvincingly (in fact, in an essentialist spirit). My sense is that Goodman hopes, by such means, to dampen the importance of intensional (really: "Intentional") complications affecting notationality, style, and "aesthetic" properties. But the effort cannot succeed. Certainly, he fails to take into account the technological innovations that have altered contemporary music beyond *any* of the familiar constraints scores might once have been thought to impose on musical identity, hence on the ontology of the arts in general.[8]

You see this very clearly in the matter of the concept of style. *If*, say, style *is* "autographic," in that it cannot be fully characterized in terms that ignore the historical *Geist* of an age or society, then of course style, even in music or (notoriously) in dance, cannot be rightly captured in any purely notational (or extensional) way. Once you grant that, then Goodman's semiotic treatment of the arts fails, because of an excessive confidence in the extensional resources of notationality—that is, because of a doubtful assurance that "aesthetic" properties do in fact lend themselves to such notational treatment. Still, to insist on that is hardly to dismiss a semiotic treatment of the arts; it is only to oblige semiotics to come to terms with its own intensional complexities.

Goodman is curiously weak on the question of style. It hardly plays a role in *Languages of Art,* where it might have counted as a serious challenge to the neat disjunction between the autographic and the allographic. It surfaces in *Ways of Worldmaking,* but it is noticeably slack there and much more tentative than would be acceptable if, indeed, the treatment of style were construed as posing a challenge to Goodman's overall views on notationality, exemplification, the scope of autographic considerations, and the most important "aesthetic" properties. What Goodman says about

7. Ibid., 118.
8. Ibid., 114. See Glenn Gould, "The Prospects of Recording," in *The Glenn Gould Reader,* ed. Tim Page (New York: Vintage, 1990).

notation (in dance, particularly) and about style shows his intentions fairly plainly.[9] "The function of a score," he says—he is thinking of Labanotation as well as the scoring of Western music—"is to specify the essential properties a performance must have to belong to the work; the stipulations are only of certain aspects and only within certain degrees. All other variations are permitted; and the differences among performances of the same work, even in music, are enormous."[10] He immediately applies the doubtful thesis to dance notation. "The significant issue," he says, "is whether in terms of notational language we can provide real definitions that will identify a dance in its several performances, independently of any particular history of production"—in effect, allographically rather than autographically.[11]

Goodman is sanguine but cautious here. But, of course, *if* style cannot be freed from a "particular history of production" or author's intentions or, more generally, from the larger Intentional features of period practices that individual authors or composers may assimilate unawares, then the entire notion of notationality will be seen to be ultimately tethered autographically, even where, provisionally, somewhat allographic criteria help us to count particular performances as performances of this or that particular work.

Consider the largest objections. For one, it is perfectly clear, on general logical grounds, that reference, denotation, identification and reidentification, *cannot* be captured in principle by *any* merely predicative means. The point was long ago remarked by Leibniz, who of course hastened to add that, in his benevolence, God would not have permitted two numerically distinct things to possess the same attributes.[12] (Leibniz included more than general attributes—in fact, everything that befell a thing—as its attributes.) The error that Leibniz remarked so gracefully is precisely the puzzle Duns Scotus faces in developing his doctrine of *haecceitas:* that is, whether in effect "this-ness" is a quiddity. (Scotus finds no grounds for affirming that it is or is not discernible, but he does not draw its most

9. For an inkling of the extraordinary technological possibilities in the contemporary musical and visual arts, see the special issue, "Perspectives on the Arts and Technology" *Journal of Aesthetics and Art Criticism 55*, guest editor, Patrick Maynard (1997).

10. Goodman, *Languages of Art*, 212.

11. Ibid.

12. See H. G. Alexander, ed., *The Leibniz-Clarke Correspondence* (Manchester: Manchester University Press, 1956), fifth letter.

important implications. He apparently believes it is not discernible in mortal life!) It surfaces again in our time in Quine's *Word and Object* and can be eluded by Goodman only if he concedes that the allographic use of scores is logically designed to serve whatever prior independent denotative and individuative competences may be counted on—which, in context, cannot be other than autographic. Second, there is no known solution for the cognitive grasp of predicative similarity (which scores require) except would-be Platonist solutions (which no one knows how to make operational), or *lebensformlich* solutions regarding the sharing of collective practices (which are too informal to be strictly allographic, which are never criterial, which are always subject to historical drift and historical salience). Furthermore, as a nominalist, as an opponent of "Platonism," Goodman undercuts whatever credibility he might have called into play in support of a strictly allographic treatment of perceptual properties.

Again, in speaking of music, Goodman says that "the verbal language of tempos is not notational. The tempo words [e.g., *allegro molto*] cannot be integral parts of a score insofar as the score serves the function of identifying a work from performance to performance. . . . On the other hand, metronomic specifications of tempo do, under obvious restrictions and under a system universally requiring them, qualify as notational and may be taken as belonging to the score as such."[13] But of course this trades on the false precision of predicative means in settling identity and on a confusion of the acoustic (entirely physical) and perceptual (experienced) properties of sound. It pretends to disjoin the autographic from the allographic. It can only suppose its charge to be defensible (the denial of "tempo words" *and* author's intentions *and* period style affecting tempo) *if* the disjunction holds (which, of course, is contrary to the facts). Furthermore, *if* one allowed the more informal use of tempo distinctions, then even tonal distinctions would on occasion be affected by that tolerance; for there is no way to make tempo and perceived tone altogether disjoint.

You begin to see the extent to which Goodman maneuvers his account of notationality in ways intended to maximize the prospects of a thoroughly extensional semiotics. This is the reason his relative neglect of style (in dance in particular) is so telling. For, once something like balletic style is canonized, we may be able (within limits dictated by autographic considerations) to treat "style" allographically. But the same can hardly be

---

13. Goodman, *Languages of Art*, 185–86.

said of the more transient and idiosyncratic styles of modern dance (outside the classical ballet—perhaps also, outside Martha Graham's somewhat frozen stylistics); style remains discernible for all that. Goodman has no answer. (There is none.)

Music and dance notation are inextricably autographic, in spite of allographic approximations. Even metronomic fixities are little more than approximative measures (short, say, of the *tours de force* of Penderewski). Goodman cannot possibly make his case: first, because he is plainly legislating in a musical way for the sake of his extensional policy regarding the numerical identity and essential nature of music, literature, and allied arts; and, second, because notation governs attributes (or predicables), and predicables cannot determine numerical identity and cannot themselves be fixed essentially (as any nominalist ought to agree). The idea that scores determine numerical identity or the essential nature of artworks of the pertinent kinds, or even the salient "aesthetic" properties of particular works, is utterly unpromising and defies actual usage.

It is surprisingly difficult to tease out what, definitionally, Goodman intends by his account of style. It's clear enough that "the discernment of style is [intended to count as] an integral aspect of the understanding of works of art and the worlds they represent."[14] But *if* music and dance are to count as allographic arts, then, on this advice, style must be able to be characterized in relatively precise notational ways. But, on the evidence, it cannot be; it cannot be, if style is, as I suggest, insuperably autographic.

Whatever seeming success we imagine we have in capturing, notationally, the style of a Twyla Tharp or a Louis Armstrong is rather like the sense in which an improvisional act in ordinary human circumstances can be *computationally simulated after the fact* but without assurance that *that* "notation" can also be counted on to anticipate the stylistically "recurrent" (but perceptually distinctive) features of an artist's "signature" in further work. Style is inherently informal, in the precise sense that we *expect* it to evolve in unpredictable ways that will serve to establish *what to count,* retrospectively, as "recurrent" (in a style) in the work of distinctly creative artists. It is always grounded in prior denotative ways involving artist, period, intention, mode of production, and the like—hence, autographically.

14. Nelson Goodman, *Ways of Worldmaking* (Indianapolis: Hackett, 1978), 40. My own reading of Goodman's treatment persuades me that he is countering much of Danto's account, as it eventually appeared in *The Transfiguration of the Commonplace,* chap. 7.

Goodman seems to support contentions of these sorts, but he obviously means them in a firmer allographic way than is actually possible. So he says: "Style has to do exclusively with the symbolic functioning of a work as such ["and only as such"] . . . Basically, the style consists of those features of the symbolic functioning of a work that are characteristic of author, period, place, or school. [But, he goes on,] unlike some other definitions, ours does not rest upon an artist's intentions. What counts are properties symbolized, whether or not the artist chose or is even aware of them."[15] The qualification is as old as hermeneutics, of course. It appears already in the mature Schleiermacher and remains (in genre and period considerations) as "autographic" as an author's specific intentions ever are. (In fact, it *is* treated "intentionally" in the hermeneut's sense.)

You will find, in Leonard Meyer's well-known definition of style (primarily intended to range over the history of Western music and notably respectful of, and influenced by, Goodman's *Languages of Art*), the following formulation: "Style is a replication of patterning, whether in human behavior or in the artifacts produced by human behavior, that results from a series of choices made within some set of constraints."[16] This has something of Goodman's semiotic emphasis, of course, though (against Goodman) it specifically features artists' intentions. Meyer favors a "statistical" approach, but he tempers it at once in ways that clearly bear on its "allographic" possibilities and subordinates its provisional promise to deeper "autographic" considerations. So he remarks (not altogether explicitly in the pertinent respects):

[First,] as Eugene Narmour has pointed out, "the higher [the style analyst] ascends in the epistemological hierarchy—from the study of the works of one composer to the study of a genre or a period— the more he must generalize"; and hence the smaller effect, whether pro or con, any particular instance will have on the analyst's hypothesis.

Second, as in other fields, hypotheses about style gain credibility through their "fit" with other facets of theory—for instance, with hypotheses about the constraints of related parameters. And, as has

15. Goodman, *Ways of Worldmaking*, 35–36.
16. Leonard B. Meyer, *Style and Music: Theory, History, and Ideology* (Philadelphia: University of Pennsylvania Press, 1989), 3.

often been remarked in connection with scientific theories, discrepant data are often disregarded for the sake of an elegant hypothesis with broad explanatory capability.[17]

More generally, there is reason to think that Goodman's strong doctrine of "notationality" conflates (perhaps confuses) the putative physical marks of an artwork or performance with whatever perceived (or "psychological") marks may be ascribed. Diana Raffman, who pursues the matter in the most sustained way I am acquainted with, shows convincingly, for instance, "that Goodman's theoretical asceticism defeats his own analysis at certain places, blinding him to the fact that artworks and artistic activity in general are shot through with the 'practical limitations' of human *psychology*. In particular, Goodman's treatment of certain musical markings as *semantically dense* is hobbled by the finite character of auditory perception."[18]

This is a remarkably neat and perceptive distinction. What Goodman means by "semantically dense" directly affects his systematic account of notationality. "The final requirement for a notational system," he says, "is *semantic finite differentiation*," which, roughly, marks the articulation of a "semantically dense" system in a way that "provides for an infinite number of characters with compliance-classes so ordered that between each two there is a third."[19]

Raffman offers the absolutely telling (and obvious) observation that, in developing his view of musical notation, "Goodman must mean . . . in distinguishing the performance [of a work] *taken as* an instance of [that] work from the performance *taken as* a sound-event [an acoustic event], . . .that the *compliance-classes* of the supplementary markings [*fortissimo*, say] are sound-event classes as such. But then [she continues] the claim that the performance [as sound-event] complies with the supplementary markings is simply false. The performance taken as a sound-event is the performance taken as an acoustic event, i.e. as a sequence of fre-

17. Meyer, *Style and Music*, 59–60. Here, ironically, Meyer specifically cites Goodman in favor of his reading, which is to say, somewhat against Goodman himself in the matter of style.

18. Diana Raffman, "Goodman, Density, and the Limits of Sense Perception," in *The Interpretation of Music: Philosophical Essays*, ed. Michael Krausz, (Oxford: Clarendon, 1993), 216.

19. Goodman, *Languages of Art*, 152–53.

quencies, intensities, attack envelopes, etc. The supplementary markings, on the other hand, specify values along *perceptual* parameters—pitches, dynamics, articulations, and so forth. In short, Goodman confuses sound-event classes *as such* with perceptual-event classes, and wrongly identifies the former as compliance-classes of the supplementary markings."[20]

On this issue, Raffman finds: "the theoretical possibility of a dense ordering of pitches would seem to require the theoretical possibility of an infinitely sensitive discriminatory capacity, and *that* seems to amount to a 'change of subject'—we are no longer talking about perception, or about *human* perception anyway. One wants to say: a 'perception' *sans* discriminatory threshold does not merit the name."[21] She herself goes on to attempt to save what can be saved by invoking a (cognitivist) "musical grammar" that is largely "stored unconsciously" and answers to "psychological" discrimination; but this (even if granted) would (she warns) still adversely affect the idea of perceptual "density."[22] "Semantic density," of course, is one of Goodman's essential marks ("symptoms," as he cautiously puts the point) of the "aesthetic."[23]

There are other difficulties with Goodman's view of the aesthetic—notably with his account of "exemplification"; but there is no need to pursue the matter further. (I have touched on it in the preceding chapter.) Style, to return to the motivating theme, is clearly impossible to capture by "acoustic" marks (in music) or bodily movements (in dance) or in any promisingly extensional way. This is of course the ineluctable challenge of the interpretive puzzle set by scores of any kind. In the strict sense in which he intends his very spare account, therefore, Goodman cannot possibly succeed.

II

Turn, then, to Danto.

I have already credited Danto with effectively challenging Goodman's insistence on the perceptual discernibility of the difference between a forg-

---

20. Raffman, "Goodman, Density, and the Limits of Perception," 219. Compare Goodman, *Languages of Art,* 179–92.

21. Raffman, "Goodman, Density, and the Limits of Perception," 221.

22. See ibid., 224–26.

23. Goodman, *Languages of Art,* 252–53.

ery and a genuine artwork. Danto uses the occasion, of course, to introduce the more general puzzle of distinguishing between different artworks and between an artwork and a "mere real thing." Given Goodman's failure to distinguish between the acoustic (physical) and "perceptual" ("psychological") properties of musical works, it seems reasonable to suppose that Goodman wishes to restrict the sense of the "perceptual"—or at least to give pride of place—to what is sensorily (or physically) discriminable. He restricts the descriptive and aesthetic importance of an artwork's properties to whatever (in Raffman's terms, say) is "psychologically" perceived—discounts whatever otherwise bears on history, style, genre, artist's intention, whatever cannot actually be restricted or reduced to the "physically" or sensorily discerned. Certainly, Goodman's error about "semantic density" supports the conjecture. But, now, by an extraordinary turn, Danto supports the opposite doctrine: *he* holds that what distinguishes artworks as such is completely indiscernible by perceptual means! That may not be believed.

To be perfectly frank, I find this a kind of comic minuet. Goodman insists that there is always (eventually) a discernible difference marking a genuine artwork, but it is restricted to what is no more than sensorily discernible; and Danto insists that what distinguishes one artwork from another or from things that are not artworks at all is something that is not in principle perceptually (sensorily) discernible. In this sense, Goodman begs the question about what it is to perceive artworks, and Danto claims (as we shall see) that there are (there exist), as such, no artworks—hence, trivially, none that can be perceived. Apparently, for Danto, it is only by the *rhetorical imputation of certain nondiscernible "attributes"* that we are ever justified in treating "mere real things" (things that are *not* artworks) *as* artworks. *Nothing really exists as an artwork.* Goodman admits real artworks, but loses (or diminishes) the run of their perceptual properties; and Danto saves what we ordinarily mean to include as the distinctive properties of artworks, but he voluntarily abandons the existence of artworks as such, and, with that, the literal relevance of ever speaking of the perceptual discernibility of *"their"* properties.

I'm reasonably confident that you will oppose this characterization. It does seem preposterous. After all, you are bound to remind me, Danto *is* an art critic, writes and speaks about artworks all the time. I don't deny it. I say only that if you locate Danto's theory of *what* he writes and speaks about when he speaks of art, you will find that he implies—and here and there he effectively affirms—that *artworks simply don't exist.* So I insist that I *am* being respectful of the precise distinction Danto is at pains to make clear—notably, in his "Artworld" paper and in *The Transfiguration of the Commonplace.* I suggest that in all of his other writings Danto never retreats from what he says here, never offers anything ampler than what these two texts contain.

Let me put before you a somewhat longish passage from the "Artworld" paper, possibly one of the best-known of Danto's statements, certainly the single most explicit of his comments on the "ontology" of art. (You must remember that, in criticizing Goodman, Danto had prioritized the "ontology" of art over Goodman's question about authentic art.) Here is what Danto says—I think we need the entire text:

> There is an *is* that figures prominently in statements concerning artworks which is not the *is* of either identity or predication; nor is it the *is* of existence, of identification, or some special *is* made up to serve a philosophic end. Nevertheless, it is in common usage, and is readily mastered by children. It is the sense of *is* in accordance with which a child, shown a circle and a triangle and asked which is him and which his sister, will point to the triangle saying, "That is me"; or, in response to my question, the person next to me points to the man in purple and says "That one is Lear"; or in the gallery I point, for my companion's benefit, to a spot in the painting before us and say "That white dab is Icarus." We do not mean, in these instances, that whatever is pointed to stands for, or represents, what it is said to be, for the *word* "Icarus" stands for or represents Icarus; yet I would not in the same sense of *is* point to the word and say "That is Icarus." The sentence "That *a* is *b*" is perfectly compatible with "That *a* is not *b*" when the first employs this sense of *is* and the second employs some other, though *a* and *b* are used nonambiguously throughout. Often, indeed, the truth of the first *requires* the truth of the second. The first, in fact, is incompatible with "That *a* is not *b*" only when the *is* is used nonambiguously throughout. For want of a word I shall designate this the *is of artistic identification;* in each case in which it is used, the *a* stands for some specific physical property of, or physical part of, an object; and, finally, it is

a necessary condition for something to be an artwork that some part or property of it be designable by the subject of a sentence that employs this special *is*. It is an *is*, incidentally, which has near relatives in marginal and mythical pronouncements. (Thus, one *is* Quetzalcoatl; those *are* the Pillars of Hercules.)[24]

I find this admirably clear. I draw your attention, however, to two features of what Danto says. First, he says (in effect) that "That *a* is *b*" may be true, *in* the sense of the "*is* of artistic identification" *if and only if* "That *a* is not *b*" is true *in* (say) the sense of the "*is*" of existence and/or identity. I don't see how that can be gainsaid. Danto means that, in asserting the first, one is *never* speaking *of* what is, *as such,* real, but only "making" attributions (in the sense of the "*is* of artistic identification") *of what is, independently, real or exists* (but is *not* an artwork). Second, he says that one can speak in this way *only if,* in speaking *of* an artwork, one restricts what one is speaking *of* to what conforms with the "*is* of artistic identification" and *only if what* is "identified" in that sense *is* "some specific physical property of, or physical part of, an [existent] object [that is *not,* as such, an artwork]."

On the argument, denotative, referential, and identificatory discourse is confined to what exists (or is predicatively real with regard to what exists), in the sense in which physical objects exist. (Perhaps one may also speak thus in speaking of mythical or fictional entities; but, here, the point is that artworks are *not* fictional or mythical, though "they" are evidently akin. Or so it seems. Think of the Pillars of Hercules.) To speak of an artwork is, apparently, to speak *of a physical object* (again, there may be looser idioms to allow: to speak of diagrams, for example, or a utensil) and to treat such an object "imaginatively" by way of the "is" of artistic identification, to impute to it intentional properties (properties I call Intentional) that it does not and cannot possess. It is also, therefore, to speak of what *is perceptually discernible*—confined to the discernible properties of a physical object; hence, *never* to speak of the perceptually discernible properties of artworks, because, of course, there are no real properties beyond what, in the original physical object, is perceptually (really, sensorily) discernible. There's the point of Danto's objection to Goodman's treatment of forgery.

24. Arthur C. Danto, "The Artworld," *Journal of Philosophy* 61 (1964), 576–77.

But, now, Danto must pay a heavy price for his precision and agreeable humor: he's somehow lost the existence and reality of artworks! I don't deny that Danto is an opponent of sorts of physicalism and physical reductionism, though he is also plainly sympathetic toward physicalism or something very close to it. He does *not* hold, for instance, that the representational or expressive attributes usually ascribed (or imputed) to artworks are directly reducible to physical attributes. No, those "properties" are (only) "imaginatively" ascribed to physical objects, which themselves lack such properties. Nevertheless, although they are "imaginatively" ascribed, not real properties at all, they are also clearly analogous (perhaps more than analogous) to the usual attributions we make of ourselves. In Danto's sense, however, they are not perceptually discernible.

I find no clear sign in Danto's entire output that *he* believes that human *persons* or selves are "identified" like artworks (by way, say, of an alternative "*is* of cultural identification") when speaking of living human bodies (or the members of *Homo sapiens*). Of course, he could never hold such a view consistently, since *he* functions as an art critic! Or, of course, *if* history has a realist import among humans, as Danto also seems to hold.[25] But if so, then there are good reasons to suppose that *if* selves are real and have the intentionally complex (that is, Intentional) properties we ascribe to them (ourselves) in virtue of linguistic competence and the mastery of a culture and its history, it cannot but be extremely difficult (perhaps impossible) to hold that selves exist and have real properties but artworks and sentences do not. For, of course, artworks and sentences are "uttered" by us: they are our mode of expression—are real for at least that reason.

Certainly, our understanding human language *cannot* be characterized in terms of "mere" sensory perception; but if we "perceive" human discourse in some sense—hear it, for instance—then how can we deny that we "perceive" the performance of the actors *and* the speeches of the characters in a performance of *Hamlet?* I see no way to make sense of that, though I admit that the "world" of the play is not the real world in which actors do really "play" the parts of the characters of *Hamlet's* "world." If you agree, then I cannot see why something similar should not hold in painting and music. We train ourselves to "perceive" the imagina-

25. See Arthur C. Danto, *Narration and Knowledge* (New York: Columbia University Press, 1985).

tive "world" of particular artworks (Vermeer's *Lady Reading a Letter at an Open Window,* say) by learning to "perceive" *the actual painting in the real world.*

I must tell you that I take Danto's theory to be flatly incoherent. I shall come back to that. But, for the moment, I would like to have you agree with me—on textual grounds—that Danto believes that artworks don't exist, are not real entities, and therefore lack the Intentionally complex properties we impute to "them" (*whenever* we treat physical objects *as* artworks, by way of the "is of artistic identification"). Artworks cannot be physical objects, for the simple reason that the first "possess" (within the imaginative idiom of the "is of artistic identification") properties that the second really (and necessarily) lack. That begins to explain the sense in which, famously, Danto declares: "to see something as art requires something the eye cannot descry—an atmosphere of theory, a knowledge of the history of art, an artworld. . . . The artworld stands to the real world in something like the relationship in which the City of God stands to the Earthly City" (Danto means the actual earthly city, not the power that opposes the City of God, which, I assume, accords with the " 'is' of religious identification").[26]

Here, I think of a blackmail argument. Why (I ask myself) should dealers, galleries, museums buy and sell paintings at all if what Danto says is true *is* true? Surely, the great prices paid for Picassos and Van Goghs would be a very grave risk if paintings *were not real*—"ontologically," to favor Danto's idiom (though not his thesis). What should one make, then, of Danto's profession as an art critic? Surely, Goodman was right to air our worries about forgeries. The strange thing is that forgeries cannot even occur in Danto's world! That is a bit unsettling when you think of the recent charge against a would-be Van Gogh treatment of sunflowers. Too much would depend on the child's-play of the critic's rhetorical imagination.

But there's a stronger argument to be had that goes directly to the incoherence of Danto's theory. (I remind you, here, of the "lesser" incoherences that will have to be addressed in due course: those, for instance, involving the relationship between selves and artworks and those bearing on connoisseurship. I shall come back to them briefly.) You may recall that I reported Danto as saying, against Goodman, at the beginning of my

26. Danto, "The Artworld," 580, 582. The original has "decry" for "descry."

discussion: "it is not clear that concepts like 'work of art' and 'forgery' are translatable into sets of simple perceptual predicates." With what has just been cited from the "Artworld" paper, you see that, for Danto, "work of art" and "forgery" are not perceptual distinctions at all. But then, we face a puzzle that Danto cannot possibly resolve. *He* says that artworks and real things may be, are often, perceptually "indiscernible" from one another; *now,* it turns out, there's nothing *to* discern. It's not that the perceptual properties *of* artworks and "real" things are (may be) indiscernibly the same; it's rather that we are *never* perceptually confronted with more than the properties of real things—which preclude the "properties" of artworks. Of course. But if that's so, then *all* of Danto's famous puzzle cases evaporate. His indiscernibility charge *never rightly arises!* I hardly dare suppose you will accept this argument straight out. Bear with me.

"There was," Danto reminds us,

> a certain sense of unfairness felt at the time when Warhol piled the Stable Gallery full of his Brillo boxes, for the commonplace Brillo container was actually designed by an artist, an Abstract Expressionist driven by need into commercial art; and the question was why Warhol's boxes should have been worth $200 when that man's products were not worth a damn. Whatever explains this explains as well, why the primed canvas of Giorgione, in our first example [an imaginary examplar of a red square, primed by Giorgione in preparation for his "unrealized masterwork 'Conversazione Sacra',"] one of Danto's set of perceptually indiscernible red squares], fails to be an artwork though resembling in every respect the red expanses which are such.[27]

The clue he offers—it's a proper clue all right—is this: "the answer to the question has to be historical."[28] Yes, of course. But what I don't see is why, or the reason for insisting that, *if* the difference in the Warhol case is (metonymically) "historical," concerned with period and intention and the rest, that difference cannot be perceptual—*must not be perceptual.*

Danto begins the second chapter of *Transfiguration* thus: "That there

---

27. Danto, *Transfiguration,* 44; see 1.
28. Ibid. The clue is meant to do duty for a nest of related questions.

should exist indiscernible artworks—indiscernible at least with respect to anything the eye or ear can determine—has been evident from the array of red squares with which we began this discussion."[29] Fine. But if the eye (or better, *we*) cannot (by perceptual means) "determine" the *actual* or *real* "difference" between an artwork and a "mere real thing," then *we* cannot ever discern the real presence of an artwork; and if there *are* no artworks discerned as such, or if there are no artworks *period*, then indiscernibility never arises as a real puzzle. *If* artworks happen to be sensorily indiscernible from real things, but exist, then artworks *must* be discernible *in some sense;* and if there is *no* discernible difference that marks an artwork as really different from a thing that is not an artwork, then there are no artworks unless (following Leibniz's well-known account) artworks *are identical with "real" things.* (Which, on Danto's argument, is false.) Artworks cannot be real enough to be denoted and individuated if they are not real enough to have discernible properties *qua* art. That is Danto's *pons.*

On Danto's theory, artworks and physical objects can't be identical, for intentional (or, Intentional) properties are attributed to the first and denied the second. But if artworks are denoted, individuated, identified and re-identified, ascribed real properties, *in* the same world in which we exist, then *they* must exist—and, moreover, they must be perceivable in some robust sense. (You will have noticed that Danto actually uses the term "exist" in speaking of the Warhol.) But they cannot be thus denoted and bought and sold if they are not real. If they are real, if they really possess sensorily discriminable properties *as well as the nonsensory but perceivable, Intentionally complex properties* we usually adduce, then it is pointless to insist that "perception" should or can be confined in such a way as to exclude the discernibility of just what distinguishes artworks from mere real things. It would be much more natural to adjust the meaning of "perceive." There is no puzzle of the sort Danto invents: the trouble, rather, lies with anyone's supposing that the "perception" of an artwork should be confined in such a way that *seeing a painting* becomes impossible. (Why ever do we look at paintings, after all?)

I don't take these remarks to be knockdown arguments: not yet. But they do prepare the ground. They nag enough to force us to admit the utter arbitrariness of Danto's way of putting things. Can anyone rightly

29. Ibid., 33.

deny that when you *look at* a familiar Vermeer, you *see* ("looking" in the right way) the representation of a Dutch interior? Or that, *listening* to a Mozart sonata, you *hear* the sonata form, not merely the sensorily discernible sounds? Would Danto wish to drive us back to sense data? We may as well ask (with H. H. Price), whether anyone really sees a tomato on the table, or only tomato-ish patches of color about which one makes a clever constructive induction leading to other sense data?

The sensory perception of the physical world is every bit as theory-laden as the perception of artworks. But that does not mean that we do not see, in the visual sense, the Vermeer, or hear, in the auditory sense, the Mozart. The eye does not "descry" anything! *We* see with our eyes, and *we* hear with our ears.

When Danto says, "To see something as art requires something the eye cannot descry—an atmosphere of theory," what he says is either false (in the obviously intended sense of "see") or an obfuscation of that sense (in discounting the role theory plays in the perception of physical objects).

We do see painted representations of things. Any refusal to admit that we do will drive us to say that we never see anyone's *doing* anything, we see no more than "bodily movements" (or, sense data answering to them), which we imaginatively invest with the intentional features of human actions. If that were true, we would never hear speech: we would hear no more than sound. We would be driven back to something like Locke's argument and the mystery of ever coming to know anything about the public world (physical or cultural). I can only guess that Danto must have been uneasy (is still uneasy) about any realist reading of culturally formed properties (style, representationality, expressivity) or their perception. But there's no way to avoid the admission if, as seems clear, *he* admits a realism of selves and history.

I say you cannot disjoin the "ontologies" of selves and artworks, because, like language and action, artworks are the culturally apt *utterances* of culturally formed selves (ourselves). To be aware of, to perceive, the presence of a society of selves, to hear and respond to their speech, to participate in their common rituals, *entails* one's being able to perceive, by means of culturally informed sensory perception, the artworks they (we) produce as well.

All right. That should be enough on the side of sheer harangue. Now for the *reductio*. Here it is: the "sensory" indiscernibility of the difference between an artwork and some "mere real thing"[30] is (must be) internal to the common conceptual space in which artworks and mere real things *are* themselves differentiated. In that sense, artworks must be "discernible." They must be discernible *if,* contingently, they are on occasion sensorily indiscernible from other works or mere real things! The occasional indiscernibility between two would-be *artworks* (say, a painting and a forgery of it or two of Danto's imaginary paintings that look sensorily indistinguishable as painted red squares) presupposes that *we are, in fact, comparing paintings.* But if we are, we will already have identified the pairs in question *as* paintings—and then their local indiscernibility will not affect, will indeed presuppose, their discernibility *qua* artworks. "Indiscernibility" signifies indiscernibility relative to things of determinate kinds; it provides no more than a distinction interior to a discourse that already concedes a larger discernibility—within which of course the first makes sense.[31]

I don't deny that, often, one has to learn a good deal of art history in order to perceive a particular artwork for what it is. Danto makes a good case for that in perceiving Warhol's *Brillo Box.* But it hardly follows that, in perceiving artworks (as in perceiving speech and action), one *adds* something entirely extra, something altogether different from, what is already present in what "the eye . . . descr[ies]"—parts of "an atmosphere of theory, a knowledge of the history of art, an artworld." No. Sensory perception is always and already freighted with conceptual elements of just these sorts (even if not specifically what is required, say, in order to perceive the Warhol properly). There in no mere "sensory" perception that we can report, except what we agree to abstract from the culturally freighted perceptual reportings that we normally learn to make.

Here, Danto makes precisely the same mistake Goodman makes (in conflating the acoustic and the perceived properties of music) but for another reason. No doubt, "a knowledge of the history of art" cannot, during perception, be located in any way among the physical changes in the retina, but that has nothing to do with "perceiving" *Brillo Box.* The "indiscernibility" alleged is to be found (if found at all) in the space of

---

30. Bear in mind the contrastive title of the first chapter of Danto's *Transfiguration:* "Works of Art and Mere Real Things."

31. I examine this matter more closely in "A Closer Look at Danto's Account of Art and Perception," *British Journal of Aesthetics* 40 (2000).

physical changes in the activated organ of the eye—*not* in full-blown perception. It has nothing to do with ("sensorily") perceiving the (physical) differences *between Brillo Box* and a "mere" Brillo box (or between Warhol's *Brillo Box* and Mike Bidlo's *Brillo Box*).

I must say in all candor that Danto ducks the ontological issue *he* raises against Goodman. That is hard to believe, because, after all, he does challenge Goodman on the issue and because he did author the "Artworld" paper. But he published the paper as a promissory note, which he has yet to redeem. You cannot find an ontology of art in Danto's work, unless it comes to the thesis that artworks simply don't exist. But think again of Danto's distinction between the "is" of identity or of existence and the "is" of "artistic identification." The two uses are utterly different (though that's not to say their separate uses may not affect one another). The "is" of existence (*a fortiori,* the usual use of the "is" of identity) is denotative, implicates the individuation and identity of particular things; whereas the "is" of "artistic identification" is obviously predicative, though not straightforwardly so. On Danto's account, it cannot be predicative in the usual sense; for it introduces Intentional attributes, and the "real" things on which it operates clearly lack such properties. Hence, "predication" in accord with the "is" of "artistic identification" is "imaginative"—not intended literally—on pain on contradiction. (I have been using the epithet "imaginative" as a stand-in for "rhetorical" and "metaphoric." That will become clearer very shortly.)

It would be a category mistake to attribute to intention-free real things real intentional properties. Hence, it must be done (if done at all) "imaginatively"—metaphorically, figuratively, rhetorically. There is no other way. But if so, then it follows at once, since physical things are real and lack intentional properties, and since the intentional (or Intentional) properties "predicated" by way of the "is" of "artistic identification" are not (cannot be) the actual properties of *such* things, that *there are no artworks that are real.* I hesitate to offer Danto my own solution—that is, a doctrine favoring physically embodied but culturally emergent (real) entities.[32] But it is a solution that links artworks and selves, that (*contra* Danto) accepts in the frankest way the thesis of cultural realism.

---

32. See, for instance, Joseph Margolis, *Historied Thought, Constructed World: A Conceptual Primer for the Turn of the Millennium* (Berkeley and Los Angeles: University of California Press, 1995).

I do find that Danto favors a realism of persons or selves. I see no evidence that he views selves as fictions or (as I maintain) cultural artifacts distinct, but not separable, from the biologically demarcated members of *Homo sapiens*. Even on that slim view, what (through cultural means) selves learn to "utter" in the way of language and action cannot fail to be predicatively real. Existent entities cannot fail to have real properties answering to what is characteristically true of them. But if that is so, then since, as painters and musicians, selves "utter" artworks in the same general way they utter speech and action, artworks must be real; and if they are real, there cannot be any conceptual barrier against admitting real artifacts resulting from such utterance and possessing the properties thus uttered. But that is what we take artworks to be.

If you allow the argument, then there is no need for a special "*is* of artistic identification." It is quite enough to admit artworks as a special kind of entity. For then, to predicate a representational or expressive property of Michelangelo's *Pietà*, say, is to make a perfectly straightforward literal predication. There's nothing left over for the special predicative work of "artistic identification." The *only* possible reason for featuring such an effort would be to draw attention to the fact that such "predication" is not meant literally (because of course, artworks are not real entities). The difference between the *is* of existence or identity and the *is* of artistic identification is, on the argument before us, nothing more than the difference between the *is* of existence and the *is* of predication. If Danto means something more, he must say what it is. (I don't believe that what he has in mind can be recovered coherently.)

I shall risk one final passage from Danto, which (I hope) will collect in one place all the complexities of his doctrine. I think it is fair to say that Danto believes himself to have been helped to grasp the difference between an artwork and a "mere real thing" by Wittgenstein's well-known question about the difference between raising my arm and my arm's rising. I cannot say that Danto subscribes to Wittgenstein's solution. He does not. But he does find that similar bodily movements may be linked to very different human actions in much the same way as indiscernibly different "red squares" may, as in his well-known thought-experiment, be found in very different artworks. Danto actually says: "The difference between a basic action and a mere bodily movement is paralleled in many ways by the differences between an artwork and a mere thing, and the subtractionistic query [Wittgenstein's] may be matched with another one here, which asks what is left over when we subtract the red square of canvas from 'Red Square' [one of the imaginary paintings of Danto's set of indiscernibly different paintings]."[33]

There are two lessons to be drawn from this: I shall come to them in a moment. But bear in mind that Danto had employed the same theme, in an earlier volume (*Analytical Philosophy of Action*), which he applies here in some remarks about Giotto's treatment of the life of Christ, in the Arena Chapel. His point, here, is that in six panels of the Arena, Giotto represents Christ with a raised arm but performing six different actions. Of the series, Danto says: "Since the raised arm is invariantly present, these performative differences [on Christ's part] must be explained through variations in context, and while it may be true context alone will not constitute the differences and that we must invoke Christ's intentions and purposes, still, we cannot overestimate the extent to which context penetrates purpose."[34]

Danto believes that Wittgenstein's answer to his own question is, effectively "zero," which he (Danto) does not accept. He opposes Wittgenstein (and, therefore, the counterpart) solution regarding artworks because *he* thinks that it would commit us to an identity between bodily movement and action and between "material object" and artwork.[35] I share Danto's objection, whether or not it happens to provide an accurate reading of Wittgenstein. But if you look carefully at what Danto says about the Giotto panels, you will see that, in opposing the identity claim, he assigns the differences among the actions (involving the same bodily movement) to the contribution of the encompassing context that we independently supply.

The implication (for Danto) is this: first, that a *bodily movement and its accompanying context are separable:* for the one lacks intentional (Intentional) features and the other is cast essentially in Intentional terms; and, second, that *action is nothing more than the "transfiguration" (not "transformation") of a bodily movement by its being imaginatively "identified" in an appropriate context.* This strikes me as unlikely, unnecessary, counterintuitive, ultimately incoherent, hardly reconcilable with the usual flu-

33. Danto, *Transfiguration*, 5.

34. Ibid., 4. Danto is quoting himself from *Analytical Philosophy of Action* (Cambridge: Cambridge University Press, 1973).

35. See Danto, *Transfiguration*, 4–5.

ency of cultural life, and no more than an odd form of dualism regarding nature and culture.

Danto's solution requires that *context* be objectively assigned "real things" that lack intentionally freighted cultural properties—by culturally apt selves, who of course themselves inhabit an Intentionalized world. (This, now, obviously makes problematic the realist standing of an action: Is Christ's *raising* his arm a real action *he* performs, or is it a rhetorical predication *we* make—and who are *we?*—of the physical movement of his arm? There is no coherent escape from this dilemma.) I have already aired my objection to affirming a realism of selves and denying realist standing to whatever speech, action, or art they utter. A simple alternative to Danto's theory might go like this: actions are real, are embodied in bodily movements, are uttered in accord with the enabling cultural practices of our society, and, as a result, really do possess and exhibit (discernibly) Intentional properties. I cannot see any good reason to oppose such a reading.

The short truth is that Danto views art as the *rhetorical* effect of an artist's treating some "real thing" metaphorically. Thus, at the end of *Transfiguration,* he says of *Brillo Box:* "the work vindicates its claim to be art by propounding a brash metaphor: the brillo-box-as-work-of-art. And in the end this transfiguration of a commonplace object transforms nothing in the artworld. It only brings to consciousness the structures of art which, to be sure, required a certain historical development before that metaphor was possible."[36] The "structure of art" is, then, in the mind of the artist (or "percipient"), *not* in any public artwork: it is an imaginative "context" *we* bring to certain "mere real things." But what Danto says here is either not ontology at all but a reminder of the sense in which understanding art is tantamount to understanding ourselves; or, if it is ontology, then it confirms what I have already said, namely, that for Danto, artworks simply don't exist.

I rest my case.

---

36. Ibid., 208.

3

THE ENDLESS FUTURE OF ART

I

The extraordinary thing about the question of art's future, of whether art *has* a future, whether it is coming to an *end,* whether indeed we can foresee its *death*—all variations of the same question—is its instant complexity. It is not a question like that now-answered question, "Does the Soviet empire have a future?" Or that still-pending question, "Does the American empire have a future?" There is no simple fact of the matter to collect. To answer pertinently, you must say what art is, or how it functions, or what the conditions are for its continued vigor and fascination; and to say what that involves is, perhaps, to say what it is to be human. These are not ordinary questions. Familiar ones, certainly, but not ordinary, not like those endlessly many questions that can be answered without ever saying (or asking): "It all depends on what you mean by art," or "What *do* you mean by 'art'?" And even then, the question may be taken in what seems to be the same sense, only to be answered in wildly different ways; or, it may be taken in rather different senses at the start, which may, nevertheless, slip past the conceptual censor in appearing to be effectively the same.

For example, to move at once beyond the usual professional coyness: Arthur Danto, who has set the question in our own time as unavoidably as any, warns us that, in attempting an answer, we must suppose that "art has the kind of history within which the question of its coming to an end makes sense."[1] Just so. He supplies a broadly Hegelian sense (he offers several other smaller possibilities that lead more quickly to his own conclusion); but, in that Hegelian sense, he explains: "History ends with the advent of self-consciousness, or better, self-knowledge"; and, correspondingly and ineluctably: "Art ends with the advent of its own philosophy."[2] There you have an answer, if not *the* answer:

> So the great drama of history [Danto continues], which in Hegel [in the *Phenomenology*] is a divine comedy of the mind, can end in a moment of final self-enlightenment, where the enlightenment consists in itself. The historical importance of art then lies in the fact that it makes philosophy of art possible and important. Now if we look at the art of our recent past in these terms, grandiose as they are, what we see is something which depends more and more upon theory for its existence as art, so that theory is not something external to a world it seeks to understand, so that in understanding its object it has to understand itself. But there is another feature exhibited by these later productions which is that the objects approach zero as their theory approaches infinity, so that virtually all there is at the end *is* theory, art having finally become vaporized in a dazzle of pure thought about itself, and remaining, as it were, solely as the object of its own theoretical consciousness.
>
> If something like this view has the remotest chance of being plausible, it is possible to suppose that art had come to an end. Of course, there will go on being art-making. But art-makers, living in what I like to call the post-historical period of art, will bring into existence works which lack the historical importance or meaning we have for a very long time come to expect. The historical stage of art is done with when it is known what art is and means. The artists have made the way open for philosophy, and the moment

1. Arthur C. Danto, "The End of Art," *The Philosophical Disenfranchisement of Art* (New York: Columbia University Press, 1986), 107.
2. Ibid.

has arrived at which the task must be transferred finally into the hands of philosophers.[3]

This remarkable statement, which one must take care not to ridicule—so as not to appear to be no more than a moral zealot instantly alerted to action by Danto's hubris—justifies its being cited at length, even if unceremoniously. It certainly confirms that the original question is no simple matter, and it elegantly demonstrates the profound sense in which its answer may well be god-like (that is, Hegelian or Dantonian), though its obvious extravagance may advise us that that reading should be avoided if possible.

Now, Danto *sees* that art has come to a crisis. The crisis is *not* an artifact of some in-group critics' manufacture. The question of art's future or end does not arise, he says, "outside the framework of a philosophy of history"; but the academic tone of the question is fortunately offset by the "urgency of art's future," which is "somehow [perceptibly] raised from within the artworld itself, which can be seen today as having lost any historical direction . . . the concept of art [it seems, it certainly seems] is internally exhausted."[4] When you think about this carefully, you realize of course that it means that the "end" of art's history, even the "posthistorical" period of art, is a part of art's history, something akin perhaps to an Escher drawing of a hand drawing its drawing of doing just that.

Victor Burgin, by contrast, who comes to his own settled version of the question at about the same time Danto does, though he apparently tested it already in the late seventies, sees the matter quite differently. Burgin was apparently confronted by the announcement of a *"crisis* in British art" at the very moment of being invited to speak, in 1977, at a conference on the topic, in London, sponsored by the Institute of Contemporary Arts. "I never did learn," he says, "what the 'crisis in British Art' was; nor, I suspect, did anyone else. In retrospect, some ten years on, I now see the ICA event, the brainchild of three British art critics, as a textbook example of what psychoanalysis terms *projection;* the crisis sensed by these critics was not in 'art' but in *criticism itself.*" Burgin goes on to cite approvingly

3. Ibid., 111. See Joseph Margolis, "The History of Art After the End of the History of Art," *What, After All, Is a Work of Art? Lectures in the Philosophy of Art* (University Park: The Pennsylvania State University Press, 1999).

4. Danto, "The End of Art," 84.

70

a remark made by Elizabeth Bruss, "retrospectively surveying the 'theory' explosion of the 1970s, [namely,] 'an increase of theoretical activity . . . arises whenever the function of criticism itself is in doubt'."[5]

Of course, on Burgin's view, Danto must be a self-selected pigeon; and on Danto's, Burgin must be blind to the Absolute Spirit's most intimate disclosures. Even their opening epigraphs convey the difference: Danto offers the line, "Art is dead," repeated often enough anonymously, but, now, determinately ascribed to the insistent utterance of one Marius de Zayas, which appeared already in 1912; and Burgin cites a correspondingly suitable line from Berthold Brecht: "The means must be asked what the end is." Burgin comes to the conclusion that *art theory* is dead, that is, a certain sort of theorizing—*not* art:

> "Art theory," understood as those interdependent forms of art history, aesthetics, and criticism which began in the Enlightenment and culminated in the recent period of "high modernism," is now at an end. In our present so-called "postmodern" era the *end* of art theory *now* is identical with the objectives of *theories of representations* in general: a critical understanding of the modes and means of symbolic articulation of our *critical* forms of sociality and subjectivity.[6]

In short, what Burgin manages to do is change the grammar of the questions: the "end-of-art" theory now becomes the end of "art-theory." By that device, Burgin transforms the question into one very much like the one about the end of the Soviet empire. But in doing that, he falls back, not altogether comfortably, to a know-nothing view of the relationship between art and critical theory.

He cannot be too sanguine about the latter question, for, if he were, he might become enmeshed in Danto's bramble—or in a theoretical bramble of his own. Burgin is suspicious of the executive role of art theory and theoretical criticism with respect to art; but, although he obviously favors a close examination of the relationship between art and its environing

5. Victor Burgin, "The End of Art Theory," in *The End of Art Theory: Criticism and Modernity* (Atlantic Highlands, N.J.: Humanities Press, 1986), 140–41. The line cited is from Elizabeth Bruss, *Beautiful Theories* (Baltimore: Johns Hopkins University Press, 1982), 32.
6. Burgin, "The End of Art Theory," 204.

culture and history, he is decidedly wary of any extended discussion of the theoretical relationship between art and culture or between art and history. Still, *we* know (and here, Danto has a point) that we cannot mark out such connections "outside the framework of a philosophy of history [or of culture or of criticism or of art]." It need not be the Hegelian monster Danto prefers, of course, but we must still risk the fatigue Elizabeth Bruss exhales.

I should add at once, however, to avoid misunderstanding, that Burgin *does* consider the *end* of art—the end of modernist art—in something like the sense in which the Soviet empire is at an end. But, in exploring that, he emphatically does not subscribe to the view that the process of art production that the modernists (preeminently, Clement Greenberg) had construed in their peculiarly narrow technological sense *is* coming to an end. It is certainly not coming to an end for those reasons (as perceived, say, by Danto, whom Burgin does not discuss) that first pass *through* Greenberg's or some other conceptual lens *to* the completed understanding of what art is all about. No, the older art that modernist *theories* deformed, by exclusive attention to the essentially "visual" technology of two-dimensional space, had and still has a deeper productive human function to perform— one that might be suggestively collected by calling attention "to the *politics of representation*" as opposed to the "'representation of politics'" or some other suitably conventional "object."[7] In this convincing sense, not only is the judgment that art is coming to its historical end (the end of its genuine history) challenged in its soul, but the very legibility of such a judgment is rendered utterly problematic.

Burgin opposes, therefore, two quite different sorts of history of art: the history of the "*art object*," which culminates in Greenberg's penultimately suicidal modernism, which, hardly incidentally, debases and alienates the representational function of art:[8] and the history of "*representations*" (which Burgin recommends, now enlarged by what he understands as "conceptual art," which (he says) "had a special relationship to this [art] object: it wanted to explode it."[9] "Art practice," he explains, "was no longer to be defined [on the second view] as an artisanal activity, a process

7. Victor Burgin, "The Absence of Presence: Conceptualism and Postmodernism," in *The End of Art Theory*, 39.

8. See Clement Greenberg, "Modernist Painting," *Arts Year Book* 4 (1961).

9. Burgin, "The Absence of Presence," 38.

of crafting fine objects in a given medium, it was rather to be seen as a set of operations performed in a *field* of signifying practices, perhaps centered on a medium but certainly not bounded by it."[10] So Burgin emphasizes, as a result, the primacy of representing the "political" (that is, whatever is of salient public interest in our day, but which cannot rightly be marginalized in Greenberg's manner) and, in catching up poststructuralist (rather than merely postmodernist) concerns, the "politics of representation." We need not follow Burgin in all this—we may if we wish—but his example demonstrates the ease with which the end-of-art theory is not merely resisted by appeal to disconfirmatory evidence but is actually exposed as no more than a cooked, "in" theory that ignores what is genuinely vital in the arts.

II

The issue at stake is not gossip, however. The answer to the question posed must be *plural,* an answer that makes sense of the entire undertaking of the arts, the human condition, history, self-interpretation, reflexive theories about all of these. No single answer will do: any presumption that it would must suffer from the burning bush syndrome. We are being asked to explain what we should understand by our own interest in producing art and in harvesting the work of the arts, and what we suppose our own capacity is for understanding our entire history. At the close of the twentieth century, the prospect is bleaker than it would have been at the century's opening. One might now quite reasonably suppose that *no* part or trend of man's history—neither conviction nor commitment nor theory nor understanding—is tidy enough to risk the sunny clarity of Danto's reading. Perhaps you will think his summary of the end of art too pessimistic. But in a way it isn't at all pessimistic, since, on the account, *art has accomplished its rational objective and therefore rationally yields to a philosophical understanding of why it has come to an end.* It comforts us in something like Spinoza's way, in the sense in which Hegel (and now Danto) offers the confirming chronicle.

But that vision cannot be right for anyone who believes that history is a *constructed narrative,* an art form of its own by which, occasionally, in the large Hegelian sense of world-history, but more usually in the finite nar-

10. Ibid., 39.

ratives of perspectived fragments, we try to understand our world and our place in it. Nor can it be right for anyone who concedes, at least since the advent of the Second World War, that progress, rationality, freedom, perennial human values, invariant and assured truth are nowhere reliably discerned: these themes are not utterly incapable of legitimation, but they are not convincing if not hard-won against the darker doctrines that claim the same evidence; they are themselves compelling *constructions* (if they are compelling), no longer assured invariant necessities, responding to the opaque, erratic, jarring, nonconvergent saliencies of historical experience.

Danto, however, claims to grasp the rational, the radically rational thread of world-history. Hegel may have been an ironist ultimately; Danto is certainly no ironist here. And Kojève, whom Danto cites with obvious approval regarding "the end of human time, or History" (citing from Alexandre Kojève's analysis of the *Phenomenology*), certainly saw that Hegel's totalized history (Spirit's understanding absolutely *all*—that is, itself finally, *and* the final legitimating conditions for understanding all) was either a conceptual disaster (which Kojève took it to be) or else an extraordinary irony (which Hegel never explicitly confirmed).[11] So Danto is singularly alone in his adherence to the Hegelian model of history that his own confidence requires. He has taken a heavy risk there.

Still, mine is a blackmail argument thus far, an argument that has said nothing about artworks themselves—or interpretation or criticism or history, for that matter. We must remember that Danto regards his argument as compelling, on evidence internal to the artworld. We must also bear in mind that, in stalking Danto (or Burgin or anyone else), we are primarily concerned to indicate what is at stake in taking a stand on the question posed—and, if we dare, *to* take a stand of our own. The issue is not a dialectical tiff between professionals.

Hannah Arendt once complained, against Marx, and evidently in favor of Hegel, that "Marx was . . . the first . . . and greatest among historians . . . to mistake a pattern for a meaning."[12] What she meant was that, in the immediate context of deliberate action, men may achieve what they pursue, but what they pursue in this way *has meaning* only in the historical context of the "process as a whole, beyond the 'narrow aims' of

11. Danto, "The End of Art," 112.
12. Hannah Arendt, "The Concept of History: Ancient and Modern," *Between Past and Future,* enl. ed. (Harmondsworth: Penguin, 1968), 87.

acting men," where "meanings, . . . like truth, will only disclose or reveal themselves [in that larger scheme of things]."[13] She may be right, but she fails to remark: first, that the would-be revelation is no more than a convincing *construction* or interpretation of its own; second, that the "process as a whole" is never the whole process in any strict and literal sense; and third, that, as the aftermath of the Second World War should have made clear, the unfolding of the "larger whole" of later history *cannot* be said to be "rational" in the peculiar sense of approaching asymptotically the Absolute Spirit's understanding. If the argument holds against Arendt, it surely holds against Danto. But we cannot be satisfied with that.

III

Look at the matter in an entirely different way. In one of his well-known reviews in *The Nation* (January 2, 1989), Danto excoriates the German artist Anselm Kiefer and the show of his work then at the Museum of Modern Art in New York. Consider Kiefer *only* as a specimen artist, one who had made an obvious bid to change the direction of contemporary art in a distinctly challenging way. Here is a bit of Danto's review: "One way of endearing oneself to the curatorial establishment while at the same time impressing the wider populace that spontaneously equates obscurity with profundity is to stuff one's work with a farce of heavy symbolism which the former can use to justify its existence by explaining to the latter."[14] Danto takes note of "the overall perniciousness of Kiefer's crackpot message"—that is (as the show's catalogue cites Kiefer): "I do not identify with Nero or Hitler, but I have to reenact what they did just a little bit in order to understand the madness. That is why I make these attempts to become a fascist." Danto goes on to condemn Kiefer's work as being a form of "symbolic art," which, according to Hegel (as Danto explicitly observes) "is the lowest order of fine art, largely because one has to learn the meaning of a symbol the way one learns the meaning of a name—by a lexical rule of the sort provided in the MoMA glossary." Danto adds,

13. Arendt, "The Concept of History," 77, 81.
14. Arthur C. Danto, "Anselm Kiefer," in *Encounters and Reflections: Art in the Historical Present* (New York: Farrar Straus Giroux, 1990), 238.

tellingly: "With art of a higher order, the power of the priest vanishes, for with great art the meaning penetrates the work, so that to perceive is to understand. Even within symbolic art itself, a distinction is available between narrow and universal symbols."[15]

This is either a scandalously prejudiced review or little more than an extremely annoyed reading of Kiefer among many others that are more impressed (perhaps even more worried by being impressed) than is Danto. In any case, *to* read Kiefer thus is to discount at a stroke (let us for the moment say, for good or ill) the possibility (that others *see*) of a turn in recent art that might show the way beyond the "end of art." What this confirms in turn is, first of all, that Danto's thesis requires a very strong convergence of informed judgments on his own general reading of art history (which can hardly be expected); second, that the thesis cannot be disengaged from detailed disputes about the quality of contemporary art, which this little piece (important beyond its subject and its length) hardly assures us is in the offing; and third, that there are no suitably strong criteria of assessment in the arts in virtue of which more favorable readings of Kiefer (which are numerous enough) would be reasonably defeated—*a fortiori*, there are no known criteria by which *to* defeat with assurance more favorable views of the future of art.

It is worth remarking that Hegel had consigned Egyptian art to the "symbolic" level. Although he was surely an extraordinary commentator on the arts (just compare him to Kant!), Hegel was obviously misled about the hieratic style of Egyptian statuary and the conventions of two-dimensional painting (which, as we shall soon see, infects Danto's thesis in a deeper way). Wilhelm Worringer, for one, has compellingly demonstrated that the Egyptians were not incapable at all of mastering their medium in order to express some suitably *geistlich* Idea; they obviously deliberately formed a certain practice of craft and art while giving ample evidence (at the same time) of their mastery of the medium.[16] The inferiority in this respect of Egyptian to Greek art is certainly doubtful. Doubts of this kind are considerably more than doubts, of course: they challenge the very idea of the legible periodization of art history; hence, the legibility of the end of art. Danto is certainly a Hegelian, but it is not always clear that Hegel is.

15. Danto, "Anselm Kiefer," 239.
16. See Wilhelm Worringer, *Abstraction and Empathy*, trans. Michael Bullock (New York: International Universities Press, 1953).

The error draws attention to the prejudice (Hegel's as well as Ernst Gombrich's as well as Clement Greenberg's as well as Arthur Danto's) of a distinctly *technological* conception of the achievements of art, of the proper focus of art criticism and interpretation, of progress in art history, and of the rational or theoretical objective of art itself, perhaps even of the objective, uniquely correct, absolute periodization of art history. All of that is implicated in Danto's appeal to Hegel, in his utter condemnation of Kiefer, and in his confidence in the validity of his own thesis. Furthermore, that one may have "to learn the meaning of a symbol" by a sort of "lexical rule" is notably unavoidable in two sorts of "higher" cases: in one, where the *successful* visual imagery and general culture of an alien society needs to be made known to our own sort of learned ignorance; the other, where the *novel* inventions of particular modern artists (of our own world) are still too unfamiliar to invite us to interpret their work with assurance. Even the classical ideal (in Hegel) must make room for this sort of difficulty. The question of just how to interpret the symbols deliberately strewn about in Kiefer's paintings—that is, *not* the symbols taken discretely and literally, but the painter's *use and intention in using* those obvious symbols—is, to say the least, contentious. Danto has no hesitation in condemning Kiefer. But it is just that apparent use, Kiefer's relatively novel way of handling the materials of his art, that has attracted such a strong sense (on the part of many critics and observers) of his genuine effectiveness.

Andreas Huyssen, for example, opposing *en passant* Donald Kuspit's criticism of Kiefer, a criticism developed along lines not very different from Danto's, observes:

> To me, a German of Kiefer's generation, the reference to laying to rest the ghosts of the past reads like a Bitburg of art criticism if not worse, and I would claim that it fundamentally misrepresents the problematic of national identity in Kiefer's work. Kiefer's painting—in its forms, its materials, and its subject matter—is emphatically about memory, not about forgetting. . . . Immersed in the exploration (and exploitation) of the power of mythic images, this work has given rise to the mystification that somehow myth transcends history, that it can redeem us from history, and that art, especially painting, is the high road toward redemption. Indeed, Kiefer himself . . . is not innocent in provoking such responses.

But ultimately his work is also informed by a gesture of self-questioning, by an awareness of the questionable nature of his undertaking, and by a pictorial self-consciousness that belies such mystifications. I take this work . . . to be about the ultimate inseparability of myth and history.[17]

Huyssen goes on to identify a considerable number of distinctly original features (as he sees it) in Kiefer's work. It is worth citing, though at the risk of the sort of detail that would only make sense to weigh standing before Kiefer's paintings:

Kiefer's focus on Germanic iconography in the 1970s still had a critical edge [that is, anticipating the recovery of the issue of national identity in West Germany in the 1980s], attempting to articulate what the liberal and social democratic cultural consensus had sealed behind a *cordon sanitaire* of proper coping with the past. And his choice of medium, his experimentations on the threshold between painting, photography, and the sculptural, also had a critical edge in the refusal to bow to the pieties of a teleologically constructed modernism that saw even remotely representational painting only as a form of regression. Representation in Kiefer is, after all, not just a facile return to a premodernist tradition. It is rather the attempt to make certain traditions (high-horizon landscape painting, romantic painting) productive for a kind of painting that represents, without, however, being grounded in the ideology of representation, a kind of painting that places itself quite self-consciously after conceptualism and minimalism. The often-heard reproach against Kiefer's being figurative and representational misses his extraordinary sensitivity to materials such as straw, sand, lead, ashes, burnt logs, ferns, and copper wire, all of which are incorporated imaginatively into his canvases and more often than not work against the grain of figuration and representation.[18]

17. Andreas Huyssen, "Anselm Kiefer: The Terror of History, the Temptation of Myth," *October* 48 (1989), 26–27. See Donald B. Kuspit, "Flak from the 'Radicals': The American Case Against German Painting," in *Art After Modernism: Rethinking Representation*, ed. Brian Wallis (New York: New Museum of Contemporary Art, 1984).
18. Huyssen, "Anselm Kiefer: The Terror of History," 35.

What this says is: first, that Kiefer *has* made technical innovations in the handling of the actual material media of painting that Danto (following Greenberg, in effect) does not see; second, that he *quotes* or alludes to representational banalities rather than merely performs those same banal symbolic gestures; third, that he integrates all such elements in an effort to commit himself, *in painting,* to the problematic of just how a national identity emerges; and fourth, that he does this by inventing a way of working that draws his audience into reliving memorially the ambiguous social process within which Nazism was actually born.

Now, this *is* an achievement, and a critical appreciation of an achievement, that goes *beyond the end of art.* The important thing is that it wins even if it loses. Because it demonstrates both that we can escape the end of art and how we can do so; and, if we agree that Kiefer has done what Huyssen says he has, then Kiefer *has* gone beyond the end of art. Q.E.D.

I can put the point another way: Danto's would-be "end of art" is meant as the end of art, *on* the assumption that Greenberg was (approximately) right about modernist art though not about art *tout court.* The "end-of-art" thesis is parasitic on a certain *art history's* being in place *ante.* But Kiefer's achievement—representational, if you please, but *not* "premodernist," as Huyssen helpfully remarks—is, therefore, not regressive in that sense in which Danto might reasonably take as confirming his own thesis.

I am not quarreling about the right interpretation of Kiefer. I am arguing, rather, that the validity of Danto's thesis about the end of art depends on the validity of reading Kiefer in accord with that thesis—so that it may be no more than a self-fulfilling prophecy. *If* you concede that there is in principle no uniquely valid characterization of a Kiefer canvas, you may be open to the suggestion that the reasonableness of Huyssen's reading brings in its wake strong reasons for doubting Danto's end-of-art theory; because it brings in its wake strong reasons for doubting that anyone can count on art's having the linear history that, in a way, Danto conspires with Greenberg to entrench (precisely because Danto disagrees with Greenberg). There is no clear separation between the periodization of art history and the interpretation of a particular painting; hence, no assurance that there is a uniquely objective characterization of any one piece. (You will, of course, have already considered that if what has been said, in the preceding chapter, about Danto's theory of art holds up, then we should have to admit an enormous gap between that theory and the end-of-art thesis. How could the latter be more than an *obiter dictum?*)

Once you see all this, you see that Danto's argument is a whistling in the dark. The vacuity of contemporary art—if it is merely barren, and no one believes that it is altogether barren—is merely its contingent vacuity or even an artifactual vacuity produced by a certain kind of cultural intransigence. *There is no historical necessity in it.* To find what is redemptive and enlarging and creative in contemporary art requires a sympathy and an imagination equal to the barely fathomed possibilities that are just surfacing in the most recent work. Danto is in a privileged but unenviable position: being called on by himself to *discern* just what *are* the dawning currents of our own age. He may be missing the mark—he has clearly missed the conceptual possibility—when he says that "Kiefer's symbols are purely external, the kind you look up in books." Kiefer's "experience," he says, "is merely that of an art student who has had no life outside art to speak of or draw upon. Joseph Beuys [Kiefer's master, Danto adds], though a symbolic artist, managed to transcend the inherent limitations of that genre by creating works so full of human meaning that one encountered one's deepest self in encountering them."[19] He commends Beuys, therefore, for the "universality" of his symbols when, condemning Kiefer, he alludes to Kant's own attention to universal themes and principles ("not a conception to which the artist [Kiefer] has a right"[20]). He commends Beuys for what, precisely, does not exceed the end of art. But Kantian universality is precisely one of the themes that the Second World War has called into permanent question in legitimative terms—which, *if* a valid move, suggests (or confirms) as well that Kiefer is calling such universality into question in a fresh way. If Huyssen is right—reasonably in reading Kiefer, more compellingly in addressing the historicity of art—then Danto is profoundly mistaken about the end of art (and Greenberg, about modernism).

In any case, Danto has hardly earned the right to insist on the reliability of such values in his own historical report on the end of art. For, *if* such invariances are as deeply contested in the historical experience of contemporary societies as they plainly are, then an effort like Kiefer's confirms the sense in which art cannot have come to the end of (its) history; it also

19. Danto, "Anselm Kiefer," 239.
20. Ibid., 242.

confirms the sense in which if that is a pertinent concern of art, then we haven't the slightest idea of what it would mean for art to end. There *is* no viable sense in which we could be approaching closure on the meaning of art, just as there is no manageable sense in which we could ever finally grasp what *is* the rationality, or the progress, or the rational self-understanding, or the rational progress, of art. All such distinctions are horizoned constructions made within a historical age blinkered by its own interests. I admit that that is not Hegel's official theory, but it is surely a plausible extrapolation from it, one that is particularly congenial to our own age's skepticism. (And if Hegel did not himself mean to allow anything of the kind, then so much the worse for Hegel.)

IV

Well, of course, this last is an overstatement. We do have Danto's conjecture after all, and it is at least coherent. What I claim, rather, is that it is utterly untenable. Let us see why this is so.

It would be foolish to assign to any one theorist the decisive role in skewing art's history in a technological direction. But, having conceded that, we may also say that there is little doubt that Walter Benjamin's 1936 essay, "The Work of Art in the Age of Mechanical Reproduction," is extraordinarily well-placed historically—as well-placed as any—to help us link the distinctive themes of late twentieth-century conceptions of art to those of the continuously accumulating history of the whole of Western art (and more). It is certainly one of the most influential and respected essays of its kind to have been written during the period of the flourishing of Nazism and of Communism and the Second World War.

For my purpose, its distinctive feature lies in its original grasp of the antagonism between the spread of a technology of mechanical reproduction, notably in photography and film in our time, and the decline in the so-called "aura" of objects of the artworld.

Benjamin's essay has its dubious themes, to be sure. For instance, it does not quite perceive the sense in which, despite the mechanical disruption of the "aura" of the live stage and older forms of art, the film, particularly when films are shown in a public hall in which experienced but anonymous viewers join in the socially shared darkness of the occasion, can actually generate a palpable "aura" of it own.[21] Grasping that, we cannot fail to see that the recoverable theme of an artwork's "aura" for our secular world is centered much more on sharing the actual context of production, performance, and reception of art, or the near "traces" of such an event's history, than on what Benjamin explicitly offers in its primary definition, namely, "the unique phenomenon of a distance, however, close it may be."[22] "Aura" is simply more inventive than Benjamin supposed.

Quite frankly, Benjamin had in mind an original cultish or ritual sense of a sacred presence (which is a notion already somewhat estranged and nostalgic, though not irrelevant); still, the intent of his definition is much broader and closer to our experience, and covers secular, even profane, occasions. "The uniqueness of a work of art [he observes] is inseparable from its being imbedded in the fabric of tradition"; and "its uniqueness" *is* "its aura"—accessible, Benjamin thinks, even through the time of a radically changed history. Thus: "This tradition itself is thoroughly alive and extremely changeable. An ancient statue of Venus, for example, stood in a different traditional context with the Greeks, who made it an object of veneration, than with the clerics of the Middle Ages, who viewed it as an ominous idol. Both of them, however, were equally confronted with its uniqueness, that is, its aura."[23] The sense of the "presence" of an artwork is surely more ramified than Benjamin allows: it may, for instance, survive mechanical reproduction, as high-fidelity recordings and "cult" films confirm; and it may collect, however debased we think the practice is, a sense of a tradition of functioning audiences very far removed from the initial history of the "presence" of particular works (as museums of African art make clear).

What is essential, however, for my present purpose is the deep duality of Benjamin's essay: it unmistakably establishes, by its attention to "aura," that it is impossible to treat the semiotic, expressive, representational, rhetorical, symbolic, semantic, linguistic, gestural, intentional significance of art entirely in terms of the mere technological novelty of any use of its (material) medium; its semiotic use (speaking metonymically) is *always*

21. Walter Benjamin, "The Work of Art in the Age of Mechanical Reproduction," *Illuminations,* trans. Harry Zohn (New York: Schocken Books, 1969), 226–38.
22. Ibid., 222.
23. Ibid., 223. See also my "Mechanical Reproduction and Cinematic Humanism," *What, After All, Is a Work of Art?*

linked to its "aura" or public "presence." And yet, the dominant theme of Benjamin's essay, the overwhelming instruction our own generation of art historians and historically-minded theorists and critics has drawn from it, is almost exclusively focused on the history of art as a history of a certain restrictedly technological achievement, whether progressively construed or not.

That is, the *reductio* (of both Benjamin's and Danto's theories) is embarrassingly obvious: there can be no direct, spontaneous, valid perception of the semiotic attributes of an artwork that is not already "aural" in some measure: to discern such attributes is to share the historical ethos in which they are palpably—consensually—present. This cannot rightly be turned into a criterion of indubitability, but the reality of artworks remains fundamentally social and communicative nevertheless. Benjamin seems not to have entirely grasped the import of his own profound intuition; he simply confused the analysis of cultural reality with the (that is, his) moral and political judgment of its different manifestations—and with the engine of technology (a Marxist and, later, a Heideggerean thesis). We cannot afford the luxury.

Now, the notion of the "technology" of the medium may—surely must—be taken in a very generous sense. But whatever else it is, the "technological" is meant to identify a rational, purposive dimension of art that is relatively isolable from the encumbrances of collective "aura" or "presence," capable of being measured in terms of progress or improvement, in spite of the fact that technology must have its own special sources. When, therefore, any artist's achievement is construed in terms of embodying or expressing a tradition, that achievement *cannot* be construed merely technologically, even if some element (say, the novel use of would-be symbols: the cubists' use of labels and newsprint and images of the artifacts of familiar city life) could be isolated *for* technological analysis—say, in Clement Greenberg's way, so as to draw attention to the temptation, "logically" resisted by Picasso and Braque and occasionally confusedly indulged by Juan Gris, to regress from the essentially abstract requirements of the picture plane to explicit representation.[24]

24. See, for instance, Clement Greenberg, No. 99. "Review of the Exhibition *Collage*," *The Collected Essays and Criticism*, vol. 2: *Arrogant Purpose, 1945–1949*, ed. John O'Brian (Chicago: University of Chicago Press, 1986), 259–63. See, also, Rosalind E. Krauss, *The Picasso Papers* (Farrar Straus Giroux, 1999).

This is the direct and reasonable consequence of adhering to Benjamin's distinction; although Benjamin, like Hegel, and like Gombrich and Greenberg *and* Danto after him, tends to pursue technology rather than "aural" presence (or cultural tradition). It is precisely for this reason that Benjamin, exaggeratedly isolating technology, speaks of the *decline* of "aura," and Gombrich, Greenberg, and Danto speak of *progress* in the rational development of painting. The most important "symptom" of the tendency to bifurcate technology and aura (in effect, the physical and cultural aspects of painting, film, music) lies with the whole point, of course, of Greenberg's modernist treatment of painting. It is also all but explicit in Danto's view of art: it is, I suggest, illustrated in Danto's review of Kiefer. It is, of course, also, the central theme of Eduard Hanslick's treatment of music as "ordered sound."[25]

But the thesis that the artistic medium is physical is, first of all, not a necessary truth; second, it is never systematically defended; third, it can be coherently replaced (as I have already suggested) by treating the "medium" as physically embodied but intentionally complex (better: Intentional—the term of art I introduced in Chapter 1); and fourth (and most important), it cannot support any practice of interpretation or history (claiming a measure of objective rigor) that admits the intentional (the Intentional) dimension of the artworld. The reason is this: interpretive rigor requires some adequation between interpretable "text," or artwork, and a particular interpretation, and the theory that the medium of the principal arts is purely physical (Greenberg regularly casts a doubtful eye on the legitimacy of calling literature art) utterly subverts any such adequation—hence, also, any would-be objective assessment of interpreta-

---

25. See, particularly, Clement Greenberg, "Avant-Garde and Kitsch," *Partisan Review* 6 (1939) and "Towards a Newer Laocoon," *Partisan Review* 7 (1940). See also Eduard Hanslick, *On the Musically Beautiful: A Contribution Toward the Revision of the Aesthetics of Music,* trans. and ed. (from 5th ed.) G. Payzant (Indianapolis: Hackett, 1980). There is a clear link between Danto's and Greenberg's views of the medium of painting. They needn't (and don't) share the same interpretation of particular painters, but they are both modernists and attentive to technological progress. It is also worth remarking how different Greenberg's conception of the avant-garde is from more explicitly Marxist views (though Greenberg professed a Marxist inspiration). Further, on Greenberg's thesis, see the three compelling papers by Meyer Schapiro collected under the general heading "Abstract Art," *Modern Art: 19th and 20th Centuries; Selected Papers* (New York: George Braziller, 1978). The first, "The Nature of Abstract Art" (1937), reviewing Alfred Barr's work, in effect defeats Greenberg's thesis even before its appearance.

tion's "corresponding" to an artwork's attributes. What we begin to see is the conceptual isomorphism that holds among theories of art, history, language, action, and human selves: in short, the strong family resemblance among all the parts of human culture.

On occasion, of course, Danto is a severe and just critic of Greenberg's formalist, even essentialist, conception of the narrow technology of two-dimensional painting. Danto criticizes Greenberg in no uncertain terms, for example, in covering for *The Nation* the great Van Gogh show at the Metropolitan Museum of Art in January 1987. The lesson to be drawn from that, however, bears as much on Danto's view of Kiefer as on Greenberg's view of Van Gogh—and concurrently identifies, for us, the extraordinarily difficult conceptual problem of distinguishing, at both a narrowly technological level and at a more integrated level of appreciation, what we could possibly mean by an artist's use of symbols:

> In Arles [Danto remarks], Van Gogh had written, "I want to paint men and women in that something of the eternal that the halo used to symbolize and which we now seek to give by the actual radiance and vibrancy of our colors." That halo is a convention by means of which artists can give visual embodiment to nonvisual qualities, namely holiness or divinity; in Van Gogh's case these numinous attributes were transmitted by radiance and vibrancy instead. This means we must learn to read the meanings in colors, which never are merely just the colors that objects have, but signify moral qualities sensed by Van Gogh in nature and in persons. Clement Greenberg once explained the surfaces of Van Gogh's work as due to his finding what went on in the canvas more interesting than what went on in the world. This is certainly a false description of the world according to Van Gogh, and distorts his artistic intentions by subjecting them to a formalism as irrelevant as so many theoretical explanations of his work.[26]

This is an extremely perceptive remark. But it is impossible to interpret it in any way that would lend credence to Danto's Hegelian (technological) pronouncement on the end of art—or, any similar such periodizing pro-

---

26. Arthur C. Danto, "Van Gogh at St.-Rémy," in *Encounters and Reflections*, 60.

nouncement. The Hegelian claim, after all, affirms a certain *historical necessity* that inheres in the phenomena of the observed world (*Erscheinungen*). At best, if it is true that the artworld is going to hell in a basket because of the debased sensibilities of our violent world (*per* Kiefer), or is on the point of realizing its rational self-eliminative apotheosis (*per* Danto), we would still lack the evidence of it, though it would surely worry us profoundly either way. On the other hand, by parity of reasoning, how do we know that Danto is correct in his condemnation of Kiefer's "use" of symbols, when he himself has shown us a fresh way of understanding how symbols may be used, as in Van Gogh, that may need to be lexically specified at first (to our own illiterate selves), so that it may eventually be seen to "embody" visually (Danto's own term) such "nonvisual qualities" as holiness or divinity? First of all, how do we *discern,* as competent critics or observers, *that* sort of embodiment (aura or presence)? Second, how can we *link,* conceptually, in a "linear" (or "spiral") appreciation of artistic "progress" (or progressive "rationality"), an artist's novel use of symbols in his material medium, in anything like the embodiment sense? And third, what, regarding such a complex understanding, would *confirm* that we *were* coming to the end of art's genuine history, that we were entering a posthistorical phase?

The curious thing is that Danto never addresses these questions. He cannot, of course. No one can. Because to pursue the theme—which is already technologically characterized in Hegel's lectures on the arts (and which must surely have inspired Benjamin as well as Danto)—there is no straightforwardly legible way to show that *there is a final moral, political, spiritual, telic, or rationally normative purpose to art that we have finally come to understand.* We cannot understand it through technological progress alone, for, *there,* "aura" is lacking; and we cannot understand it through the appreciation of "aura," for, *there,* telic progress either makes no sense or is no more than the obvious prejudice of some philosopher.

There you have the superb nonsense of Hegel's master vision. There is no end *of* art, because there is no end *of* human existence. It's immensely open. There is no teleology of history or culture. There may well be an end to *man*—and to his art. But that is a contingency we must live with forever. (The same difficulty, remember, had surfaced in Hannah Arendt's conception of history.)

If, then, we take Kiefer at his word—remember, I offer him as a specimen only—then we must consider carefully whether he has not indeed combined Benjamin's themes of the alienating power of our age of mechanical reproduction with the recovery of the "aura" of an art that arises out of just such elements: the deliberately banal "use," for instance, of the banally evil symbols of the Nazi past, *in order* (as he says) *to* "embody" them in a fresh memorial recovery of the (original) "aura" of the world in which they first functioned so fatefully—now reclaimed within the historical "aura" of our own "responsible" world. Imagine that, and you will have formed an interesting possibility Danto has not defeated, has not shown us how to defeat, has not even seriously considered, and could not rightly assess along the lines of his own dogma. As soon as you acknowledge the possibility, you see the profound banality of our own familiar notions of art—largely technological. And, of course, the import of doubting that art has a legible "end."

The American philosopher of science, John Stachel, makes a very pretty point about the relationship between the so-called "formal" sciences of mathematics and geometry and logic and the so-called "empirical" sciences of physics and astronomy, to which the first are said to be "applied." "The whole hierarchical organization of the sciences into logic, mathematics, the empirical sciences—each earlier term supposedly founded independent[ly] of, and serving as part of the foundation for, the later ones—must be rejected [Stachel says] as the consequence of an incorrect starting point in the division of formal and empirical sciences."[27] Stachel is objecting, of course, that the conceptual "separation" falsifies the true relationship between the "two" sorts of science and, as a result, falsifies the very nature of scientific accomplishment. We are faced, in the context of the theory of art, in the context of its history and interpretive focus, with a misunderstanding of a very similar sort. There *is* no independent "technological" dimension of art focused primarily (or even first) on the mastery and innovative use of its material medium: there is only an indissoluble cultural achievement of some sort, by noting which we *may*, for this or that purpose, abstract (but hardly separate), within "the process as a whole" (in Hannah Arendt's phrase), this or that technological or

27. John Stachel, "Comments on 'Some Logical Problems Suggested by Empirical Theories' by Professor Dalla Chiara," in *Language, Logic, and Method*, ed. Robert S. Cohen and Marx W. Wartofsky (Dordrecht: D. Reidel, 1983), 92. See also Mary Tiles, *Mathematics and the Image of Reason* (London: Routledge, 1991), chap. 5.

craft feat. But if we agree to that, then we oblige all the Hegelian thinkers to tell us (please!) *what* the teleology of History or Reason or Human Existence is, and how they know what it is. They have no answer. Not having an answer to that, they have no account at all of the detailed rigor of describing, analyzing, interpreting, comparing, assessing particular artworks along either of the two supposed "dimensions" we have borrowed (for convenience of exposition) from Walter Benjamin. Benjamin, we realize, exaggerates the disjunction between aura and technology for his own purpose.

Danto, as we have seen, declares that "The historical stage of art is done with when it is known what art is and means." But when is that? It might be thought to be when the technological possibilities of representing (or otherwise semiotically conveying) the human condition are known to be exhausted. That would require a "hierarchical organization" (to use Stachel's phrase) of technological mastery and the representation or expression of the human "presence" or "aura" (to use Benjamin's). (The distinction distantly reminds one of the crude Marxist contrast between "substratum" and "superstructure"—but it is not the same.)

There is no question that Danto *is* tempted by such a bifurcation, through his leanings toward something like the unity of science model.[28] That is just the difficulty of his notorious notion of "the 'is' of artistic identification."[29] But then, there is also the sort of thing we have seen Danto say about Van Gogh—against Clement Greenberg, for instance— which, taken seriously, is incompatible with the other. If Danto holds to the bifurcated first model (in some way), then it is at least clear why he supposes it makes sense to speak of the end of art. But he offers no supporting theory at all and no compelling evidence. And if he holds to the unified second model (in some equally unspecified regard), then there is no way to support his thesis, except, perhaps, in the sense (which Kojève dangles before us) that Hegel really did suppose *he* understood the ultimate meaning of Napoleon's career, impenetrable to Napoleon himself. There are no other options.

Let us, therefore, look a little more closely at the "second model." Two

28. See, for instance, Joseph Margolis, "Ontology Down and Out in Art and Science," *Journal of Aesthetics and Art Criticism* 56 (1988).

29. See Arthur C. Danto, "The Artworld," *Journal of Philosophy* 61 (1964); see also Chapters 1 and 2 above.

clues are all I can afford. They are not really separate clues, but two ways of entering the same conceptual space. The ulterior theme is simply that painting, the arts, all of human activity for that matter (including theory), are forms of *praxis* that have no fixed antecedent cognitive or productive resources. They are culturally constructed capacities, emergent, embedded, empowered, variably interpreted, effective in and only in the enabling social processes of the historical form of life in which they are formed. Our habits of thought, of action, of production tacitly internalize our "second nature" and provide for the transformation of that nature and the form of life in which it is formed, impressed on the biological template of the species—a template obviously both soft- and hard-wired. It functions distributively, reciprocally, reflexively, open-endedly, and in a historically changing way all at the same time. To state things thus is, perhaps, to combine Marx and Wittgenstein: to treat historical *praxis* as the encompassing context of all that is distinctly human, indissolubly so, legible in terms of the conditions of production and reproduction, and effective in the exercise of spontaneous practices that reflexively alter the tacit form of those same practices at later moments in a society's life.[30]

The point of the intended clues is to secure the sense in which we cannot separate in any intelligible way the technological use of the medium of painting (or of literature, for that matter) from the "representation" (if we may use the term benignly) of the perceived "presence" of our own form of life. It is our *praxis* that unites the two: *that,* we may say (anticipating a fair objection), explodes at once the absurdity of the familiar hierarchical Marxist ordering of "substratum" and "superstructure."[31]

There are two themes, therefore, that we must keep before us: one affirms that the meaningful structure of artworks, of whatever we treat as a work of art, or art *tout court,* gains and holds its particular form or internal order only to the extent that, between the fine structure of the society in which it is originally formed and the fine structure of the society in which we claim to discern that form, its "aura" or "presence" may be said to be recovered—even if it is, horizonally, very much altered from the original; the other affirms that, in any plausible such recovery, which

30. See Joseph Margolis, "The Novelty of Marx's Theory of *Praxis*," *Journal for the Theory of Social Behavior* 19 (1989).

31. See, for instance, Terry Eagleton, *Criticism and Ideology: A Study in Marxist Literary Theory* (London: NLB, 1976).

cannot fail to have its own open history, the bifurcation of technological achievement and a society's self-referential representation makes no sense. Marx's generic notion of *praxis,* then, now no longer restricted to specifically Marxian or Marxist models—suitable, say, for Foucauldian or Weberian or Aristotelian or other adjustments as well—supplies the most ramified picture we have of their integral unity.

Consider, then, a modest first clue. Michael Baxandall, in a carefully tuned account, examines and weighs the possible difference in the explanation of what is accomplished in the building of a bridge (the historical Forth Bridge, built, by Benjamin Baker, to cross the Firth of Forth, at Queensferry, toward the end of the nineteenth century, in order to facilitate north-south traffic to the centers of Scottish life and, ulteriorly, to connect Scotland more effectively with England) and the explanation of a painting (Picasso's *Portrait of Kahnweiler* is Baxandall's choice, adjusted in a thoughtful way by close comparison with the explanation of Chardin's *A Lady Taking Tea* and Piero della Francesca's *Baptism of Christ*).[32]

Baxandall begins with a deliberately oversimplified sense of what may be called the "rational teleology" of the building of the bridge, which he finds leaves out an enormous number of pertinent details, the grasp of which permits us to see how it is that the explanation of "historical objects" (the Forth Bridge) and the explanation of "pictorial objects" (the Kahnweiler *Portrait* and the other paintings) ineluctably converge, in different ways and to different degrees, depending on differences in (what I am calling) the forms of life in which these "objects" are first produced and later examined and appreciated.

"I started," Baxandall says, "from a very low and simple theoretical stance that historical objects may be explained by treating them as solutions to problems in situations, and by reconstructing a rational relationship between these terms."[33] The formula Baxandall starts with is precisely the one that Gombrich, for instance in discussing Constable's achievement, ends with.[34] In fact, in a spirit unmistakably approaching glee, Gombrich cites Constable's haunting reflection (in 1836): "Painting is a science and should be pursued as an inquiry into the laws of Nature.

---

32. Michael Baxandall, *Patterns of Intention: On the Historical Explanation of Pictures* (New Haven: Yale University Press, 1985).
33. Baxandall, *Patterns of Intention,* 35.
34. E. H. Gombrich, *Art and Illusion: A Study in the Psychology of Pictorial Representation,* 2d ed. (New York: Pantheon, 1961).

Why, then, may not landscape painting be considered as a branch of natural philosophy, of which pictures are but the experiments?"[35] With very little adjustment, a similar pronouncement could be formed from Clement Greenberg's conception of modernism (of course, utterly at variance with Gombrich's taste: compare their remarks for instance, on Jackson Pollock!); and, one would suppose, *if* his notion of the historical fulfillment of the philosophical teleology of painting makes sense, a similar pronouncement could be formed from Danto's remarks. (Recall Kiefer!)

In any case, Baxandall offers a very clear impression of the complex way in which the simple idea of the bridge's being "a concrete *solution* to a problem" leaves out, as he mildly puts it, "much of the circumstantial matter one wanted to bring in"—which confirms the misleading simplicity of the would-be "problem" and "solution," the sense in which those terms convey and mask oversimplifications of the dense currents of historical and praxical life within the context of which the Bridge was built.[36] One of the decisively misleading features of the study of the Bridge and of similar studies of paintings, for instance, is focused on the idea of an explicit commission—in the case of the Bridge, an explicit contract; in the case of painting, something very similar in the commissions of patrons *before* the painter begins his work (as with Piero but *not,* typically, Picasso—even in the Kahnweiler *Portrait,* which was never actually commissioned).

Baxandall's point is that the artist's *intention* (even the bridge-builder's intention) is difficult to fathom in the complex setting of his culture; that what a painter paints, particularly when (as in the modern world) he is not explicitly bound to a commission but "markets" his work as best he can, is not readily legible; and that, as Baxandall puts it, "painting is a less pure art than bridge-building in that *how* is much more clearly contaminated by *why.*"[37] Of course, to the extent that this is so, the bifurcated (first) model of art and interpretation (that we considered earlier) cannot possibly work, and technological studies must be "contaminated" by historical "presence."

Baxandall suggests in a light way a sense of the fluid "market" in

35. E. H. Gombrich, "Experiment and Experience in the Arts," in *The Image and the Eye: Further Studies in the Psychology of Pictorial Representation* (Oxford: Phaidon, 1982), 215.
36. Baxandall, *Patterns of Intention,* 35.
37. Ibid., Chap. 4 and 49.

which, say, Picasso worked. He calls it *troc,* the small world of exchange the structure of which is too subtle and fluid to be entirely captured by any supposed larger rules of the market: "I am particularly anxious," he says, "not to elaborate anything like systematically regarding *troc* because its appeal for me lies in its simplicity and fluidity: it is no more than a *form* of relation in which two classes of people, both within the same culture, are free to make choices in the course of an exchange, any choice affecting the universe of the exchange and so the other participants." But he adds at once, thinking of Picasso's *Kahnweiler:* "while the basic relation of *troc* is simple and fluid, in any particular case it is partly encased in actual market institutions that are less so. The *forms* of these institutions are part of the painter's Brief [that is, his supposedly well-formed intention or purpose in painting] because they embody latent assumptions about what painting is. And the forms of the institutions are not pure expressions of immediate aesthetic impulse in a culture. Often they represent survivals from earlier moments: institutions are inertial. Often they reflect patterns and practices current in the markets of other manufactures and goods—clothes, antiques, precious metals, lectures on art, wines and so on—not specially developed for pictures."[38]

To put the point more provocatively: Baxandall, who clearly means to practice art history in an entirely canonical way (though he exhibits great skill and tact in that regard), acknowledges the difficulty of fixing the artist's intention. We, on the other hand, under none of Baxandall's compunctions, may insist not only on the difficulty of discerning the artist's intention (confronting Danto's reading of Kiefer, say) but also the prospect of plural and diverging histories and interpretations that may never come to rest in a single reading (against Baxandall's own reading of Picasso's *Kahnweiler*). A philosophical theorist, possibly one attracted to Foucault's complications, might well doubt what a nonphilosopher (Baxandall) takes no notice of or certain philosophers (Danto) clearly refuse to countenance.[39] Baxandall's candor counts against two of Danto's doctrines, therefore: against Danto's reliance on the artist's intentions in identifying artworks in the first place (discussed in Chapter 2), and against Danto's

---

38. Ibid., 48–49.

39. Compare, in this regard, Baxandall's own candor, in *Patterns of Intention* (14), which shows his own inclination to view intention as a plausible artifact—a little surprising, but welcome enough. (Perhaps we should not make too much of this.)

theory of the end of art history (in Danto's Hegelian account of art and its application to Kiefer in particular.)

The interesting point is that it is *here,* reflecting on Apollinaire's role in *troc* rather than as a critic, that Baxandall identifies the "ideology" of "the good Artist . . . who pushes on to new modes [of perception and painting]."[40] For my own purpose, it is not so much that Danto may be entirely wrong about Kiefer as that, right or wrong, he *could not perceive* the technological banality of Kiefer's work except within some ambience of *troc* and ideology in which, first of all, the bifurcated model that seems to support the Hegelian pronouncement is entirely outflanked, and, secondly, any suitable model must make room for the *ongoing* process of historical appreciation before the dawning of which the "full" meaning of what has been done and made cannot be located at the very moment in which it first obtains. This is in fact a finding in accord (thus far at least) with Danto's well-known theory of history: particularly, with the difference between history and chronicle.[41]

The second clue, which we may treat rather briefly, is drawn from Peter Bürger's provocative account of the avant-garde, developed quite sympathetically in accord with a Marxist sense of *praxis* and explicitly opposed to the bifurcating tendencies of the Frankfurt Critical theorists, particularly Adorno and Benjamin, as well as Lukács.[42] Bürger opposes the disjunction of the concepts of "productive forces" and "productive relations" from an encompassing analysis of a unitary society—*and* the transferring of that bifurcated notion to the analysis of the production of art—on the grounds (which he claims to find in Marx) that the concept of productive forces "unambiguously refers to the totality of social relations that govern work and the distribution of the products of work."[43] He then applies the point in a powerful way to Benjamin's genuine discovery of the difference between the production of art with and without "aura"; for, as he correctly notes, the absence of "aura" in bourgeois art *does not entail the validity of the bifurcated model:*

40. Baxandall, *Patterns of Intention,* 57.

41. See Arthur C. Danto, *Narration and Knowledge* (New York: Columbia University Press, 1985).

42. Peter Bürger, *The Theory of the Avant-Garde,* trans. Michael Shaw (Minneapolis: University of Minnesota Press, 1984).

43. Ibid., 30.

the historical conditions for the possibility of self-criticism of the social subsystem "art" cannot be elucidated with the aid of Benjamin's theorem; instead, these conditions must be derived from the disappearance of that tension that is constitutive for art in bourgeois society, the tension between art as institution (autonomy status) and the contents of individual works. In this effort, it is important not to contrast art and society as two mutually exclusive spheres. For both the (relative) insulation of art from demands that it serve purposes, and the development of contents are social phenomena (determined by the development of society as a whole).

Given these distinctions, Bürger moves compellingly to two findings that are entirely decisive for the issue we have been considering: first, "technical development must not be understood as an independent variable, for it is itself dependent on overall social development. Second, the decisive turn in the development of art in bourgeois society must not be traced monocausally to the development of technical reproduction techniques."[44]

There you have—in a way that is hardly merely Marxist—the utter defeat of the end-of-art theory, of Hegelian final histories, and an expression (incidental, of course) of the profoundly open spirit in which the function of art *is* indeed human self-understanding, a project that cannot come to an end but may well come to a close.

In a word, Danto is quite right in holding that "The end of art, meaning the end of a certain narrative of the history of art, is always [cast] in terms of an internal history. . . . It can make no *external* predictions, but only a forecast from within."[45] To claim, however, that the history of art really *has* come to an end is to forecast that there *will* be nothing yet to come in the world of art, external to the narrative in which art ends, that would ever force us, by the sheer power of its having been produced and recognized for what it is, to turn from that once-reliable history to another. *Or,* even more tellingly, that would force us to reinterpret the very past and promise of the art history that appeared to confirm the end-of-art thesis. Danto admits that this sort of defeat has already happened at least twice before: once to Vasari and once to Hegel, and he sees his own vulnerability in this regard. *He* believes, however, that he has a narrative of a deeper

44. Ibid., 31–32.
45. Arthur Danto, "Narratives of the End of Art," in *Encounters and Reflections,* 339.

94

"technology" than the others, freed for instance from "Clement Green-berg's tyranny" (*via* Frank Stella, apparently)[46] as well as from Vasari's and Hegel's limitations. But that is a sunny sort of optimism.

The required narrative is almost more Hegelian than Hegel: art has "come to an end by turning into something else—namely, philosophy."[47] But the objection, here, is *not* that there will be another "external" irrup-tion, like those that doomed Vasari's and Hegel's stories (which Danto himself supplies), but that the real history of art *is not a narrative* at all (which, on Danto's clever view, *must* therefore come to a close or end) but an open process *on which we impose one narrative or another.* The fatal error, which we want to have as clearly formulated as possible, lies in Danto's having conflated the two senses of "history": that of the actual Intentional life of a society or of some strand within it and that of the story that we say represents it accurately. The first has *no* assignable end, but the point of the second is to capture the first in a story that *does* have an assignable end. That is why, speaking of the 120 years following Hegel's last course in aesthetics, which witnessed the achievements of "the Impressionists and Cézanne, Picasso and Matisse," Danto declares that *that* post-Hegelian history "*culminates* in Pollock and De Kooning."[48]

But the actual process of that part of the artworld does not *culminate* in Pollock and De Kooning: it does so only in Greenberg's narrative, which Danto to some extent accepts. On his own Hegelian hook, Danto is content to follow Andy Warhol, who, he says, "demonstrates . . . that anything, if a work of art, can be matched by something that looks just like it which is not one, so the difference between art and non-art cannot rest in what they have in common—and that will be everything that strikes the eye."[49] But the argument fails. Art, on Danto's own view, and on any plausible view, does *not* consist in what, "retinally," strikes the eye or in what may be "retinally indiscernible" as between art and non-art.[50] It

---

46. Ibid., 340.

47. Ibid., 342.

48. Ibid., 335–36; italics added. (I should perhaps seize the occasion to remark that I have been using the term "intentional" here, in its familiar sense, more or less nontechnically. I do use a related term, "Intentional"—written with a capital "I"—as a term of art in other essays in this volume.)

49. Ibid., 344.

50. See the wording in Danto, "Narratives of the End of Art," 333; and in Margolis, "Ontology Down and Out in Art and Science." See also Chapter 2 above.

concerns something the "eye cannot descry."[51] It concerns "presence" or "aura," in the sense we have adjusted from Benjamin in order to oppose any technological bifurcation of art. In that sense, once again, there cannot be an end to art just as there cannot be an end to philosophy—or to human history. To treat the distinction between art and non-art as a matter of art-theory, and to treat art-theory as itself a creature of (philosophical) history, is, effectively, to make it impossible to confirm once and for all that art has come to the end of its history or that we are now, objectively, in a "post-historical" age. Or does Danto suppose that art is post-historical but philosophy is not? A paradox confronts us on every reading.

Having said all this, I must risk a short addendum. Danto, who is an exceedingly clever man, has written a brief piece, "Art after the End of Art," which appears in a new collection of his essays, *Embodied Meanings* (1994), that continues the *Kehre* of "Learning to Live with Pluralism" of the *Beyond the Brillo Box* volume.[52] To do full justice to the turn in Danto's thinking would rightly require a fresh beginning.[53] I would have to distort the argument of this essay to make room for that. Nevertheless, this chapter was originally written for an international conference in Finland (1990), which was actually titled "The Future of Art," in which I replaced Danto (who couldn't make the meeting). The reversal is too delicious to resist nibbling at. The timing of Danto's new paper suggests that "Art after the End of Art" may also have reviewed (in part at least) the end-of-art thesis in the company of my original paper.

In any case, I must insist on a few judgments that run the risk of being deflected by the turn of Danto's recent adjustment. My thesis is that there is no end to art because there is no end to history, no end to the history of art, no end to the history of philosophy, no end to the history of mankind. (I don't deny that there may be an end to the human species.) I say there is no end to art or to the history of art because there is no robustly real history that art's end belongs to. (Art has its history, or histories, of course;

51. See Danto, "The Artworld." See also Joseph Margolis, "A Closer Look at Danto's Account of Art and Perception," *British Journal of Aesthetics* 40 (2000).

52. See Arthur C. Danto, "Art After the End of Art," in *Embodied Meanings: Critical Essays and Aesthetic Meditations* (New York: Farrar Straus Giroux, 1994); and "Learning to Live with Pluralism," *Beyond the Brillo Box: The Visual Arts in Post-Historical Perspective* (New York: Farrar Straus Giroux, 1992).

53. See Margolis, "The History of Art After the End of the History of Art."

but there is no prior or independent history that art belongs to.) Danto certainly did write a narrative, which he called "the" history of art, in which the end-of-art thesis confirmed the end of art! But that's neither here nor there. In his narrative, he does claim that, necessarily, art had come to an end. He still believes it; but you may not believe that he does, when you read those genial papers, "Learning to Live with Pluralism" and "Art after the End of Art." How so?

The answer is this. We are *now*, Danto claims, in a *post-historical* period of art. That is, we are necessarily now in a "post-historical" period in which there is no longer any necessarily historical direction for art to take! One remark of Danto's may serve to make this clear: "I think of post-historical art as art created under conditions of what I want to term 'objective pluralism,' by which I mean that there are no historically mandated directions of art to go in, at least so far as the history of art, considered internally—as Greenberg [and, I should now add, Danto in earlier statements] certainly considered it—is concerned."[54] I put it to you that Danto's thesis is that the *present* "post-historical" period of art follows, by historical necessity, the "internal" necessity of the history of art that has brought itself to an end. It is now part of the same "narrative" of art that art has turned "post-historical"! The new necessity is "externally" linked to the other—but also internally. That explains Danto's reversal of Malevich's pronouncement, his generous embrace of "pluralism" as necessarily, now "post-historically," correct, by which the unique historical correctness of art in the historical age has been superseded—in being continued. My complaint is that there never was (and there is not now) a "Hegelian" history—objectively "there"—to which art ever belonged; and that, as a consequence, we are not *now in* a "post-historical" age.

Or perhaps Danto means, in his ingenious way, to signal, by affirming the end of art in our "post-historical" age, that we are now clearly (perhaps have always been) in a historical process in which we have never reached and could never reach the "end of art." In that case, the whole idea was a pleasant spoof.

Notice that the subtitle of *Beyond the Brillo Box* already speaks of a "post-historical perspective." There is no such perspective, because there never was a historical world that, in the Hegelian way, came to an end.

---

54. Danto, "Art After the End of Art," 328.

Art came to an end only in Danto's narrative, and in that same narrative we are (now said to be) in a post-historical age, an age in which there are no longer historical "ends"—except that one! (Kiefer clearly had not heard the news about either narrative.) I cannot see how anything has changed.

PART TWO

4

THE METAPHYSICS OF INTERPRETATION

I

In speaking of human beings and their world in all the ways in which that has interested them reflexively (ourselves, of course), I find it impossible to avoid endorsing two dicta of compelling power. The first is nowhere contested as far as I know; but the second is often viewed with great suspicion, though it seems as certain as the first. I draw from their conjunction two relatively bland conclusions: one, that in principle, humans can understand one another—their language, behavior, art, history—despite cultural differences and different origins (though there are no determinate conditions or criteria for fixing mutual understanding, or for fixing understanding in a way that can be shown to be uniquely valid or objective or universally confirmed); the other, that our understanding of the human world is, intrinsically, ineliminably interpretive (where the natural world cannot be understood except through the mediating work by which we understand ourselves and our human world). What's bland in these findings is what appears in the principal clauses; what's quarrelsome appears in the parentheses. I am interested in the parentheses more than the main clauses.

The dicta on which both depend are these: first, that

there are no natural languages for which there are no competent bilinguals—hence, that there are no cultures for which there are no interculturally competent persons; and, second, that persons or selves, that is, the actual denotable entities that manifest linguistic competence, are themselves contingently formed "artifacts" of the native enculturing processes of variously viable historical societies.

I admit that the second dictum is philosophically contentious, and I admit that many discussants would rather collect the facts I bring together here by entirely different means. Featuring them as I do, I suggest that they have an explanatory power that is lacking in all the alternative conceptions known to me. But, of course, in making the assertion, I am not making the case. Let me add, therefore, that I collect the import of all the foregoing in a single motto: selves, I say, are self-interpreting texts.[1]

The single most important clue that keeps us from deriving overly sanguine theorems from the mere motto or from what it may be thought to entail is this: that, though we can understand one another's meaning, there is no prior (or independent) meaning that we grasp or understand in virtue of which we do understand one another; that, though we can understand the differences between our own culture and another's, there are no determinately demarcated independent cultures that we grasp or understand in virtue of which we do understand one another; that, though we can perceive a common world and reason according to common rules and principles, there is no separable world that we neutrally perceive and no rules of reasoning that we first neutrally grasp or understand in virtue of which we do share a common world or reason in a common way.

What I mean is: what *is* common, objective, universal, meaningful, rational, or the like is a somewhat idealized artifact postulated in a revisable way *within* the space of our own artifactual competence in understanding ourselves and our world, both with regard to its cultural and its natural manifestations. I don't mean by that that we actually construct or make physical nature as such or even (the whole of) our cultural world by mere linguistic fiat. That would amount to a preposterous form of idealism. But we *do* construct a sense of what the independent natural world is determinately like, as well as of our encompassing cultural world—where we *do* in part make and alter the latter by continual linguistic and related interventions. Many find this last idea a baffling puzzle. It is indeed a

1. On the sense of "texts," see Chapter 6 below.

contested finding. It is also a premise on which the ontic theory of interpretation rests.

I should say, however, on pain of paradox, that there is no way to mark
what *is* an actual part of the real world that is not conceptually dependent
in any way on what *we* can defensibly claim is such; and what we can
claim and defend *is* indeed a function of our own artifactual and changing
history. My suggestion is that we acknowledge that the *ontic* independence
of physical nature is *epistemically* dependent on the conditions of understanding ourselves and our cultural world; that every viable realism is a
constructive realism (a constructivism); that ontic and epistemic questions
are, however different, inseparable;[2] that the cultural world is very different, *qua* real, from the physical world, because its Intentional, not its
embodying, features are ontically constructed ("mind-dependent") and because it provides real epistemic conditions on which any objective or
realist account of the natural world itself depends; and, finally, that, as a
result, constructivism entails the ineliminability of interpretive "intermediaries" at every point of understanding ourselves and our world, hence
some form of cultural realism.

One effective way to flag the misconceptions we must avoid in recovering objectivity in the "constructivist" way is this: meanings, cultures,
rules, traditions, histories, minds, reasons, acts, utterances are all nominal-
izations of what is first predicated of existent selves (societies of selves);
they are not, or not straightforwardly, independent entities. Even artworks, which, for commercial and legal reasons, are usually detached as
denotata apt for attribution, are open to being construed as entities—
grammatically congealed from what creative humans happen to "utter" as
by speaking or cutting marble or executing a bodily movement or writing
bad checks—that is, predicatively. The equivocation bears in an essential
way on the "nature" of cultural entities—*a fortiori*, on the logic of their
interpretation.

The point is that there is no way to construe "cultural entities" (artworks or selves) as entities on a *par* with physical entities, if that means
that their description must conform, *a priori*, with whatever logical or

---

2. This goes entirely against the realism defended, for instance, in Michael Devitt, *Realism and Truth*, 2d ed. (Princeton: Princeton University Press, 1991). I offer Devitt only as a
particularly transparent specimen of the dominant metaphysical tendency in recent Anglo-
American philosophy.

conceptual constraints are thought to limit what could possibly be true or said of physical objects: for instance, that physical objects cannot (taken pair-wise) occupy the same place at the same time or cannot (individually) have validly ascribed to them incompatible properties or can (as a commonplace set of things) exist even if human beings had never existed. Cultural entities are a breed apart because they have "natures" (if they do have natures) that include such properties as expressiveness, representationality, semiotic import, signification—which behave in a distinctive way and which is partly what we mean when we say they are intrinsically interpretable (or "mind-dependent"). Their nature is radically different from whatever we suppose the nature of physical objects is: for instance, they appear to possess properties that are determinable but not determinate (in the physical way), that change as a consequence of their histories—including the history of their interpretation—and are "objectively" real even though they are "mind-dependent" in some way. Nothing of this kind occurs among things that are entirely physical.

I collect all this by defining cultural entities as having *Intentional* "natures," where, by "Intentional," as already remarked, I mean any of a set of attributes that belong to the collective life of a human culture in the way of sharing a language or tradition or ethos or history (all of which, properly construed, are attributes). This hardly constitutes a full metaphysics, but it does yield a sense of the importance of insisting that what might count as an objective interpretation—in art or law or history, for instance—is impossible to identify without attending to the peculiar metaphysics of the cultural world. Nevertheless, many discussants, Monroe Beardsley and Richard Wollheim, for instance, are committed to modeling the theory of artworks (hence, the logic of interpreting art) on the metaphysics of physical objects.[3] They concede that interpretations are open to objective standing, but they insist that they must conform with the strictures of a bivalent logic.[4] They might be Fregeans, Aristotelians, Kantians,

---

3. See Richard Wollheim, *Art and Its Objects,* 2d ed. (Cambridge: Cambridge University Press, 1980).

4. Among recent essays in the theory of interpretation in the arts, I may mention the following at least that are opposed in varying degrees and in different ways to my own approach: Annette Barnes, *On Interpretation: A Critical Analysis* (Oxford: Basil Blackwell, 1988); Robert Stecker, *Artworks: Definition, Meaning, Value* (University Park: The Pennsylvania State University Press, 1997); and Michael Krausz, *Rightness and Reasons* (Ithaca: Cornell University Press, 1993).

positivists, Quineans, or pretenders to whatever common sense requires. But they would not willingly admit that bivalence *was* "metaphysically" or "methodologically" or "semantically" contestable.[5] They would insist that it was metaphysically neutral, even necessary![6] But how could that be shown?

My own conviction is this: that, in the matter of interpreting artworks (and more), there is no way to ensure a uniquely valid interpretation for any particular work; that there may be many valid interpretations if any can be shown to be objective; and even that valid interpretations of the same work or the same *denotatum* may not be reconcilable in any single interpretation. After all, the idea of objective but incompatible interpretations is not demonstrably incoherent or inconsistent; but the argument cannot be made without attention to the distinctive nature (or metaphysics) of interpretable *denotata*.

In fact, the most interesting heterodox theorem that I can mention that features the metaphysical difference between physical and cultural entities bears on the fact that the individuation and numerical identity of artworks and selves, the principal exemplars of what it is to be a cultural entity, are themselves thoroughly Intentional—not reducible to the conditions of the individuation and identity of the entities in which they are embodied. As a

---

I may perhaps risk mentioning a title I have read in manuscript only, Paul Thom's *Making Sense: A Theory of Interpretation*, which, more or less in agreement with E. D. Hirsch (at least to this extent) eschews, in the context of a general theory of interpretation, all metaphysics and methodology. The book has now been published as *Making Sense: A Theory of Interpretation* (Lanham, Md.: Rowman & Littlefield, 2000).

5. The prejudice in favor of bivalence, largely in the Fregean spirit, is the cornerstone of Dummett's treatment of the relationship between semantics and metaphysics, in the matter of *any* range of objective claims about the real world. See Michael Dummett, *The Logical Basis of Metaphysics* (Cambridge: Harvard University Press, 1991).

6. This is the view of the Fregeans, Dummett, for instance, and Robert C. Stalnaker, *Inquiry* (Cambridge: MIT Press, 1984). In the theory of literary criticism, it is straightforwardly championed in Monroe C. Beardsley, *The Possibility of Criticism* (Detroit: Wayne State University Press, 1970); and in E. D. Hirsch, Jr., *Validity in Interpretation* (New Haven: Yale University Press, 1967). There is no serious worry—on the part of either Beardsley or Hirsch, arguing from altogether different premises—that an exceptionless bivalence might be metaphysically inapt or inappropriate. The prejudice is very widespread and very blandly defended: rather, I may suggest, like the casual claim, made by both Donald Davidson and Hilary Putnam, that Tarski's semantic conception of truth (committed to bivalence and extensionality) is also, plainly, "philosophically neutral"! Tarski himself seems to have had no such illusions. See Alfred Tarski, "The Concept of Truth in Formalized Language," *Logic, Semantics, Metamathematics,* 2d ed., ed. John Corcoran, trans. J. H. Woodger (Indianapolis: Hackett, 1983), particularly §7.

consequence, they are individuated as they are (particular artworks within an "artworld," selves within a society) in virtue of sharing an ethos or culture; and their "natures" are alterable as a result of changes in the collective (Intentional, historical, *geistlich*) features of the culture they share. They are individuatable but not entirely free-standing in the way physical objects are said to be; their natures are not determinately bounded in the way physical natures are said to be, though not in any way that makes their numerical identity problematic. It is, precisely, the peculiarity of their nature's being determinable but not determinate (in the manner of physical objects) that accounts for their interpretability *and* for their interpretability's yielding objective interpretations that *do not* accord with the insistent bivalence (excluded middle, *tertium non datur*) that Aristotle makes so much of in *Metaphysics* Gamma and that nearly the whole of Western philosophy adopts with him.

II

There are many casually adopted doctrines, favorably linked to the canon already mentioned, that are prejudicial to the thesis I am now beginning to firm up, that are themselves distinctly doubtful or contentious but rarely made to submit to direct challenge. I have mentioned the most important of these; namely, the presumption that in all matters concerning what is real—the realist reading of interpretation or, more generally, the realist reading of predication—bivalence rules unconditionally. I have also hinted at other clues that I shall collect shortly. But let me offer, first, two specimen views opposed to mine, both utterly undefended, both presumably realist, neither clearly true, each open to stalemate, and each plainly governed by prior metaphysical convictions—all of which should confirm that they cannot possibly be self-evident or simply neutral.

In one, Monroe Beardsley, speaking primarily of literary interpretation, unceremoniously affirms that "there are a great many interpretations that obey what might be called the principle of 'the intolerability of Incompatibles', i.e., if two of them are logically incompatible, they cannot both be true. Indeed, I hold, [he adds] that all of the literary interpretations that deserve the name obey this principle."[7] Read in context, Beardsley adopts

7. Beardsley, *The Possibility of* Criticism (Detroit: Wayne State University Press, 1980), 44.

two linked policies: one, bivalence regarding interpretations; the other, a tolerance for "plural" interpretations consistent with bivalence.

In the second account, Nicholas Wolterstorff, also discussing the arts, though from a very different point of view—a view not primarily addressed to interpretation but concerned enough to "avoid various absurdities" regarding interpretation—advances two formidable principles: one, the

> *Principle of Exemplification:* Everything x is such that for every property P and every time t, x has P at t only if x exists at t;[8]

the other, the

> *Principle of Completeness:* For everything x and every property P, x either has P or lacks P.[9]

Here, Wolterstorff commits himself to the following at least: first, the complete determinateness of whatever exists; second, the conviction that the determinateness of what is real is strictly constrained by an exceptionless use of bivalence.

Beardsley's and Wolterstorff's doctrines are certainly self-consistent, but I cannot find the least effort on their part to defend their claims against competing views. Each, I take it, believes that his own doctrine is necessarily true. But since my own thesis (briefly sketched) is clearly *not* self-contradictory and applies to the same domain as theirs, their own modal claims are at least *prima facie* false! In any case, I argue that bivalence may be fairly challenged in realist contexts wherever entities possess Intentional natures; for pertinent attributes that may be objectively ascribed to artworks, texts, histories, discursive events, acts, and the like are: (*a*) determinable in a *sui generis* way (without being determinate in the conventional sense), (*b*) intrinsically interpretable, and (*c*) alterable as a result

---

Very recently, a view of interpretation quite sympathetic to Beardsley's New Critical doctrine has been advanced by William C. Dowling, *The Senses of the Text: Intensional Semantics and Literary Theory* (Lincoln: University of Nebraska Press, 1999), by way of what can only be described as an implicit Platonism (though Dowling would object). I return to Dowling in the Epilogue.

8. Nicholas Wolterstorff, *Works and Worlds of Art* (Oxford: Clarendon, 1980), 115.

9. Ibid., 137, 140.

108

of their ongoing histories and history of interpretation. (Concessions such as these cannot yield self-evident truths.)

Even this much permits us to review three very different theories of interpretive objectivity. The most unyielding, which may be called *objectivism,* holds that, ideally, description is contextless, satisfies something very much like Wolterstorff's two principles; and, applied in interpretive contexts, entails equating interpretation and description (or some suitable surrogate). Broadly speaking, this *is,* also, Beardsley's position.[10] For Beardsley holds that "literary works are self-sufficient entities, whose properties are decisive in checking interpretations and judgments": so much so that he concludes that "the literary text, in the final analysis, is the determinacy of its meaning"; that is, in interpretive "elucidation," we try "to report discovered meaning in a literary text."[11]

The sense is that interpretation is nothing but the elucidation of the meaning of a literary text—which is to say, "there really is something [meaning] in the [text] that we are trying to dig out, though it is elusive."[12] If meanings are construed as properties that behave, logically, in the way physical properties do (which Beardsley's theory pretty well requires), then Beardsley is effectively committed to the doctrine that interpretation = description; hence, that though there may be many partial interpretations of a given literary text, ideally all valid readings must be part of one uniquely correct "description" (or elucidation) of what is determinately and independently real. In this sense, Beardsley is no "pluralist"; or if he is, he views pluralism as little more than a tolerance for diverse but incomplete interpretations within an ideally adequate interpretation.

E. D. Hirsch is similarly committed to a strong use of bivalence and objectivism. Hirsch, however, is not an objectivist regarding literary *texts,* but only of "authorial *will.*" (I concede that Hirsch's thesis would normally not be said to fall under the range of "objectivist" views, because, of course, it adverts to the mental and the intentional.) Texts, Hirsch holds, are heuristically constructed by discerning the authorial will that informs a string of words. "A determinate verbal meaning," he says, "requires a determining will. Meaning is not made determinate simply by virtue of its

10. See, on objectivism, Richard J. Bernstein, *Beyond Objectivism and Relativism: Science, Hermeneutics, and Praxis* (Philadelphia: University of Pennsylvania Press, 1983).

11. Beardsley, *The Possibility of Criticism,* 16, 37–39.

12. Ibid., 47.

being represented by a determinate sequence of words. . . . Verbal meaning is whatever someone has willed to convey by a particular sequence of linguistic signs and that can be conveyed (shared) by means of those linguistic signs."[13] Furthermore, Hirsch says, "When . . . I say that a verbal meaning is determinate I mean that it is an entity which is self-identical. . . . it is an entity which always remains the same from one moment to the next—that is, it is changeless."[14]

This is an extraordinarily strong statement, which, I daresay, suggests (if it does nothing else) the reasonableness of considering nonobjectivist alternatives regarding the "metaphysics" of interpretation. For it is very difficult to believe that if the meanings of "texts" or verbal utterances, taken without regard to their utterer's intentions (Beardsley's approach), cannot be determinately fixed once and for all, such fixity can be assured by recovering their utterer's intention (on any theory of such intention).[15] Hirsch, I should add, is prepared to concede—in accord with the familiar doctrine favored by the Romantic hermeneuts—that "an author almost always means more than he is aware of meaning, [though it remains true] that meaning is an affair of consciousness."[16]

It's here, of course that Hirsch opposes the historicist version of hermeneutics advanced by Hans-Georg Gadamer, which calls into fundamental question all fixity of meaning, determinate authorial intent, and (most important) the very idea that any would-be interpreter of a piece of uttered discourse could convincingly claim a fixed or changeless competence in discerning its (changeless) meaning. One might conceivably have made such a claim in speaking of the barest sensory perception. But perception of *meanings*? Hardly! In any case, any such claim would need to be properly secured; and, if defended, would implicate one metaphysics or another. Retreating to the classic complaint, Hirsch insists that if authorial intent were not changeless, interpretation would be impossible.[17] Nonsense!

In the same spirit as Beardsley's objectivism, but for very different reasons, Hirsch has no particular tolerance for pluralism except by way of

---

13. Hirsch, *Validity in Interpretation,* 31, 46.
14. Ibid., 8.
15. See ibid., 46.
16. See ibid., Appendix II; and Hans-Georg Gadamer, *Truth and Method,* trans. Garrett Barden and John Cumming (New York: Seabury Press, 1975).
17. See Hirsch, *Validity in Interpretation,* 133–39, 144, 155.

extraneous accommodations of readers' or authors' interests imposed one way or another on prior objective interpretation ("intrinsic criticism"). Hirsch distinguishes here between intrinsic "meaning" and variable "significance."[18] Beyond that, Hirsch's own account is unintentionally subversive of both his own doctrine and Beardsley's. For one thing, he is surely right to insist that the meaning of a text requires *some* objective grasp of what speakers are doing or intending in what they write or say; and, for another, it is surely doubtful that we could ever fix uniquely, timelessly, objectively, any speaker's "will" or intention in speaking as he does. But if that is a genuine difficulty, then objectivism must fail. That is, objectivity could hardly be more than a reasoned conjecture (or, better: a proposal) of some sort, though, of course, it could be *that*.

If you allow this much, then *pluralism* signifies two very different doctrines at least—read in the realist way. One would be little more than a relaxed version of objectivism itself, in which, for various reasons, interpretations (or descriptions) were normally partial and incomplete, or approximative or informed by divergent interests—however guided by objectivism's original goal. The strongest philosophical expression of this kind of "pluralism" appears, famously, in Charles Sanders Peirce's fallibilism and Karl Popper's falsificationism,[19] which Peirce happens to have influenced.

The other form of pluralism is more a conceptual possibility than a fully established theory and practice. But it would have to be a two-story doctrine—no matter how thin or attenuated—if, indeed, it favored bivalence, even if not in accord, say, with anything as strenuous as Wolterstorff's completeness principle. In that sense, pluralism would concede a "first story" that, as either descriptive or interpretive, remained contextless, independent, determinate, bivalent, but also always incompleteable *at* that first story; so that a second story would always be needed (to "complete" a particular interpretation—*not*, for that reason, to "complete" the *object* "interpreted"). At the second story, however, what would have to be added would be objectively determinable but not determinate in the

18. Ibid., 8.

19. See Charles Hartshorne, Paul Weiss, and Arthur W. Burks, eds., *Collected Papers of Charles Sanders Peirce*, 8 vols. (Cambridge: Harvard University Press, 1931–34, 58), 5.565–66; and Karl R. Popper, "Introduction, 1987," in *Realism and the Aim of Science*, ed. W. W. Bartley, III (Totowa: Rowman & Littlefield, 1983); see also Joseph Margolis, "Peirce's Fallibilism," *Transactions of the Charles S. Peirce Society* 34 (1998).

same sense the first story was, *not* bivalent therefore in the sense of Wolterstorff's completeness principle, and yet (for all that) confined (for antecedent metaphysical or methodological reasons) by constraints consistent with a bivalence operative at the first story.

For example, one might suppose that the "ordinary" meanings of words and phrases in natural-language use occupied the "first story" but that a well-formed interpretation of an actual text literally permitted (possibly required) a freer use of the cultural options that belonged to the interpretive tradition to which the text in question belonged or was submitted (a psychoanalytic interpretation of *Alice in Wonderland,* perhaps). In that case, Beardsley's disjunction between "interpretation" and "superimposition" and Hirsch's between "intrinsic meaning" and "subjective significance" might be redeemed in the pluralist's two-story way.[20] (Beardsley would not concur, of course. Neither would Hirsch.) Beardsley uses the term "superimposition" (as opposed to "interpretation" proper) where, instead of "bring[ing] out of [a] work something that lies momentarily hidden in it[, we favor] ways of *using* the work to illustrate a pre-existent system of thought"; or, where we attribute to the work "connotations and suggestions [that] are not a part of [its] meaning but something psychological and personal" or something further that depends on such an attribution.[21] Beardsley, it must be said, offers not the slightest sketch of a criterion adequate for confirming any such disjunction.

Pluralism in either of these senses is, you realize, inseparable from a deeper objectivism (or "monism," as some prefer). In general discussions of philosophical realism, the closest one comes to something akin to the second version of pluralism may be found in Hilary Putnam's so-called "internal realism" (which Putnam has now pretty well repudiated); also, Nicholas Rescher's (self-titled) idealism.[22] Neither is an altogether suitable

---

20. If I understand him rightly, Stecker holds a view similar to the one suggested here regarding the preference of objectivism (Stecker's "critical monism") and its compatibility with pluralism (Stecker's "critical pluralism"), which he manages by way of favoring "truth" for monism and "acceptability" (short of truth) for pluralism. See Stecker, *Artworks: Definition, Meaning, Value,* chap. 8, particularly 134–38, 148–55. Stecker remains opposed to relativism in most of its current forms but is noticeably shy about linking his logical and methodological policies to the "metaphysics" of artworks. I regard that as a way of reducing philosophy to ideology.

21. Beardsley, *The Possibility of Criticism,* 43–44, 48–49.

22. See Hilary Putnam, *The Many Faces of Realism* (LaSalle, Ill.: Open Court, 1987); and Nicholas Rescher, *Pluralism: Against the Demand for Consensus* (Oxford: Clarendon, 1993).

analogue. In the theory of history, interpretation takes a very modestly pluralistic form, along the lines of the first option, in Arthur Danto's theory.[23] In the theory of art, perhaps the most sustained effort along the lines of the second option appears in Michael Krausz's theory of interpretation, particularly at the point at which Krausz speaks of the "indeterminacy" of musical compositions.[24] (Krausz, however, treats the interpreted "objects" as inherently "incomplete." That is what I wish to avoid.)

In mentioning these possibilities, I mean to draw attention, first, to the important consideration that, though there are undoubted differences among interpretive practices regarding artworks, sacred texts, legal documents, histories, face-to-face conversations, scientific theories, and the like, the argument in hand is addressed to cultural *denotata* in general, not yet sorted in any more specialized way; and, second, that, regarding this entire range, it is easy to provide a declension of coherent options ranging from objectivism through pluralism to relativism that could admit objective claims, though not without conceding very different metaphysical and epistemological alternatives. For the moment, I emphasize the need for a proper defense of the inviolability of bivalence, if it is to be invoked in fashioning interpretive policy. (An attack on bivalence, it must be said, does not depend, however, solely on the fortunes of Intentionality.)

III

I must make a detour here. The declension of the metaphysics of a text begun in the previous section proceeds a little too smoothly. I stand by the distinctions offered there, but they presuppose a series of more fundamental assumptions that I've only hinted at and now must air. Let me put these before you in a tabular way, perhaps a little too abstractly. They should help in distinguishing between natural and cultural entities, but I apply them to discourse in general.

First, then, we may concede the truism that nothing can be interpreted that cannot "first" be described.[25] Hence:

23. See Arthur C. Danto, *Narration and Knowledge* (New York: Columbia University Press, 1985).

24. See Krausz, *Rightness and Reasons*.

25. Many have chided me for apparently violating this truism, but they have misjudged the argument. See, for instance, Robert Stecker, "The Constructivist's Dilemma," *Journal of*

1. The usual distinction between description and interpretation does not require that the logical priority of the first over the second signify as well the temporal detachability of the first from the second.

I am prepared to accept the constraint. But I insist that affirming the inseparability of description and interpretation (along, say, lines that would not preclude Nietzsche's notorious doctrine[26]) does *not* as such violate the logical priority of description over interpretation. *Once* (as I have already urged) you concede that every viable realism is a constructivism, the difficulty dissolves and objectivism is stalemated.

I maintain that epistemic neutrality (in the objectivist's sense) is impossible to vindicate: it would require foundationalism or epistemic privilege, which hardly anyone believes can be sustained, and it would require a principled disjunction (not a mere distinction) between ontological and epistemological issues that would reactivate all the puzzles of skepticism belonging to the early history of modern philosophy ranging from Descartes to Kant, which constructivism easily obviates. In a word, the *objectivity* of description is as much constructivist as is interpretation.[27] (As we shall see, this first move disqualifies certain easy complaints against relativism.)

Please notice that the objectivity of *nature* is, on the argument, an *epistemic* artifact of conditions on which—despite the fact that interpretive questions normally do not arise in nature, or do not arise in the same way they arise in cultural contexts, or arise (by courtesy) in the sense that nature cannot be objectively described except within the conceptual terms of one theory or paradigm or another—the objectivity of the natural sciences is bound to be inseparable from the objectivity of cultural description and interpretation. I emphasize the point, so that it may be clear that

---

Aesthetics and Art Criticism 55 (1997); and Richard Shusterman, "Beneath Interpretation: Against Hermeneutic Holism," *The Monist* 73 (1990).

26. See Friedrich Nietzsche, *The Will to Power,* ed. Walter Kaufmann, trans. Walter Kaufmann and R. J. Hollingdale (New York: Vintage, 1967), §481.

27. I believe this to be the essential discovery Kuhn hit on in developing his account of "paradigm shifts," which he could not strengthen convincingly. That is, Kuhn saw that the history of science led inexorably to a constructivist view of realism in science; but he opposed the idea in part, and in part was unable to explain the sense of how, abandoning "strict" *neutrality,* we could ever reclaim *objectivity*! See Thomas S. Kuhn, *The Structure of Scientific Revolutions,* 2d ed. enlarged (Chicago: University of Chicago Press, 1970), section X.

item 1 of the tally I'm offering is *not* due to any merely narrow doctrine about the interpretation of artworks: it follows rather from a much larger reading of the inseparability of ontic and epistemic issues.[28] (You realize, of course, that this is part of a pay-down on the promise of the Preamble.)

But I need to reassure you as well that the loss of objectivist neutrality does not jeopardize the prospects of a workable sense of objectivity in any sector of inquiry. On the contrary, there is no viable alternative, and the fear that anarchy must ensue is a vestige of objectivist fears that were never justified in the first place. Hence:

> 2. Referential and predicative practices are normally fluent and successful, in terms of objectivity, in natural-language discourse; but that does not entail that, though they function in tandem, the conditions of success of the one are the same as those of the other.

It is a truism that to denote any thing is to denote something of a kind, and that to predicate something of any particular thing presupposes something sufficiently determinate to support predication. Once again, I accept all that, but I also insist that a *denotatum* may be numerically determinate, though its "nature" need not be comparably determinate (for all and any of its properties or for properties of certain kinds) but only determinable, sufficient for objective attribution. For one thing, reference, reidentification, or denotation cannot, in principle, be secured by any predicative means.[29] (I have raised the issue in an earlier chapter.) For another, apart from implicit or explicit Platonism (which is epistemically inaccessible on any known account), the determinacy of attributes is a function of the consensual fluency of discursive practices, not of any cognition of their independent determinacy. And, for a third, Intentional attributes, viewed as intrinsically interpretable, are inherently determinable but not determinate in the manner of physical attributes.

Objectively, in nature, physical properties do not change as a result of interpretation, whereas Intentional properties sometimes do or at least may. Hence, though a natural property—"red," say—may be (is often said to be) at once determinately "red" and open to some further, more precise

---

28. For a fuller account, see Joseph Margolis, *Historied Thought, Constructed World: A Conceptual Primer for the Turn of the Millennium* (Berkeley and Los Angeles: University of California Press, 1995). The technical arguments backing all the items of the present tally are offered there, though not in the linear order of the tally itself.

29. See W. V. Quine, *Word and Object* (Cambridge: MIT Press, 1960).

determination of *that* "red,"[30] the would-be determinate "meaning" of a poem is not, similarly, determinably some further, more precise determination of *that* first meaning. No, *its* objective standing, both as the determinate meaning it is and as whatever further determination may be objectively assigned as its successor, is never more than what is accorded, separately, objective standing within some consensual (but noncriterial) interpretive practice.

On the argument I am recommending, our cognitive powers function very differently with respect to natural and cultural attributes, though all general properties are never so completely determinate that they cannot be treated as determinable in some further respect (even alterable, in the case of cultural attributes, as a result of being interpreted). In any case, the objectivity of natural properties depends on acknowledging the objectivity of cultural properties, and the determinacy of the second entails the determinacy of the first. For cognate reasons, only entities defined in terms of natural properties can be said to have determinate *natures* or to be of "natural kinds," though admitting that is not to endorse essentialism. By contrast, cultural entities lack "natures" or "natural-kind" natures. This explains why it is entirely possible for *denotata* apt for interpretation to change their "natures" as a result of being interpreted, while not thereby jeopardizing their individuatability (or "number").

This line of reasoning goes entirely contrary to the tradition spanning Aristotle and the unity of science program.[31] But neither Aristotle nor the unity theorists pay particular attention to the ontological peculiarities of Intentional entities. Furthermore, to admit these possibilities helps to confirm that the logic of interpretation (for instance, bearing on bivalence) cannot be disjoined from whatever we count as a defensible theory of the interpretable "nature" of Intentional entities.

I hinted earlier that predicated "meanings" are quite different from physical properties; here, I give some reason for believing that that need not adversely affect their objectivity, which must be consensual, more or

30. In fact, the determinacy of "red" is more problematic than is usually admitted. The adoption of technical conventions obscures the problem, and cultural diversity confirms the variety of ways in which it may arise. For a particularly clear account of the complications, see Eleanor Rosch, "Principles of Categorization," in *Cognition and Categorization*, ed. Eleanor Rosch and Barbara B. Lloyd (Hillsdale: Lawrence Erlbaum, 1978); and Melissa Bowerman, "Learning a Semantic System: What Role Do Cognitive Predispositions Play?" in *Language Acquisition: Case Readings*, ed. Paul Bloom (Cambridge: MIT Press, 1996).

31. See Aristotle, *Metaphysics*, Book Gamma, in *The Complete Works of Aristotle*, 2 vols., ed. Jonathan Barnes (Princeton: Princeton University Press, 1984).

less in Wittgenstein's sense of the *lebensformlich*.[32] This supports and leads directly to the next item in my tally:

> 3. Intentional properties, like other general properties, are deter-
> minate or determinable relative to our interests and consensual
> practices; but, unlike natural properties, they cannot claim realist
> standing on grounds *other than* those of conforming with our con-
> sensual practices—there being no Intentional structures in nature
> apart from our practices in virtue of which their determinacy could
> possibly be confirmed or constrained.[33]

It is a truism that the "meaning" (or Intentional structure) of artworks, histories, discourse, human acts cannot be objectively ascribed in any way in which such *denotata* are detached from the Intentional life of the home societies in which (in accord with our predicative idiom) they are first uttered and identified. This begins to explain the benign sense in which the admission that interpretation logically presupposes description does not, as such, entail that the description (of the cultural *denotatum* in question) is detachable from the conditions of objective interpretation, that is, ca-pable of first being fixed in some noninterpretive way. For example, the non-Intentional description of the *marble* that embodies Michelangelo's *Moses* is *not* (as such) a description *of* (hence, does not impose a descrip-tive precondition *on*) the Intentional interpretation of the *Moses*. To insist that it is (and, accordingly, does) ignores the difference between natural and cultural entities. (Also, of course, to deny that the Intentional is, as far as we know, confined to the human world *is not* to affirm that the *intentional* is confined to the human. But it does mean that attributions of the latter are "anthropomorphically" modeled on attributions of the former.)

I have already alluded to this puzzle. For example, if "meanings" are confirmable only and entirely by reference to consensual practices, then, although that affords a basis for the objective standing of Intentional properties, it prevents us from being able to prove that meanings can never

---

32. See Ludwig Wittgenstein, *Philosophical Investigations,* trans. G. E. M. Anscombe (Oxford: Basil Blackwell, 1953).

33. The most perceptive grasp of the general determinate/determinable distinction ap-pears in *Collected Papers of Charles Sanders Peirce,* 5.446–49. Peirce would not favor the distinction of the Intentional; it goes somewhat against his notion of Thirdness.

be diversely or incompatibly interpreted—objectively. Only the pretense of cognitive privilege could claim to fix the meaning of a text that way (Beardsley's view) or the authorial intent with which a verbal utterance is said to have been originally uttered (Hirsch's view). Failing that, meanings cannot but be variably (consensually) determinable; the putative determinacy of any text's meaning will then be an artifact of such consensus (subject always to further constructivist divergence).

IV

Very similar findings hold with regard to the interpretation of artworks and the practice of interpreting constitutional law. Both confirm therefore the amplitude of item 3. You will find, for instance, in an essay by Supreme Court Justice Antonin Scalia, addressing the interpretation of the American Constitution, precisely the same objectivist options Beardsley and Hirsch apply to poetry, with due regard to the complexities of legal as opposed to literary texts. (I believe these findings apply convincingly to the whole of cultural life.)

Scalia is a "textualist" on his own say-so. He holds a view remarkably close to Beardsley's: that is, in favor of the plain legibility of texts and the exclusive authority of their fixed literal meanings—which entails the unqualified rejection of the *separable* intent of the original drafters of the Constitution (which would have signified "authorial intent" in Hirsch's sense). Scalia also takes note of the "aspirational" or "interested" orientation of judges, legislators, commentators, and ordinary persons bent on seeing the law "applied" according to their own interests—which corresponds very nicely to Beardsley's pejorative distinction between "meaning" and "superimposition."

Here are some of Scalia's summary remarks about "textualism" (or "originalism"), that is, objectivist theories of interpretation:

> A text should not be construed strictly, and it should not be construed leniently; it should be construed reasonably, to contain all that it fairly means.[34]

34. Antonin Scalia, "Common-Law Courts in a Civil-Law System: The Role of United States Federal Courts in Interpreting the Constitution and Laws," in *A Matter of Interpreta-*

My view that the objective indication of the words, rather than the intent of the legislature, is what constitutes the law leads me, of course, to the conclusion that legislative history should not be used as an authoritative indication of a statute's meaning.[35]

In textual interpretation, context is everything, and the context of the Constitution tells us not to expect nit-picking detail, and to give words and phrases an expansive rather than narrow interpretation—though not an interpretation that the language will not bear.[36]

What I look for in the Constitution is precisely what I look for in a statute: the original meaning of the text, not what the original draftsmen intended.

But the Great Divide with regard to constitutional interpretation is not that between Framers' intent and objective meaning, but rather that between *original* meaning (whether derived from Framers' intent or not) and *current* meaning. The ascendent school of constitutional interpretation affirms the existence of what is called The Living Constitution, a body of law that (unlike normal statutes) grows and changes from age to age, in order to meet the needs of a changing society. . . . it is the common law returned, but infinitely more powerful than what the old common law ever pretended to be, for now it trumps even the statutes of democratic legislatures.[37]

Scalia holds that "original meaning" is straightforwardly recoverable; that speakers' intentions are not separable from what is textually uttered; that separable intentions about what *is* uttered are interpretively irrelevant; that (apart from ambiguity) diverging plural interpretations nowhere apply; that the separable history of legislation, political concerns,

---

tion: Federal Courts and the Law, Amy Gutmann, ed., with commentaries by Amy Gutmann et al. (Princeton: Princeton University Press, 1997), 23. See also Scalia's "Response," in the same volume, 145.

35. Scalia, "Response," 29–30.
36. Ibid., 37.
37. Ibid., 37–38.

the specific application of the law, the public's interests, and even changes in the meaning of words (up to current meaning) have no standing in determining the objective meaning of the Constitution or of particular statutes.

Scalia is appealingly candid, and I have no wish (or competence) to engage him in specifically legal wrangles. But he *does* raise (and fails to answer) a number of conceptual issues that bear directly on the meaning of "original meaning" and its fixity under actual historical conditions. I daresay hardly any reader of Scalia's essay, aware of his reputation, would not be surprised by the unlikely simplicity and confidence of his *obiter dicta.* The difficulties posed by his text are so familiar in literature (in the arts at large, in history and sacred texts and ordinary conversation) that it would be hopeless to suppose such puzzles could be resolved by mere affirmation or that they were very different in the law.

Let me mention some difficulties with Scalia's textualist norms that Scalia himself cannot meet in the objectivist's (or textualist's) way any better than Beardsley can or Hirsch or Wolterstorff. The most glaring is simply that there is no obvious *textualist* sense in which *the very sense of what it is to institute a written constitution* (say, the American Constitution) can be shown to justify, or justify exclusively, the textualist reading of the supposed compliance of enacted statutes.

The actual history of alternative conceptions of interpreting the Constitution (briefly summarized by Scalia himself) clearly supports the charge. Furthermore, the Constitution nowhere explicitly says *that* it should be read as Scalia says it should![38] Even if you favored Scalia, you could never hope to defend his notion *by* textualist means. Texts normally lack such clauses, and would not be transparent if they included them. (They would generate a most awkward regress.)

In this connection, Chief Justice John Marshall's original 1803 decision, in *Marbury v. Madison,* which sets out the Supreme Court's adjudicative role, was little more than tautological in declaring that the strictly "judicial" (as opposed to the "political") aspects of enacted law fall to the judiciary rather than to the legislature. (Even that was contested at the time.) Marshall's opinion—affirming the High Court's right to judicial review and its power to declare invalid Congressional statutes on Consti-

---

38. Ibid., 135. See also Laurence H. Tribe, "Comment," in *A Matter of Interpretation.*

tutional grounds—depended ineluctably on the supposed original intent and purpose of a *written* constitution, *not* on any explicit authorizing statement within the body of the text.

Furthermore, at the very moment of Marshall's rendering his decision and during the interval in which the Federalists and Jeffersonians were known to hold opposing views about what a written constitution signified (whether, say, a compact among sovereign States or the deliberate imposition of a higher Federal power on the powers of the States—to stay with the details of American Constitutional history)—the *textual* sense of the Constitution could not have been reliably or exclusively read in the way Marshall did: Marshall's own purpose seems to have been to make sure that the Jeffersonian reading would not prevail! (There were, apparently, infelicities in the *Marbury* case that should have disqualified the Court's right to take it up or to take it up in the way it did.)[39]

I am prepared to argue, analogously, that there is and can be no reliable sense in which a literary text should or must or even could be straightfor-wardly read in the textualist way (as Beardsley insists). On the argument, every objectivist version of interpretive rigor collapses, without entailing that all rigor and objectivity must collapse as well.

Here is a second objection. *If,* as is plainly true, the Constitution may be amended, then it is entirely possible that laws judged admissible (or inadmissible) under an amended Constitution might not, need not, have been so judged under the Constitution prior to amendment. If so, then an Amendment might be judged (even by the Supreme Court) to authorize the *legislature,* without further amendment, to make laws that, in effect, *con-tinue* to "amend" the Constitution by legislative initiative! That seems in fact to have happened in the career of the Fourteenth Amendment (1868). The Amendment features the "due process" clause and the clause guaran-teeing "equal protection of the laws." But of course it was used very early to uphold segregation in *Plessy v. Ferguson* (1896) because, apparently, segregation was judged not to violate the "civil" or "political" rights of citizens (as opposed to other social concerns, like education and public accommodations).

More to the point, under section 5 of the Fourteenth Amendment, Congress was authorized to "enforce" the Amendment "by appropriate

---

39. See, for instance, the helpful summary offered in Robert H. Bork, *The Tempting of America: The Political Seduction of the Law* (New York: Simon & Schuster, 1990), 28.

legislation." The Court, judging the constitutionality of literacy tests under the Amendment, actually conceded that Congress might, justifiably, interpret the Amendment differently from the Court. It found, for instance, in *Lancaster v. Northampton Election Board* (1959) that literacy tests did not violate the Amendment; yet it upheld, in *Katzenbach v. Morgan* (1966), a Congressional ban on such tests. The decision has been judged to threaten *Marbury v. Madison and,* as a result, to suggest a very plausible way in which no single interpretive principle could possibly prove adequate for such a complex history as that of Constitutional law.[40] (The analogy with the history of the continuous interpretation of a literary text should be obvious. Procedurally, interpretation and amendment are entirely different; but, logically, they behave very similarly relative to a given text.)

There are also arguments to the effect that the intent of the Fourteenth Amendment was in some measure racist. But my own point is the deeper hermeneutic one: if we concede the two objections just advanced, it seems entirely reasonable to hold, with regard to both Constitutional and literary matters, that the Intentional content of given texts may be changed by interpretive history, without ever losing a workable sense of objectivity and rigor. But if so, then, once again, objectivism proves impossible to defend: that is, its modal presumption.

Here is another difficulty. Scalia raises the important question of the bearing of new technologies on the right application of the Constitution. "How," he asks, "does the First Amendment guarantee of 'the freedom of speech' apply to new technologies that did not exist when the guarantee was created—to sound trucks, or to government-licensed over-the-air television? In such new fields," he says, "the Court must follow the trajectory of the First Amendment, so to speak, to determine what it requires—and assuredly that enterprise is not entirely cut-and-dried but requires the exercise of judgment."[41] Many will be reminded here of First Amendment problems posed by the technical difficulty of controlling the use of the Internet in purveying hard-core pornography, without abridging freedom of speech.

You must bear in mind two considerations. For one, it is entirely

---

40. I have relied here on Cass R. Sunstein, *The Partial Constitution* (Cambridge: Harvard University Press, 1993), 42–45, 149–53.
41. Scalia, "Response," 45.

possible, on textualist grounds, to arrive at a coherent policy by merely concluding that the First Amendment has no application to such technologies. But that would be judicial suicide. If, alternatively, we insisted (with Scalia) on "following the trajectory of the First Amendment," the resolution of the new puzzles would inevitably exceed the resources of the most sanguine textualism, for there would then be no changeless condition to apply. Secondly, Scalia holds that the "whole purpose" of "a constitution" (*a fortiori,* the American Constitution) "is to prevent change—to embed certain rights [for instance] in such a manner that future generations cannot readily take them away."[42] Admirable, I suppose. But it raises the same textualist question *Marbury v. Madison* raised. I set that aside as having already been sufficiently aired. But try to follow Scalia's logic regarding the "trajectory of the First Amendment." On Scalia's proposal, the Court's strategy would be analogous to the use of the common-law principle, *stare decisis,* which Scalia defines as "the principle that a decision made in one case will be followed in the next," and which he then criticizes in the following terms: "It is an art, or a game, rather than a science, because what constitutes the 'holding' of an earlier case is not well defined and can be adjusted to suit the occasion."[43]

Scalia had in fact opened his essay with the promise to explain "the science of construing legal texts," which he claimed has been neglected largely by way of favoring *stare decisis* and similarly defective policies.[44] But he does not seem to have realized that the "trajectory" of the First Amendment, in fact the "trajectory" of any clause of the Constitution, applied to new technologies, would oblige us to proceed in the constructivist way—rather than by textualist discovery—to propose the "right" extension of the Amendment's meaning. It must inevitably yield a "pragmatic" artifact,[45] unless Scalia could provide Platonist criteria adequate for deciding the right extension of the Constitution's meaning.

Two consequences follow: for one, Scalia's textualism is itself a closet

---

42. Ibid., 40; see also 44–45.
43. Ibid., 7–8.
44. Ibid., 3.
45. Scalia does, it is true, treat *stare decisis* as a "pragmatic *exception*" to "origination"; but he does not explain what that implies. See Scalia, "Response," 139–40. Stanley Fish makes a pertinent observation on a related issue, in a very breezy bash at Ronald Dworkin, in *Doing What Comes Naturally: Change, Rhetoric, and the Practice of Theory in Literary and Legal Studies* (Durham: Duke University Press, 1989), 94.

constructivism, an "evolutionism" (as he himself calls it), a version of the "Living Constitution" he abjures; if that is so, then, for another, Scalia must admit that what holds for new technologies holds for new social conditions and new histories as well. But if the textualist doctrine fails in Constitutional law, it is hard to see how it could succeed anywhere else. Here, again, literature and Constitutional law go hand in hand.

V

Turn back, then, to the declension from objectivism to the two versions of pluralism already sketched. I said that, in the arts, Michael Krausz's so-called "multiplism" was the most sustained version of pluralism I could find. I repeat the point with some misgiving: for Krausz does not regard himself as a pluralist (in the sense given); in fact, his formulation has a distinct sympathy for relativism, which I take to be incompatible with the pluralisms already discussed. In light of that, I must add another item to the tally of assumptions or constraints I provided earlier.

I am not at all clear about Krausz's distinction between "multiplism" and "singularism": in particular, (*a*) about *what* would provide an objective basis for choosing either policy over the other (since both are coherent options); (*b*) about *how* either choice would affect the processing of evidence leading to an objective assessment of particular interpretations (their being "right" interpretations or not); and (*c*) about *what* regarding the would-be "objects" of interpretation would justify the objective standing of particular interpretations, without reference to the "ontology" of the objects in question (that is, would, according to Krausz, justify interpretation's being "right" or not but never "true" or "false"). Hence, I am not clear about how Krausz would distinguish between his multiplism and the pluralism I have sketched (unless he held that interpretations according to the first may be "right" but never "true," whereas interpretations according to the second aim at being true).

Here is what Krausz offers by way of a near-definition:

> The singularist holds that the range of ideally admissible interpretations should be singular, that the range of contending interpretations should be conclusively narrowed to a limit of one. He or she construes rightness in an exclusive way, and takes the rightness of a

given interpretation to be logically incompatible with the rightness of alternative interpretations. He or she requires that the single right interpretation should conclusively unseat alternative interpretations. . . . In contrast, the multiplist holds that singularist conditions may obtain in some but not all cases. The multiplist holds that nothing mandates that an interpretation must answer to a singularist ideal. Rather, such ideals are shaped by historically variable circumstances. The multiplist allows that the range of ideally admissible interpretations may be multiple. . . . The multiplist does not construe rightness in an exclusivist way. On the other hand, while he or she allows that ideally there may be tension between competing interpretations, such tension should be logically weaker than contradiction. The multiplist further allows for non-conclusive grounds for comparing and rationally preferring contending interpretations. The multiplist holds that the standards appropriate for the evaluation of one interpretation might not be fully commensurable with the standards appropriate for the evaluation of another.[46]

As I understand Krausz, singularism and multiplism are options under the notion of (what he calls) "praxial ideality" rather than "ontology" (the latter's options being exhausted, apparently, by "realism" and "constructivism" or, as seems apparent, "idealism"). It's for this reason that, in the passage cited, Krausz does not speak of the truth or falsity of interpretations but only of their being "ideally admissible" (or inadmissible) relative to well-established social practices; hence, also, of "rightness" rather than of truth.[47]

Krausz claims to remain "agnostic" about the relationship between "ontology" and "praxial ideality,"[48] but that seems to deprive him of grounds for a strong reading even of "admissibility" and "rightness." If true, this would seriously weaken the force of his position: first, because, as he acknowledges (and as we shall see more clearly shortly), *whatever* truth-values may be accorded particular interpretations depend essentially on what values may be accorded them in view of interpretive practices

46. Krausz, *Rightness and Reasons,* 27.
47. See ibid., 8–9.
48. Ibid., 6–7.

applied to "objects" of some determinate kind or other; second, because "rightness" is nowhere defined in this regard and, as a result, claims collected as singularist and multiplist are not marked off in any evidentiary way in terms of the conceptual difference between "truth" and "rightness."[49] (There is a similar difficulty in Nelson Goodman's *Ways of Worldmaking*. We need to know how the objectivity of a practice can be fixed without reference to the actual nature of what is being judged.)

I must add a third consideration here: singularism seems to be governed by an analogue of bivalence, whereas multiplism seems to be in accord with something akin to a relativistic logic; but without a sense of the "nature" of interpretable artworks, the first can only be a purely formal constraint, and the second provides no sense in which the intended tolerance (for options "logically weaker than contradiction" but such as "might not be fully commensurable with the standards" for others) can be explicitly provided.

It would be easy to resolve this matter by appealing to the distinction between bivalence and a many-valued logic, but that would go contrary to Krausz's intention. We may without prejudice, however, admit part of its lesson. Thus:

> 4. The admitted ubiquity of negation and noncontradiction as formal constraints on the logic of discourse does not entail our adhering to bivalence in testing truth-claims.

It is a familiar truism that affirming that Caesar crossed the Rubicon is tantamount to affirming that "Caesar crossed the Rubicon" is true. But it is also possible (certainly it is coherent) to affirm—in (say) interpreting Wordsworth's "A Slumber Did My Spirit Seal"—both Cleanth Brooks's and F. W. Bateson's incompatible interpretations[50] without risking self-contradiction, even where interpretation is viewed in realist terms.

---

49. There is a hint, in Krausz, that he has some sympathy for Nelson Goodman's preference of "rightness" over "truth," but it is an extremely oblique reference. See Krausz, *Rightness and Reasons*, 141; see also Nelson Goodman and Katherine Elgin, *Reconceptions in Philosophy* (Indianapolis: Hackett, 1988).

50. For a review of the interpretation of Wordsworth's Lucy poem, though from his well-known Romantic position, see Hirsch, *Validity in Interpretation*, 224–35. Hirsch, incidentally, says very clearly that "verbal meaning always exhibits a determinate structure of emphasis" (230), which, in context, signifies that, apart from ambiguity and the like, words *are* determinate in meaning. But is meaning straightforwardly "determinate" if it validly supports incompatible readings? Hirsch does not answer satisfactorily.

126

It doesn't matter (here) whether the actual interpretations of Wordsworth are strong enough to be proved valid. (The interpretations of the Lucy poem are in fact disputed, but I am prepared to believe that the infelicities alleged are largely minor and replaceable.) The important point is the modal issue: one *can* engage the argument without supposing that to confirm both interpretations would be self-contradictory. Contradiction, consistency, coherence, relevance do bear on sound reasoning of course, whether one subscribes to a bivalent or a many-valued logic; and it is true enough that, in admitting negation and contradiction, one *can* always "cook up" a bivalent formulation for expressing same, regardless of the "logic" one ultimately favors. But that is an innocuous, purely formal trick that has nothing to do with the supposed modal need to adopt bivalence in all realist contexts. In interpretive contexts, to support the validity of incompatible readings need never force us (on formal grounds alone) to support self-contradictions.

The paradigmatic mistake is surely Aristotle's—in *Metaphysics* Gamma. Robert Stecker has recently provided a very pale version of the same error (though without anything like Aristotle's metaphysical backing), in holding (on the strength of Stephen Davies's reading of my own theory) that my "ontology of art [which I have been summarizing piecemeal] is compatible with bivalence."[51] Not in the sense intended!

My account is indeed compatible with bivalence, but in two very bland respects that are far from Stecker's purpose: first, because one can always (as I say) paraphrase matters of formal negation and contradiction *ad hoc* in accord with a bivalent formula, even where, as when one prefers a three-valued logic, the inferences of a two-valued and a three-valued logic may not be the same; and, second, because no conflict need arise in the conjoint use of a many-valued and a bivalent logic if the affected truth-claims are suitably segregated (even *ad hoc*) within a particular interpretive practice. The two need never collide. (Otherwise, what Stecker and Davies say about compatibility is flatly mistaken.) In any case, there is no convincing demonstration that realist interpretations can always be suitably cast in bivalent terms, that is, preserving what may be affirmed in the relativistic way. That must be false, since, though the two interpretations

51. See Stecker, *Artworks: Definition, Meaning, Value*, 228 n. 11. See also Stephen Davies, "Relativism in Interpretation," *Journal of Aesthetics and Art Criticism* 53 (1995).

of Wordsworth *are* indeed admissible (as Hirsch concedes in airing the matter), Brooks's and Bateson's interpretations remain incompatible—in the strong sense that what they say *of* the Lucy poem *cannot be jointly true of one and the same poem,* or *cannot be integrated in a single consistent interpretation.* Neither Stecker nor Davies addresses the issue directly.

The bearing of this last consideration on the declension I began much earlier is straightforward enough: the option before us cannot be reconciled with either objectivism or pluralism or cast in objectivist or pluralist terms. It's another kind of cat altogether. In my idiom, it is simply *relativism:* schematically, the thesis that, in realist interpretations (at the very least), truth-claims or truth-like claims that would, on a bivalent logic, yield contradictory or incompatible claims, need not do so when construed in terms of a many-valued logic. (The claim that contrary or incompatible interpretations are valid need not, of course, be inconsistent. I call such claims or judgments "incongruent."[52]) You may name the pertinent many-valued values grades of "aptness," "reasonableness," "plausibility," even "probability," so long as you do not construe them as bivalent or tethered to bivalent values (for instance: as plausible or probable *relative to truth.*)[53]

The essential point remains a "metaphysical" one, if you concede that what I have collected as items 1–4 of the tally offered (above) defines a sense of "metaphysics" (or "ontology," to favor Krausz's term), that has nothing to do with affirming First Philosophy, transcendentalism, privileged knowledge of a reality altogether independent of the conditions of human inquiry, pretensions of modal necessity *de re* or *de cogitatione,* and so on. In short, *any* conceptual analysis, under realist terms of reference and predication, of what it means to make a valid claim about the prop-

---

52. See, further, Joseph Margolis, *Interpretation Radical But Not Unruly: The New Puzzle of the Arts and History* (Berkeley and Los Angeles: University of California Press, 1995); *What, After All, Is a Work of Art? Lectures in the Philosophy of Art* (University Park: The Pennsylvania State University Press, 1999); and, more compendiously, "Plain Talk About Interpretation on a Relativistic Model," *Journal of Aesthetics and Art Criticism* 53 (1995). I shall rely on these accounts for a detailed sense of relativism and will not pursue relativism's logic here.

53. Michael Krausz, though explicitly sympathetic with this thesis of mine, unaccountably commits the mistake just flagged. In fact, he does so inconsistently, since he acknowledges my intention *not* to allow the reading he finally relies on. See Krausz, *Rightness and Reasons,* 62–65.

erties of any *denotatum* is (on my reading) a metaphysics.[54] Any such analysis is plainly continuous with the work of "descriptive" or "revisionary" philosophy addressed to the sciences and ordinary discourse.[55]

It is just possible, then, to claim that relativism *is* a version of pluralism, because, of course, it's quite true that relativism would admit the validity of plural interpretations. But saying only that would ignore the decisive fact that *such* "plural" interpretations may be "incongruent": that is, such that, on a bivalent logic but not now, they would be, or would yield, contradictories or incompatibles. Thus, if you allow, as most theorists would (with care), that musical performances of scored compositions reasonably count as "interpretations" of the music and justify formulating associated discursive claims,[56] then, obviously, relativism is rampant in the music world! (This would not be possible on the objectivist's or pluralist's account.) What is of decisive importance is that the defense of relativism *is* metaphysical and realist in the sense I have already explained. In fact, I cannot see the point of distinguishing between an "ontological" and a merely "praxial" approach to relativism, as Michael Krausz seems to favor,[57] *if* a relativistic treatment of interpretations is to be reached in the realist way; if it is not, then, for my money, the issue is entirely idle. To deny relativism realist standing seems to me to deny it evidentiary standing in the serious sense that is normally contested. (The same is true of multiplism and singularism.) That is the reason I have made so much of the peculiar nature of Intentional attributes.

I cannot be entirely sure of Krausz's doctrine here. Speaking of interpretation, Krausz offers the following: "I have remained agnostic about whether the very idea of a practice-independent object in cultural practices is coherent. The ontological realist affirms that it is; the ontological constructivist affirms that it is not: the praxial constructivist leaves the matter

---

54. If you wish an exemplar, I can mention none better than Strawson. See P. F. Strawson, *Individuals: An Essay in Descriptive Metaphysics* (London: Methuen, 1959), which was the first compelling recovery of metaphysics in Anglo-American philosophy following the onslaught of the positivists and the post-Tractarian Wittgenstein.

55. It is also, in this sense, an effective rebuttal of Richard Rorty's enormously influential but (to my mind) completely arbitrary and failed effort to dismiss philosophy. See Richard Rorty, *Philosophy and the Mirror of Nature* (Princeton: Princeton University Press, 1979).

56. For a sense of this, see Krausz, *Rightness and Reasons,* chap. 1.

57. See, for instance, Krausz, *Rightness and Reasons,* 147: "praxial ideality" seems to be intended to be entirely outside "ontology" (or metaphysics); but if it is, it is indifferent to realist questions.

open. Yet, even if the idea of practice-independent objects in cultural practices is coherent, there is no way to inspect such objects. They can do no praxial work."[58] (I should say, rather, that they can do no work anywhere!) Of course, there is something troubling about Krausz's appeal to a "practice-independent object" wherever he speaks of ontology: cultural *denotata* cannot be "practice-independent" in the same sense in which they are Intentional entities; but they can be judged to be "independent" entities on the strength of a constructivist ontology.

I have implicitly urged, against "praxial ideality," the important thesis that ontic and epistemic questions are inseparable. I should add the following corollaries: first, *any* objectivist view of "practice-independent objects" (which surely includes objects independent of epistemic practice) is impossible to defend, because it generates insuperable skeptical difficulties of just the sort Descartes and Locke famously produced; second, no constructivist alternative need deny that "natural" or physical objects *are* "practice-independent," in the ontic sense, if it but concedes that if they *are* they *are* so on the sufferance of being epistemically dependent; third, specifically cultural or Intentional entities *cannot* be practice-independent in either ontic or epistemic terms; and, fourth, distinctions of these three sorts define what we mean by the realist standing of truth-claims or truth-like claims of any kind. But, if so, then there is nothing left for "praxial ideality" to be agnostic about.

Ontic "determinacy" is another matter. The reason I speak of the *sui generis* "determinability" of artworks and other cultural *denotata* rather than of their "indeterminacy" is that Intentional entities are not actually indeterminate—or, more specifically, "indeterminate" in the sense Krausz seem to favor, that is, in accord with the "incompleteness" of an artwork that performers (of music, say) or interpreters (of texts) may validly "complete." They are, rather, "determinable" (predicatively) in a realist sense not matched in physical nature: that is, in a sense restricted to their Intentionality. Krausz speaks of "indeterminacy" in both nature and culture.[59] I am not entirely sure of his usage, but I assume that, given that he treats musical performance as interpretation, what he means by indeterminacy regarding cultural entities is somewhat akin to the thesis I am espousing. (He obviously means more.) Still, difficulties arise if we concede that

58. Ibid., 146.
59. See, for instance, Krausz, *Rightness and Reasons,* 146, 150, and generally in chap. 7.

"an ontological realist construal of a work of music may allow that Muti's and Commissiona's interpretations are both admissible on the grounds that the ontologically real work is sufficiently indeterminate to answer to both." "This possibility," Krausz says, "suggests the logical compatibility of ontological realism with multiplism, and it constitutes part of the argument for the detachability of ideality from ontology."[60]

Clearly, Krausz views "indeterminacy" chiefly in performative terms. But then he grounds indeterminacy in the (ontological) "incompleteness" of what musical scores signify and thus favors the work of performers in "completing" what was "indeterminate" before. (That is a formula rather like Roman Ingarden's and Wolfgang Iser's, which are more than difficult to defend.) If this is the right way to read Krausz's doctrine, then I suggest we substitute "determinability" for "indeterminacy" (in the ontic sense) and simply treat musical performances as tantamount to epistemically defended "determinations" of *such* determinability (in the sense of supporting objective claims or objective interpretations about a particular work). It avoids all the familiar paradoxes and infelicities of incompleteness. (Everything that exists must be "complete" enough to exist!)

Let me offer in evidence (and in closing these reflections) Robert Stecker's recent objections to "relativistic" interpretation, directed chiefly against Nelson Goodman, Stanley Fish, Krausz, and me:

> Relativism [Stecker says] is committed to the claim that . . . interpretations are to be (and can only be) evaluated as true or false relative to the assumptions from which they start. . . . [Against the objection that that is "implausible," since our practice ought not be arbitrary, the relativist] may always *ask* for the justification of competing assumptions, conventions, or rules. What the relativist will deny [however] is that nonarbitrary *answers* will always be forthcoming.[61]

Read literally, what Stecker says here is entirely innocuous, in the sense that the evaluation of any truth-claims cannot fail to be made "relative to the assumptions from which they start"; although, of course, Stecker intends something more ominous, namely, the "relationalist" theory of truth

60. Ibid., 147.
61. Stecker, *Artworks: Definition, Meaning, Value,* 141–42.

usually applied to Protagoras but nowhere demonstrated either against Protagoras or here or as unavoidable. (It is an objection that, if cast in formal terms, deserves a serious answer, but Stecker does not provide the formal objection. I set it aside, therefore, though it is inseparable from Stecker's larger argument.)[62]

Stecker continues by way of singling out Stanley Fish's "relativism," but what he says clearly bears on the matter I have just pursued in Krausz's company. Here is what he says: "According to Fish's *theory,* critical activity *constitutes* its objects. (This claim, which can only be based on [Fish's] prior claim that we have no interpretation-independent access to the objects of interpretation, does not, in fact, follow from the prior claim. . . .) An interpretation [Fish holds] can be more or less adequate to the assumptions or rules on which it is based. Furthermore, these assumptions can be criticized in the light of other assumptions. However, since such criticisms have their own assumptions, such critiques do not bring about progress, only change. This is Fish's theory, his relativism."[63]

Two observations are in order: one, already remarked, warns that the denial of epistemic privilege will seem to yield "arbitrary" results when seen from the objectivist's standpoint; the other, which relates to different versions of constructivism (Krausz's, Goodman's, Fish's, my own), is quite capable of admitting *both* that "there is no interpretation-independent access to the objects of interpretation" *and* that, nevertheless, we *do* have objective access to those same objects. Stecker does not concede the possibility and misreads constructivism in accord with the objectivist's bias. My own stand—against both Stecker and Krausz—is this: for one thing, constructivism need not be a form of relativism at all (witness Kant); for a second, constructivism is (on an argument already sketched) the only form a viable realism can take; for a third, the realist standing of cultural entities cannot be "independent" in anything like the way physical reality is said to be; and, for a fourth, the "mind-dependence" of the cultural world (if you allow the phrase as a convenience) does not entail its "indeterminacy" or "incompleteness" (in the sense examined a moment ago). If all this holds, all of Stecker's objections fall away.

62. But see Joseph Margolis, "Relativism and Cultural Relativity," in *What, After All, Is a Work of Art?*

63. Stecker, *Artworks: Definition, Meaning, Value,* 238. See Stanley Fish, *Is There a Text in This Class? The Authority of Interpretive Communities* (Cambridge: Harvard University Press, 1980), chap. 16.

Krausz is quite clear on *this* matter. As he says: "Relativism denies the viability of grounding [interpretive] claims [any claims in fact] in ahistorical, acultural, or absolutist terms. Relativism is often motivated by the recognition of cultural or historical diversity, but that recognition cannot be equated with relativism. Cultural or historical diversity is logically compatible with either relativism or antirelativism."[64] Of course.

I can now put my argument in a nutshell: the impossibility of confirming any form of objectivism or epistemic privilege, joined to the distinctive nature of Intentional entities and properties, makes it impossible to disallow, as either arbitrary or self-contradictory, the *realist* reading of the relativism I espouse. The rest of the argument is broadly "empirical": Which metaphysics, we may ask, best fits the practice and conceptual puzzles of interpretation? I have offered a reasonable answer. I do not think there is a uniquely right answer to be had.

64. Krausz, *Rightness and Reasons,* 62–63. I would be remiss if I did not acknowledge receiving Michael Krausz's new book, *Limits of Rightness* (Lanham, Md.: Rowman & Littlefield, 2000), in the middle of proofing the edited transcript of *Selves* just before sending it off to the printer. I'll risk one comment on the basis of a first quick scan of Krausz's new book, which extends and strengthens the argument of *Rightness and Reasons.* In his conclusion, Krausz straightforwardly says: "The issue of singularism versus multiplism is logically detachable from realism, constructivism, and constructive realism" (149). Here, I think we may identify a benign equivocation on the term "detachability." Krausz clearly means, by "detachability," to maintain that neither singularism nor multiplism is "entailed" by the (mere) choice of any of the metaphysical options just listed and that none of these options "entails" as such either singularism or multiplism (see, for instance, 94–95). I myself don't happen to use Krausz's term in any useful way, though I would say that a ramified version of any of the metaphysical options offered *would* in all probability "entail" some constraints on the theory of interpretation—and vice versa. In that sense, the denial of "detachability" might mean no more than that *there cannot be a viable theory of interpretation that is not "adequated" to one's metaphysics,* for without meeting that condition one's theory of interpretation would have no relevance or application at all.

5

THE DEVIANT ONTOLOGY OF ARTWORKS

I

As far back as 1980 (in fact, earlier), I introduced the notion of "embodiment" to distinguish the metaphysics of artworks and cultural entities in general, according to the formula: "the 'is' of embodiment . . . is not to be collapsed into the 'is' of identity."[1] I meant it to displace Arthur Danto's better-known formula—viz., that the "'is' of artistic identification" is not the same as the "'is' of identity."[2] I meant it as an irony, because, as I have already remarked, Danto never rendered a full account of what he meant. Now, a dear friend of mine, Eddy Zemach, has chided me (in his recent book, *Real Beauty*) for having introduced, by the formula just given, a "gnomic" relation—that is, a relation that is conceptually "unhelpful" because its "logic" is lacking. Zemach signals an unwillingness to entertain conceptual improvisations that begin by acknowledging a profound ontic difference between what

1. Cited in Eddy M. Zemach, *Real Beauty* (University Park: The Pennsylvania State University Press, 1997), 159–60. The remark appears in Joseph Margolis, *Art and Philosophy* (Atlantic Highlands, N.J.: Humanities Press, 1980), 43–44.

2. See Arthur C. Danto, "The Artworld," *Journal of Philosophy* 61 (1964).

is culturally real and what is physically real—without, that is, invoking dualism. I am still committed to defending the embodiment doctrine as a strategy for featuring the strangeness of artworks and other cultural objects (selves, notably) when it is supposed that physical objects are the paradigms of what should count as a real entity.

Zemach correctly reported that, in invoking embodiment, I maintained (I confess I still hold) that one particular may (be said to) "instantiate another particular."[3] Certainly, I meant by that to offer something in the way of a distinctive (even provocative) "metaphysics" of art (and of culture in general), apt, for instance, for the special puzzles of description and interpretation that arise in the cultural world.

By this device, I hoped to collect, in one motto, at least the following doctrines and to lay the ground for a coherent defense: first, that cultural phenomena are "emergent" with respect to (not reducible to) physical and biological nature; second, that cultural phenomena exhibit certain *sui generis* properties that their "embodying" medium lacks; third, that these distinctive properties (which I denominate "Intentional") are indissolubly embedded ("incarnate") in the properties of their embodying (non-Intentionally qualified) medium; and, fourth, that since the embodied and embodying entities share physical or biological properties (the non-Intentional properties indicated), we may speak of one particular's instantiating another.[4] Very simply put (though it's hardly a simple matter), Michelangelo's *Moses* is "instantiated" by way of Michelangelo's art (and more), in the block of marble Michelangelo worked: he made the sculpture "emerge" from the marble in a way in which it remains inseparable from its natural medium but acquires Intentional properties thereby that no mere physical entity can literally possess. The *Moses* is instantiated in the marble because it is embodied in it.

The economy thus gained brings together, by a single stroke, the avoidance of dualism, the admission of the conceptual distinction of cultural reality vis-à-vis physical reality, and the minimal peculiarities of the ontology of artworks. What I claim is that no philosophy of art or culture is

3. Zemach, *Real Beauty*, 160; Margolis, *Art and Philosophy*, 22.

4. This resolves, in fact, the notorious incoherence of Strawson's account of "basic particulars," since, now, we can admit that two "basic particulars" (in Strawson's sense) *can* occupy one and the same place, if one is "culturally emergent" with respect to the other. See P. F. Strawson, *Individuals: An Essay in Descriptive Metaphysics* (London: Methuen, 1959). The difficulty appeared in Strawson's original account (and of course obtains here as well).

likely to be viable if it does not come to grips with these considerations. Most analytic accounts ignore the charge. But, in saying all this, I freely admit two further caveats: one, that I am enlisting the term "instantiate" for a substantive rather than a predicative use; and, the other, that though I would be willing to speak of embodiment and incarnation as "part"/ "whole" distinctions of some kind, they are not (cultural complexities in general are not) mereological distinctions (in the familiar sense Zemach favors).

Zemach broaches an essential puzzle the resolution of which was meant (for my own part) to contribute an argument supporting embodiment. I need to reclaim that puzzle and its resolution: they are as important now as they ever were.

He says (not accurately, but discerningly):

> Relativists believe that there is no way for us to identify the interpretandum, the artwork X itself, through the veil of its interpretations. Being what we are, we are necessarily biased: we cannot see the work as uninterpreted, and each reader constitutes the interpretandum differently. In a word, interpretation is all there is; the interpretandum is a myth. . . . Interpreters impute (as Margolis says) their interpretations to the interpretandum, and different interpreters impute different interpretations to the work, but that does not obliterate the work X as it is in itself. The properties X has as such are those shared by all its instances, so if you know X's occurrences, you know what X is as such.[5]

What Zemach reports here is, I'm bound to say, false about art and my theory. You have only to consider that, regarding engravings (Dürer's, for instance, which I have always puzzled over), there may be no set of properties (neither physical nor Intentionally incarnate) that *all* correctly pulled instances of a particular Dürer could be reasonably said to share— that would not be too much like an artwork's least common denominator—to have much relevance for any pointed discourse about the arts. I offer this only as a clue. There are more important considerations that need to be laid out. But you surely see that Zemach has put his finger on a nagging concern that has occupied a great many philosophers of art

5. Zemach, *Real Beauty*, 155–56.

(many whom I've already mentioned) in related ways: for instance, Beardsley, Hirsch, Ingarden, Iser, Goodman, Danto, Wollheim, Krausz, Stecker, and Davies, besides myself.

I'll dwell a little longer on Zemach's formulation, if I may. If you review his implied objection, you will see that it rests on the presumption that if artworks are real entities, they must have their properties *apart* from interpretive imputation, which our descriptive efforts must be able to address *ante;* that to "impute" (to be able to do no more than impute) properties by alternative perspectived means (what amounts to "bias," in Zemach's idiom) signifies that there *are* no artworks at all, that artworks are not real, or that they are contrived *ad hoc,* or that there is a multitude of artworks matching (one for one) a multitude of alleged interpretations. On my reading, of course, that would risk collapsing the difference between my theory and Danto's—which is the reverse of my intention. It is also, I daresay, a *non sequitur.*

Against Zemach, I would say: (i) that artworks *are* real *but* have significantly different natures from those of physical entities; (ii) that their natures include a range of properties that disallow any criterial or epistemic disjunction between "perceiving" and "imputing" (or between "describing" and "interpreting") the objective properties of given artworks; (iii) that the "objectivity" of all referential and predicative discourse cannot but take a constructivist form, so that invoking (ii) in cultural contexts is not questionbegging; (iv) that admitting (ii) and (iii) makes it impossible to disallow the pertinence of a relativistic account of objective (truth-)claims; (v) that acknowledging the reality of physical entities in general *presupposes* and *entails* the reality of cognizing selves (persons, ourselves); and (vi) that what distinguishes artworks from physical entities is generically the same as what distinguishes selves from physical entities (the members of *Homo sapiens*), however specifically different selves and artworks (or other cultural entities) may be from one another (for instance, in possessing or lacking consciousness). Treat this, please, as an addendum to the tally collected a moment ago regarding "embodiment."

I don't find a compelling argument in any account known to me to the effect that all real entities are nothing but physical entities or that truth-bearing (or truth-like) discourse about the cultural world is logically modeled (denotatively and predicatively) in the way discourse about physical entities is (or necessarily is). On the contrary, I hold that artworks *are* real and have very different "natures" from physical entities; so different, in fact, that the first are "embodied" in the second—uniquely so, conformably with the vexing thesis that one particular (a particular of the physical kind, say) can instantiate another (a particular of the cultural kind) by way of (cultural) emergence.

I see no troublesome paradox in so speaking, and no better idiom in sight. We invent the ontologies we need for purposes that arise, just as we invent our mathematics, seeking only to make them plausible and coherent and serviceable. The idea (Zemach's) that a real entity is, in all cases, determinate in all its properties, intact apart from our inquiries and interventions, and that that is the minimal condition on which interpretive objectivity rests, is, in my opinion, a recipe for conceptual disaster. We must, in any case, accommodate what is distinctive of the cultural world. If you demur, I must ask you where the dialectical advantage lies.

The importance of the quarrel rests with the possibility that, first of all, what's generically true of artworks is true of selves—and everything else that belongs to the world of human culture; and, second, that if the entities of physical nature are *said* to be real, then (on pain of paradox) it cannot be denied that cultural entities are real as well and must be embodied in the sense I suggest. There's the challenge. *Epistemically,* we cannot admit determinate physical entities without admitting the reality of selves; but the reality of selves is inseparable from the *ontic* standing of the cultural world.

This is sometimes cast in a derogatory way, as by affirming that to insist on the epistemic dependence of the determinacies of the physical world on the work of inquiring "minds" is tantamount to espousing some form of idealism. But that is simply a blunder: it's not idealism but constructivism that follows from the post-Kantian exposé (for instance) of all the paradoxes and skepticisms and *reductios* the "Cartesian" realism spanning Descartes and Kant engenders. *That* the *cultural* world is "mind-dependent" is also not idealism in the classic sense; for both concessions entail no more than the infelicity of ever having opposed "realism" and "idealism" disjunctively. It is only the inertia of philosophical prose that makes the ghost of idealism seem to hover over inquiries that have exorcised idealism long ago.

Certainly it is clear that, unlike what may be argued regarding physical objects, cultural phenomena (language, artworks, institutions, practices) *cannot* have their properties "apart" from human selves or human societies, in the sense in which we say physical objects are "independent." The Intentional properties of cultural things *do not,* for that reason, depend arbitrarily on whatever any one or several of us suppose they are. They may rightly claim *some* sort of objectivity; yet even the existence and nature of human selves (the enlanguaged, encultured, "second-natured" members of *Homo sapiens* who acquire, in infancy, the aptitudes that mark them as, and transform them into, the cultural "artifacts" we call selves or persons) cannot possibly be what they *are,* entirely "apart" from the similarly second-natured societies in which they are first formed: I would say, "uttered." Short of some reductive or eliminative physicalism—which I claim cannot work—it is hardly strange to suppose that artworks and selves invite (even oblige) us to concede that something like the embodiment relation holds among cultural entities *if* we insist on characterizing physical objects in something like Zemach's way!

II

Let me come to the nerve of the quarrel and urge a concession any ontology of art should allow: namely, that artworks characteristically possess representational, expressive, symbolic, semiotic, stylistic, genre-bound, traditional, and historical properties. I have named such properties "Intentional," meaning by that to equate the Intentional and the cultural (or, the culturally meaningful—or, the intrinsically interpretable).[6] That permits me to accommodate the notion of the "intentional" which Brentano and Husserl developed, while escaping the methodological solipsism and the acultural and ahistorical cast of their particular theories. All that is easily recovered under terms keyed to our acquisition of a first language. It is presupposed (I suggest) in all our talk of art, but also in theorizing about the nature of human selves—which, as I say, motivates my ontology of art. I mean to capture all this by the term "Intentional."

I suggest as a formal, uninterpreted condition that properties must be

6. For a fuller sense of the "Intentional," see Joseph Margolis, *Historied Thought, Constructed World: A Conceptual Primer for the Turn of the Millennium* (Berkeley and Los Angeles: University of California Press, 1995).

adequated to their *denotata;* that is, whatever properties we attribute must be consistent with the conceived "nature" of the things to which they are ascribed. In the sense intended, it would not be controversial to hold that, when read literally, sentences like "The stone smiled" would fail the adequation test. John Searle claims (without benefit of argument) that mental attributes may be directly predicated of the brain (thoughts and memories, for instance), though he does not show that they are physical attributes.[7] I cannot support this way of speaking though I would not endorse physicalism either: it's just that, on the usual view, physical objects lack Intentional properties or are assigned them rhetorically or figuratively. If so, then Searle must be stonewalling. Danto, as we have seen, assigns Intentional properties to "mere real things," but he does so rhetorically. Hence, he does not fail the adequation test in any technical sense. (He simply sacrifices the realist standing of the "artworld.")

Zemach is on stronger ground. He believes that those who, like myself, speak of *imputing* Intentional properties to artworks imply thereby that there are no such entities (they don't *exist*); or, alternatively, that, if there are artworks, they lack Intentional natures or their distinctive properties are entirely reconcilable with physicalism. (Why else, he wonders, should we "impute" such properties to them if they are "there"?) Zemach ignores the obvious answer: namely, that Intentional properties are distinctive in such a way that no one, modeling artworks on physical paradigms (Zemach himself), would (*a*) admit such properties in the adequational and realist sense, or (*b*) admit their descriptive and interpretive oddities in discourse correctly deemed to be objective.

I say the cultural world has *emerged* in a *sui generis* way from the physical and biological world, possibly by small biological increments through which our cognizing competences develop to such a point that *we* can claim to discern an "emergent" world (the cultural world) that we find we cannot explain in terms restricted to physical nature alone. The reality of the cultural world is never really in question, whatever we suppose its analysis may yield. It manifests itself in the mastery of natural language and whatever language makes possible in nonverbal ("lingual") ways (as in dancing, the preparation of food, making love). It is exclusively identified (as is, indeed, the physical world) *by* encultured selves, who are

---

7. See John Searle, *The Rediscovery of the Mind* (Cambridge: MIT Press, 1992).

themselves the preeminent entities of the cultural world (indeed, of "both" worlds).

The important point is that cultural phenomena (or entities) are (i) real, as real as physical phenomena, (ii) causally efficacious in physical and cultural contexts, (iii) distinguished by their possessing Intentional properties, and (iv) adequationally sufficient for justifying the objective standing of interpretive and legitimative inquiries that go beyond the causal. Furthermore, adequated to embodiment, mental, linguistic, stylistic, and related (Intentional) properties may be said to *have* both physical and Intentional features, such that their Intentional features are indissolubly "incarnate" in their physical features and, as a result, are "discernible" only *in* their incarnating features. (Here, the term "Intentional" is benignly equivocal.)

It is in this sense that I treat the "is" of embodiment as an entitative analogue of the "is" of predicative instantiation, which I restrict to the cultural world. The device is a convenience facilitating reference, predication, numerical identity, reidentification; hence, also, description, interpretation, explanation, evaluation, and the like. Except of course that I am not willing to scant a realist reading of conditions (i)–(iv) of the tally given above.

It follows from all this that: (*a*) *to* denote an artwork as the referent of descriptive and interpretive discourse, *and* (*b*) *to* go on to describe and interpret such a *denotatum*, is (*c*) to concede that, as opposed to physical entities, there is no principled distinction between the *description* and *interpretation* of artworks on the one hand and *imputations* to that effect on the other. Whether introducing "imputation" is ultimately idle or misguided depends on what the connection is between Intentional and non-Intentional properties. *If*, as I say, reference and predication are epistemically informal—so that there are no perceptual or other directly discerning powers by which their success can be criterially confirmed— then there cannot be a principled disjunction between description and imputation. Q.E.D. And if that is admitted, then "objectivity" cannot fail to take a constructivist form.

There is no escape from the consensual informality of natural-language discourse. There is no algorithmic connection between discourse about the physical and cultural worlds. Reference and predication are epistemically hostage everywhere. If so, a relativistic treatment of description and interpretation cannot be ruled out *a priori*. Hence, reference and predication are affairs not of *savoir* (the right exercise of a definite cognitive faculty) but of *savoir-faire* (a consensually tolerable measure of practical success). If, more pointedly, reference cannot be fixed predicatively or causally, and if Platonism is never accessible in predicative matters, then the informalities of reference and predication apply everywhere—and no principled disjunction obtains between discerning and imputing what we take to be objective, anywhere. Here, what we mean by "objectivity" is not lost: it must be redefined under argumentative pressures.

III

Let me mention without ceremony the least contestable clue favoring the theory I support: viz., we first learn to speak, living as children among linguistically competent adults; but there is no way to account for our fluency (in learning and using language) by any general inferential strategy that proceeds *from* reliably first fixing certain physical marks (sounds, say) *to* the determinate Intentional features of linguistic utterances (meanings, say). That would, in effect, be methodological solipsism, faulted by self-referential paradox. It would also preclude "emergence" in favor of what is now fashionably called "supervenience," which claims a necessary algorithmic invariance linking the mental or Intentional and the physical.[8] What holds here holds for artworks as well.

Herbert Feigl, as remarked in an earlier context, was fond of speaking, in conversation at least, of the "many"/"many" problem, that is, of the puzzle, that, for any determinate physical movement, there were indefinitely many significant actions that might be "associated" with (I would say, "embodied" in) that movement (signaling or pretending to signal, for instance); that, for any action, there were indefinitely many alternative bodily movements that might convey the same action (greeting another, say); and that there were no legible rules or laws coordinating the two sets.[9] (Feigl worried about the prospect, but reported the possibility never-

---

8. See, for instance, Jaegwon Kim, *Philosophy of Mind* (Boulder: Westview Press, 1996), 10.

9. I have never found the expression in Feigl's papers; but it is, of course, the central worry of his important book, *The "Mental" and the "Physical": The Essay and a Postscript* (Minneapolis: University of Minnesota Press, 1967).

theless.) The "many"/"many" problem obviously applies to language as well.

If you add to this the insuperable informality of reference and predication (*and* the informality of fixing the "contexts" of reference and predication), you will find that you are committed to some form of constructivism in adopting any realist view of physical and cultural phenomena.[10] This means, very simply, that what is real—however *ontically* "independent" we suppose the real to be—is *epistemically* dependent on human conditions of understanding and belief. In this sense, *the realist reading of what is real* is itself an interpretive posit: the internal accusative, so to say, of interpretive "intermediaries," subject therefore to the historical drift of our conceptual schemes. But that hardly makes physical *reality* "mind-dependent."

I emphasize the point because it is regularly supposed (certainly by Zemach[11]) that we cannot *interpret,* in any sense that may be called objective, what is not antecedently *described* or describable. But that fails to concede that what is taken to be descriptively reliable, the condition on which "interpretation" is supposed to perform its characteristic labor, *is,* on a constructivist theory (which, I claim, we cannot escape), itself the upshot of an interpretive posit. Epistemically, we "constitute" the intelli-

---

10. I give the full argument in *Historied Thought, Constructed World* and, by pieces, in other places. See Joseph Margolis, *Interpretation Radical But Not Unruly* (Berkeley and Los Angeles: University of California Press, 1995).

11. The disjunction is implicit in Arthur C. Danto, *The Transfiguration of the Commonplace* (Cambridge: Harvard University Press, 1981); also, in Richard Wollheim, *Art and Its Objects,* 2d ed. enlarged (Cambridge: Cambridge University Press, 1980). See also a succinct version of this overly easy presumption (partly directed against my own view) in Richard Shusterman, "Beneath Interpretation: Against Hermeneutic Holism," *The Monist* 70 (1990).

Of course, the principal figure in the philosophical wings who has disputed the appeal to interpretive or epistemic "intermediaries" (or, misleadingly, "*tertia,*" in Richard Rorty's idiom) is Donald Davidson, writing in support of his "naturalizing" of realism. See Donald Davidson, "A Coherence Theory of Truth and Knowledge," in *Truth and Interpretation: Perspectives on the Philosophy of Donald Davidson,* ed. Ernest Lepore, ed. (Oxford: Basil Blackwell, 1986). See also Richard Rorty, "Pragmatism, Davidson, and Truth," in the same collection. But Davidson has now admitted that the theory he advanced (which he has yet to redeem or replace) rested on a "blunder" (his own term). But if that is so, though I cannot spare the space here for the full argument, then the entire attempt to "naturalize" the cultural world (which, in effect, I sketched in Chapter 1) is put at mortal risk. See Donald Davidson, "Afterthoughts, 1987" appended to a reprinting of the paper of his mentioned (just above in this note), in *Reading Rorty: Critical Responses to Philosophy and the Mirror of Nature (and Beyond),* ed. Alan R. Malachowski (Oxford: Basil Blackwell, 1990).

gible world we claim to describe objectively: that is, what is often called the "sense" of *both* the natural and the cultural worlds; ontically, we posit what we take to be the reality of physical nature as it is apart from our positing it thus *and* apart from what we claim to discern as culturally real. The very *reality* of the cultural world is ontically inseparable from our enlanguaged interventions in the world; and the *realist* standing of independent physical nature remains epistemically (not ontically) dependent on the conditions of human inquiry.

The denial of this benign antinomy produces instant and insuperable paradox; and, as I say, its affirmation is not a form of idealism. I see no difficulty there. Culture, but not nature, is infused with Intentional properties; and Intentional properties are intrinsically apt for interpretation. There is, therefore, a dual sense in which we speak of interpretation: first, constructively, that is, in terms, *pace* Kant, that cannot be disjunctively first assigned cognizing subjects and cognized objects but depends instead on (as the analysis of reference and predication shows) some prior symbiosis within which epistemic and ontic distinctions are first "constituted"; and, second, objectively, *within* the terms of the first, by which we claim to discern the meanings and significative structures of human "utterances," the nominalized acts, speech acts, histories, practices, institutions, artifacts, machines, technologies, artworks thereby constituted. But if that is so, then, once again, there can be no principled disjunction between description/interpretation and imputation.

In Anglo-American philosophies of art, as in Anglo-American philosophy in general, discourse about physical nature is regularly taken to be paradigmatic of "objective" inquiry, so much so that the right analysis of the ontology of art and the logic and methodology of interpretation are thought to be rightly governed by the exemplars of the first. That is certainly the assumption shared by Beardsley, Danto, Goodman, and Zemach. But it utterly fails to capture or eliminate Intentionality. The question of the ontology of art is best managed, I suggest, by adhering to the following two elementary constraints: one, that the logic and methodology of describing and interpreting artworks should be adequated to their supposed nature; the other, that artworks have an Intentional nature. I cannot imagine a more sensible way to begin, but I admit that that alone settles very little. I, for instance, think it impossible to avoid drawing certain radical conclusions from the inherent complexities of Intentionality. Others obviously do not: chiefly, I believe, because they adhere to certain entrenched views about bivalence and interpretation, *a priori* conditions of objectivity, canons governing discourse about "reality," all of which betray a taste for the presumptive paradigms of physical nature.[12]

All this is threatened in the profoundest way by admitting the epistemic puzzles regarding reference and predication and Intentional attributes. I could add cognate difficulties about context, the historicity of thinking, truth and knowledge, the distinction between the subjective and the objective, and our understanding of what is real. But, for the sake of a lean challenge, I put all that aside.[13] There remains an "adequational" theorem that the theory of interpretation must surely conjure with: namely, that, if artworks are construed entitatively (as individuated *denotata*), then (*a*) artworks may and must be assigned numerical identity, however problematic their nature; and (*b*), compatibly with (*a*) and in virtue of their Intentionality, artworks possess determinable but not strictly determinate "natures."

The theorem is almost universally neglected. There are very few sustained analyses of the ontology of art in English-language philosophy that are not effectively committed to either a physicalist paradigm or some frank Platonism.[14] Both seem to me inadequate for the same reason: viz., the nature of Intentional properties.

I hold that cultural entities form a *sui generis* run of real things implicated, as ontically different, *in* the very analysis of physical nature. For *knowledge* is itself a cultural artifact. We cannot, without admitting that,

12. I offer in evidence the recent views of Stephen Davies and Robert Stecker. See Stephen Davies, *Definitions of Art* (Ithaca: Cornell University Press, 1991); and Robert Stecker, *Artworks: Definition, Meaning, Value* (University Park: The Pennsylvania State University Press, 1997). The strategy of these two books should be viewed in the light of a symposium, in which Davies and Stecker respond to a paper of mine outlining the general form of a relativistic account of interpretation. See my "Plain Truth about Interpretation on a Relativistic Model," Davies's "Relativism in Interpretation," and Stecker's "Relativism about Interpretation," all three published in *The Journal of Aesthetics and Art Criticism*, LIII (1995). The point I wish to stress is that the relativism I propose is intended to support (has always been explicitly linked to) a ramified account of what an artwork is. I single out Davies and Stecker because of their confrontational style—which I enjoy; but the truth is, there are many discussants who, like them, favor bivalence and objectivity and the rest and who show a similar disinclination to venture into the ontological thickets.

13. See Margolis, *Historied Thought, Constructed World,* for a further reading of these matters.

14. See, for the most developed recent account of the Platonist stripe, Nicholas Wolterstorff, *Works and Worlds of Art* (Oxford: Clarendon, 1980). On the first option, you may of course take Beardsley, Danto, and Zemach as reasonable specimens.

give a convincing account of the central puzzles of art and criticism; for instance, of these: How is an artwork individuated and numerically identified, if it is not merely a physical object? In what sense is it possible that artworks remain real, in spite of the fact that Intentional properties are not determinate or fixed in whatever way we suppose physical properties are? What does it mean to say that the properties of artworks are inherently interpretable, in spite of the fact that we cannot defend a principled distinction between what they are and what they are imputed to be? In what sense can we rightly say that the imputed properties of artworks remain objective (or real), if divergent ascriptions, possibly even incompatible interpretations, may be validated? And in what sense can the Intentional properties of artworks be objectively assigned if they can be altered or affected by the changing history of their ongoing interpretation? You cannot find any parallel among canonical physical objects.

I favor certain heterodox possibilities here, and I claim to be able to provide a unified and plausible answer to all these questions in relativistic and historicist terms—for instance, in accord with the interpretive work (*not* necessarily the theories) of such figures as Stephen Greenblatt, Michel Foucault, Roland Barthes, Harold Bloom, and Stanley Fish.[15]

All this is mere scaffolding, I admit. But I anticipate that the answers I have still to air will drive us back to the distinctions we already have in hand. So let me collect the scattered parts of the doctrine already introduced. Here is a convenient tally: (1) physical nature and culture are distinguished primarily in terms of what lacks and what possesses Intentionality; hence, the cultural is *sui generis* and cannot be reduced to the physical; (2) cultural entities are embodied in natural or physical entities and their properties are correspondingly incarnate in natural or physical properties; hence, cultural entities exist in the same sense physical objects do and their properties are as real as physical properties are; (3) Intentional properties are inherently interpretable, determinable but not determinate in the way we suppose physical properties are; hence, whatever we believe the logical features of truth-bearing discourse are (when addressed to physical entities), it must be clear that physical exemplars are not likely to provide the best or even suitable paradigms for defining objective discourse about cultural entities; (4) the individuation and numerical identity of (adequated) cultural entities differ markedly from the individuation of

---

15. See, further, Margolis, *Interpretation Radical But Not Unruly.*

physical entities, and their "natures" accordingly are such that we cannot defend any principled distinction between discerning and imputing natures (or properties) to them; hence, the description of cultural entities is already interpretive or imputational; and (5) the objective ascription of Intentional properties is compatible with conceding divergent imputations (or descriptions) that, applied to physical objects, would produce contradiction and paradox; it is also such that objectively imputed properties may actually be altered by the ongoing process of interpretation and reinterpretation; hence, the criteria of objective description cannot be the same in nature and culture, though they are logically reconcilable. You see by this tally that conceding cultural realism threatens to dismantle all of our canonical views of reality.

IV

Turn back, then, to the most strategic considerations. These fall into two baskets: one, regarding reference and predication, which confirm the impossibility of disjoining ontic and epistemic questions, hence the unavoidability of a conjoint realism involving nature and culture; the other, regarding the Intentional complexities of cultural entities themselves (within the space of the first), hence complexities that cannot fail to lead to heterodox concessions about the logic of truth-claims, the constructed nature of objectivity, and the replacement of physicalist paradigms of reality.

About the first basket, I remind you of the following findings, which have been touched on elsewhere: for one, reference cannot be captured by predicative or causal means at all, hence cannot be captured in any rule-like, criterial, or algorithmic way; for another, since there is no invariant rule by which to confirm successful predication, predicative objectivity must be consensual in a sense more or less akin to the *lebensformlich* regularities Wittgenstein sketches in his short account of human practices.

These findings may be more powerful than we actually require, because they affect all parts of discursive inquiry equally—confirm, in fact, the epistemic dependence of truth-claims about physical nature *on* a realist reading of selves and other cultural entities. You see, therefore, that a principled disjunction between description and imputation (even in the absence of Intentional properties) signifies a form of cognitive privilege;

alternatively, the rejection of privilege (in effect, of the vestiges of Cartesian privilege) confirms that a viable realism must be a constructive or constructivist realism. There is no principled way to assign the apparent "structures" of the intelligible world to what, disjunctively, is "brute" and what, conceptually "invented."

You begin to see how much may have to be revised to make room for the ontology of artworks. It's one thing to admit that the world of human culture and human minds evolved from cosmic sources that originally lacked Intentionality altogether. It's quite another to grasp that *whatever* is posited to exist and to be real is insuperably dependent (epistemically but not necessarily ontically) on *our* being the competent agents and investigators that we are. Our description of the real world is endogenously encumbered by the epistemic conditions under which *we* function, in spite of the fact that, within such terms, we have good reason to believe that we have indeed evolved from independent prior conditions that lack altogether the Intentionality of our cultural world. I see no paradox there. I say only that the *realism* of the physical world presupposes and entails the *reality* of the cultural world! That is my bottom line: a theorem I find implicated in the strongest way in the philosophical span that runs from Galileo and Descartes to Kant and Hegel. No philosophy can bypass its lesson.

I have already remarked that we cannot fix the "number" even of physical objects except consensually—in effect, by relying on Intentional and interpretive means. But, if, in addition, we turn our hand to identifying an artwork that (a) is embodied in, but is not identical with, any physical object, (b) exists only as an Intentionally qualified object such that (c) its Intentional properties are not the same as whatever physical properties they are incarnated in, you cannot fail to see that we cannot succeed except by having interpretively posited a suitable *denotatum at* the (physical) site at which conditions (a)–(c) can be said to be satisfied. You see, therefore, that, at the point of individuation and attribution, a good deal of interpretive imputation will have been impossible to avoid.

Even if we claimed to be clear about the "number" and "nature" of the embodying physical object and the incarnating physical properties in which a particular artwork is embedded, there would be no rule (recall Feigl!) by which the number and nature of that artwork could thereby be emergently (or, better: superveniently) fixed. That is what the "naturalists" regularly ignore (Quine and Davidson for instance).[16] Think of the diverse performances of a Mozart sonata or the printings of a Dürer engraving or the bearing of the history of interpretation on the identity and reinterpretability of *Hamlet* or *Las Meninas* or *Sarrasine* or *Miss Lonelyhearts* or (Duchamp's) *Fountain*.

There is a conceptual gap between the number and nature of what embodies and incarnates artworks and the number and nature of what is embodied and incarnated as artworks and their Intentional attributes. That is the key to the second basket of difficulties promised. *Those difficulties cannot be overcome except consensually,* within the changing practices of the societies in which they arise. But they are also uniquely cultural. We are free, of course, to theorize as we please about what to count as an artwork—and why. But when, for instance, I conjecture that Max Ernst's *Jeune fille poursuivie par un rossignol* justifies ascriptions (imputations) of a psychoanalytic sort or even looser attributions drawn from the reception of Freudian materials, I am theorizing in accord with the *sui generis*—the ontological—latitude I argue cannot be avoided and cannot be brought to closure on any uniquely valid interpretation. There's the clue to the second basket of difficulties. There's no point to quarreling about whether interpretation should follow a bivalent or a multivalent logic, if the parties to the dispute ignore the implicated puzzles.

V

I apologize for the busyness of all this labor. The truth is: English-language philosophies of art have largely avoided addressing the ontic complexity of art's Intentional "nature." It would have been quite impossible to make plausible the logical peculiarities of artworks in terms of an ontology that simply shunned the Intentional. (Famously, in accord with W. V. Quine's *Word and Object.*) But the ontic admission of Intentionality has an extraordinary effect on the standing of more canonical views. I have, therefore, found it necessary to provide some evidence of the sheer coherence of

16. See W. V. Quine, "Epistemology Naturalized," in *Ontological Relativity and Other Essays* (New York: Columbia University Press, 1969); and Davidson, "A Coherence Theory of Truth and Knowledge."

the model of cultural realism that I propose. There is a contest there that deserves a fuller inning.

I come, finally, to the deeper oddities of art's interpretable nature. The most important runs as follows: viz., that, ontically, the individuation of a particular artwork need not: (*a*) presuppose the necessary fixity of its nature, or (*b*) presuppose that its being determinate in "number" entails its being determinate in "nature." The two issues are inseparable of course but have entirely different weights.

Let me step back a little for the sake of a further gain. I have shown that both reference and predication owe their usual determinacy to the informal (collective) tolerance of discursive practices; hence, that there cannot be any criterial appeal to *haecceities* or fixed essences anywhere in nature. Furthermore, what holds here for non-Intentionally qualified entities must hold as well for culturally qualified entities. I have also argued that Intentional properties are determinable but not antecedently determinate in whatever crisp way we suppose holds for physical exemplars. That is as far as we have gone.

But, now, consider that our Intentional attributes *are alterable because they are interpretable!* If true, that would be ontologically stunning— absolutely unique. It would explain at once why the properties of artworks were determinable but not determinate in the *sui generis* respect I am urging. It would explain the logical barrier against the reduction of the cultural world to the physical world. It would also explain what precisely is meant by segregating the determinacy of the "number" and "nature" of cultural entities: in effect, by violating the canonical view (Aristotle's, most anciently), which affirms that the determinacy of individuation is necessarily a function of the determinacy of the nature of what is being individuated. All of our ontological intuitions are put at risk, therefore. And yet these possibilities are almost never aired. All of the most contested puzzles of objective criticism and interpretation depend, I am persuaded, on the resolution of this master question. I rest my case on it.

In any event, the objectivity of general properties cannot be secured— avoiding Platonism in all its protean forms—unless (borrowing casually from Wittgenstein) we locate it in a *lebensformlich* way: meaning by that (more precisely) that predicative objectivity is (i) collective, (ii) consensually tolerant, (iii) not criterial, (iv) grounded in the discursive practices of an enabling society, (v) constructed or constituted critically, (vi) subject to historical drift, hence also (vii) discernible or imputable in a way that precludes reliance on any antecedent disjunction between would-be "subjective" and "objective" ingredients contributing to predicative knowledge. To this general catalogue, we may now add the special features of Intentional properties: namely, that they are (viii) intrinsically interpretable, (ix) alterable because interpretable, hence also (x) determinable *sui generis*, that is, not determined in the way non-Intentional properties are said to be. This defines in good part what, epistemically, is defensible in speaking of the "natures" of things and of the natures of cultural things in particular. I know of no comparably explicit account.

There is no other avenue for securing objectivity *anywhere,* if the puzzles of reference and predication are as I suppose they are! Hence, to offer a constructivist account of descriptive objectivity for the interpretation of artworks is *not* to fall away from a stricter canon, as many suppose (Zemach for instance). *There is no such canon,* but there is objectivity enough for all our needs.

There is another nest of complications to consider, affecting attributes. Properties are all of course general—make that item (xi) of our tally—that is, plurally instantiable if instantiable at all; but, now, they are also (xii) instantiable in a historicized way, not merely in accord with the drift of history. Applied to Intentional properties, this means that interpretable predicables are alterable not merely because they are interpretable or subject, *qua* interpretable, to the drift of history, but because they are (xiii) interpretable in historicized ways. Item (xiii) marks, I would say, the most radical feature of the logic and ontology of interpretation. For, if you grant (xiii), you cannot but concede that the objective treatment of the interpretation of Intentional properties is distinctly hospitable to a relativistic logic.

Failing Platonism, no descriptive practices can escape the drift of history. But history, of course, is blind. There are no epistemic grounds for fixing the historical drift of epistemic practices: except retrospectively, that is, from a vantage that cannot possibly identify itself historically in timeless terms. (You see the paradox.) Practices change with use, we know; but we cannot judge except synchronically, except systematically. (Diachrony, as opposed to historicity, is, for instance, no more than a synchronic category.) Nevertheless, we remain aware that, with the passage of time, we shall "surely" change our epistemic assessment of what has gone before—including our assessment of our cognitive competence *ante.* That is the ordinary state of affairs, of course, but it says nothing to the purpose regarding historicism.

The picture changes radically when we consider Intentional properties. Non-Intentional predicates do change with historical change all right: for instance, as with the meaning of "gold," signifying a basic element.[17] But we normally collect *such* changes in terms of the theoretical work of the natural sciences or in some comparable way. There is no need and no occasion for introducing historicity there. We simply replace one "objective" *predicate* by another that improves our inquiries, according to our lights. To allow historicity, we should have to think not of "gold" but, say, of the related property of scientific *thought*: roughly, "applying the predicate 'gold' as thus and so defined relative to this and that evidence and theory." That is, historicity applies directly only to Intentional attributes, though, of course, every attribute is Intentionally specified.

Specifically Intentional attributes are intrinsically significative; hence, when *they* change historically, we mark their significative drift retrospectively. Doing that, as in interpreting Shakespeare's use of the "great chain of being," we treat Intentional properties in specifically historicized ways. To judge in the *historicist* way presupposes that what we mean by "knowledge" is (*a*) an artifact of our reflecting on our cognitional history, and (*b*) that we neither require nor can defend as necessary a commitment to the neutral standing of any determinate form of would-be knowledge.

Under these conditions, the historicist characterizes cognizing competence as (*c*) a second-order posit of how *our* self-ascribed cognitional powers serve (according to our lights) as a corrective for similar such posits made (in past presents) through the history of such theorizing. The point is that doing that is essential to the *sui generis* objectivity of interpretive criticism. There is nothing comparable in speaking of the "objective" or "independent" physical world; although what we say there will be affected by what we say here.

Thus, for instance, it is generally acknowledged that the early forms of Cubist painting (in Braque's work) were deliberately built up from the forms Cézanne originally developed in his still lifes and landscapes. But, then, the "meaning" of the so-called geometrizing tendencies in Cézanne

---

17. See, for instance, Hilary Putnam, "The Analytic and the Synthetic" and "The Meaning of 'meaning,'" *Philosophical Papers,* vol. 2 (Cambridge: Cambridge University Press, 1970).

(poorly characterized thus, it must be said) will have been retrospectively affected by the *later* history of painting, now including and going beyond Braque's and Picasso's cubism. The attribution will be a function of our dawning sense of the possibilities of new ways of painting as a result of going beyond the canons of past history.

The logical oddities of Intentional properties are most noticeable there: determinable Intentional properties, for instance, will not be able to be progressively determined in the same linear way non-Intentional properties (red, say) are said to be. In the one case, the *predicable* actually changes *for historicist reasons;* in the other, the meaning of the *predicate* changes or is replaced *historically* (where the property in question remains—is said to remain—unchanged). Of course, this is not meant to preclude changes over time in the phased nature of a particular creature or of kinds of creatures (for instance, the growth of a particular horse over a lifetime or the evolution of the modern horse, or, for that matter, the appearance of a mutant strain of microbes suddenly rendered immune to antibiotics).

As philosophers of art, we are likely to take very different stands on what to make of historical change and historicity. My own view is that interpretive objectivity will be strongly imputational, hospitable to divergent "meanings," and inclined to make room for the actual alterability of the historical past. I judge this to be the counterpart of Thomas Kuhn's historicizing of scientific "paradigms," once we give up canonical notions of "perceptual neutrality."[18] Kuhn was unable or unwilling to sustain the argument, but the conditions of its coherence are exactly the same in the natural sciences and the arts. The idea that the historical (*not* the physical) past is actually alterable by interpretation, not merely subject to a change of verbal (or, as in music, performative) interpretation, is bound to startle anyone who favors one version of objectivism or physicalism or another. Small wonder philosophers avoid Intentionality if they can. (Of course, they cannot.)

Thus, in interpretive contexts, we construe the meaning of an artwork as ranging, reinterpretively, over the historicized import of selected *prior* interpretations. For instance, the "meaning" of *Hamlet* is, *now*, a function of how the play is to be objectively reinterpreted in the light of how *we* reconstitute the history of its past interpretations! The significance of

18. See Thomas S. Kuhn, *The Structure of Scientific Revolutions,* 2d ed. enlarged (Chicago: University of Chicago Press, 1970), section X.

Hamlet's procrastination has, as we now see matters, definitely passed through a phase of Oedipal interpretation, which may now have waned in terms of cultural plausibility. We cannot fix our own historicized perspective, our "horizon" so to say: that is for others to determine. But we are aware, inferentially, that we must be occupying what, from a later historical vantage, will be defined as that perspective. We construe the objectivity of our interpretations in terms of how we reconstruct (historically, blindly, but pertinently in "story-relative" terms) our relationship to the interpretive work of the past. There is no other way to proceed: there is no sense, comparable to the "independence" of non-Intentionalized reality, in which the meanings of artworks are thought to be independent of the drift of human history. (That is the nerve of the imputational thesis.)

The underlying argument is entirely straightforward: artworks are Intentionally qualified; what is so qualified is intrinsically interpretable; interpretation cannot fail to fall within the historicized tolerance of actual practice; historicity signifies the actual alterability of Intentional properties by interpretive means; there, conformity never functions criterially but only consensually; as a result, interpretation can never preclude, on principled grounds, the validity of divergent, even incompatible, interpretations.

Reflections like these change in an extraordinary way our conception of what is real and what, objective. In fact, my argument is, ultimately, a *reductio*: for, to reject Intentionality is to reject our own existence and the tribunal of experience; and to admit our existence—an odd source of reluctance—is to discover that we cannot, conformably, deny the reality of history and art.

6

SELVES AND OTHER TEXTS

I

Paradigmatically, texts are the intrinsically inter-pretable utterances of (human) selves; derivatively, any-thing is a text if and when suitably "anthropomor-phized," modeled on the paradigm of human thought and behavior. This is the linchpin of my proposal bridging artworks and selves within the analysis of the cultural world. I shall allow it to expand a bit extrava-gantly at first, in order to suggest its amplitude and resources. But then I shall confine it to what is needed for a more limited purpose. The cries of a newborn infant, for instance, are not texts, except derivatively, in the sense in which infant behavior and psychology are heuristically described (as they must be) in accord with the model of the linguistic competence of self-conscious selves apt for reporting their thoughts, their intentions, their experiences, their undertakings. In this sense, too, the world is a possible text, or is texted, if we concede that its intelligible structure is inseparable from the conditions under which we understand our-selves: even the realism of the physical sciences may be said to be texted if realism is interpretively constructed (or constructivist); *not*, if we claim to know the world neutrally, or to know it as it is independently, or to know it as it is invariantly structured. In any case, to say the world is texted in this sense—epistemically—is not to fall back to any form of idealism, only to concede (and to avoid thereby) the insuperable paradoxes of the Cartesianism that spans Descartes and Kant and is rampant once again in Eurocentric philosophy.

We ourselves are texts, if we view ourselves—our thoughts and deeds—as the individuated expression of the internalized enabling structures of the larger culture in which we first emerge, are first formed, as the apt selves we are, apt for discovering how the language and practices of our society course through our every deed. In this sense, selves are the paradigmatic agents of linguistic and lingual uttering; also, metaphorically (historically), they "are" the legible utterances of their age: Goethe, Napoleon, Rousseau, Goya, for instance.

One might say that every generation "utters" its own offspring, not in the sense of merely producing offspring but in the more pointed sense of facilitating their formation as "second-natured" (encultured) selves of this or that particular ethos. Formed thus, selves continue to "utter" and alter and transform themselves reflexively, by interpreting and reinterpreting and effectuating their evolving potentialities in speech and deed.

Viewed this way, Freud's and Marx's and Foucault's theories of the human condition converge on the texted nature of human life, but they do so by featuring the would-be mechanisms of change by which we understand life's meanings, not mere change itself. In this regard, their theories are very different from those offered by such figures as Lévi-Strauss, Gadamer, and Bourdieu, who pretend to isolate objective meaning without attention to the dynamics of social life or who reduce dynamics to kinematics. "Text" is a term of art that may be made to do service for a very wide range of undertakings spanning the interpretation of artworks and human histories. What unites them is a common sense of the conditions under which "meanings" are generated and discerned and made effective in cultural life. The trick is to grasp how the epistemic puzzles of objective interpretation are indissolubly embedded in the causal forces of historical change itself *and* how change in the cultural world is inseparable from the play of those same epistemic puzzles.

I have in mind answering the interpretive puzzles—both epistemically and ontically—but only in order to bring my answers into functional accord with the question of how to understand and explain human history. I am aware that I am barely broaching the larger issue. Its answer, however, cannot avoid the dynamics of generated meanings. The analysis of meanings has also been distorted therefore, by urging an overly simple analogy between the predicative standing of Intentional attributes and the standing of physical attributes. Viewed that way, one can hardly grasp the sense in which the objectivity of interpretation mediates between the objectivity of the natural sciences and that of the judgments of practical life. Yet that *is* the key to bridging the lesser difference between our understanding of art and our understanding of ourselves. (I seize the occasion to add at once that, by "lingual," I mean only to mark the various nonlinguistic or nonverbal forms of utterance that presuppose and depend upon linguistic competence and cognate powers, and thereby manifest many of the same interpretable structures that language manifests—as in art and action—in making love and war and sculptures and food and clothes. Both lingual and linguistic utterance must be construed, of course, in "bodily" terms.)

I agree here somewhat with the spirit of Pierre Bourdieu's analysis of the *habitus*, except that I construe the mechanisms of enculturation and of the continuing transformation (and self-transformation) of agents and practices *dynamically*, in terms of cognitively effective powers (no matter how subterranean); whereas (on my reading) Bourdieu never ventures beyond the *kinematic*, as in his empirical sociology. In that sense, Bourdieu's theory is tautological, though not uninstructive. Still, the validity of the societal model must be supported dynamically. (I am thinking, here, of the analogy of comparing Copernicus and Newton on the movement of the planets.) Bourdieu treats the *habitus* of a salient practice as "generative" *of* that practice through the "body's dispositions"—*somehow* without attention to the actual microprocesses of human behavior cast in causal and epistemic terms at once.[1] The result is dangerously close to the explanation of opium's inducing sleep by its dormative powers. (The explanation need not be vacuous, of course, but its dynamic factors must be properly supplied.) The analysis of what to make of the valid interpretation of art helps us, I believe, to see what is required (but missing in

---

1. See, for instance, Pierre Bourdieu, *Pascalian Meditations,* trans. Richard Nice (Stanford: Stanford University Press, 1997), 142–46. For my own part, I much prefer the less mysterious, less abstract "kinematics" of the account of cultural practices in Michael Oakeshott, *On Human Conduct* (Oxford: Clarendon, 1975), chap. 1.

Bourdieu) in order to explain the automatic fluency of social life. Here, you begin to see the strategic advantage of formulating what to count as the objective description of the life of historical societies based on the requirements of validating objective interpretations in the arts. The two undertakings are, finally, very much the same.

To press the point: it would not be unreasonable to say that selves were also self-interpreting texts, meaning by that that selves view themselves as perpetually interpreting subjects as well as tacitly interpretable, often interpretively problematic, objects, each role reciprocally affecting and potentiating the other through an evolving history that is in part constructed by that same duality. Grant only that the temporal careers of selves and societies and what they do and produce have histories or are histories in this sense, and you have before you the most compendious picture of texted reality that can be imagined. Canonical usage, I concede, does not favor such an accommodation. But if you construe speech and art and action as the interpretable utterances of culturally apt selves, then you cannot rule out the propriety of our speaking of selves as texts, by way of their interpreting their own "utterances," which, being texts as well, merge with the evolving cultural processes that continually alter the potentiated powers of the primary agents of cultural change (selves, of course). Ultimately, putting matters thus poses, but hardly answers, the question of the conceptual relationship between physical nature and human culture (reductionism, for instance).

Much that is suggested here in the way of enlarging the scope of the theory of texts may be thought extravagant, perhaps even flatly false. But you must bear in mind that humans are the only creatures that view themselves at once, ambivalently and intransparently, as both cognizing subjects and cognized objects: the only creatures capable of reporting and interpreting their own public utterances, the only creatures that acquire by enculturation a functional second nature as linguistically apt selves, the only creatures that address the world directly and discursively in terms that are inseparable from the theorizing and interpretive categories through which they understand themselves and what *they* utter and produce, the only exemplars of historical and creative careers. It is in this sense that selves serve as the paradigm of cognitive and mental life; for, of course, the bare question of how to analyze cognition and mental life arises only reflexively: only in a society of selves. We have no alternative option here.

It is entirely reasonable to recommend that we confine the principal work of understanding and interpreting texts to the most absorbing linguistic utterances we can identify—or (perhaps better) to the entire world of art, or (perhaps) to the world of history. But, as you consider such enlargements, you realize that, just as there is no strict demarcation between a man and his act, there is none between a functioning self and that self's utterance. We scan even ourselves as the phased, significant, often mysterious or surprising precipitates of our own Intentional acts—acts that ineluctably embody the vagaries of our incompletely fathomed culture. Think of Beethoven or Alexander the Great or Van Gogh or James Joyce or Jean Genet.

Beyond all that, the detailed theory of texts will inevitably remain hostage to a choice of axioms of knowledge and reality: for example, to what, disputatiously, we are prepared to take as given in the way of objectivity, necessities, invariances *de re* and *de cogitatione,* cognitive privilege, universality, flux and closed systems, divergent and incommensurable conceptual schemes, communicative success, conditions of truth and understanding and legitimation, and norms of rationality and worth. It seems obvious that one cannot demonstrate the validity of a theory of texts—as if by way of a scrupulous analysis of a particular sector of the independent world: for instance, in the arts, with respect to poems and novels (literary texts) or, by analogy, with respect to paintings and the performance of notated music (visual and musical texts, say) or, more directly, with respect to human histories and social practices (historical and sociological narratives).

But the very idea of a study of texts as of determinate, stable, well-boundaried *objects* relatively unaffected by their undergoing interpretation is open to serious challenge for many reasons: for one, because, predicatively, texts are the utterances of selves, and, nominalized, only formally, never completely, detachable *denotata* of effective interpretation (sentences, paintings, deeds, histories); for another, because, in the world of culture as distinct from physical nature, there is no plausible pretense of a disjunction between cognizing and cognized, except distributively and for convenience of reference—for, there, we are forever bound to inquire into ourselves; for another, because whatever the interpreted structure of uttered texts may be, it can never be independent of the interpretive resources of the self-examining selves that undertake the task; for another, because the interpretive powers of individual selves are never completely known to those same functioning selves, who are (themselves) no more than a small self-conscious part of the tacit, collective, effective competence of one or another enabling society; for another, because the reciprocal historical influence of interpretive power and the palpable precipitates of prior interpreted structures (the work of historical memory) substantively affects the evolving interpretive resources shaped for subsequent utterance and interpretation; and, for still another, because interpretive scope and focus and fluency are always endogenously limited by the historically contingent horizon under which, tacitly and divergently, they are affected and made effective.

It is not as a theorem of the theory of texts but as a reasonable presupposition of it that we affirm that general practices cannot be cognitively fixed by way of Universals or Platonic Forms or Husserlian *eidé* or anything of the kind; nor, conformably, that "meanings" or what may be called "Intentional structures" (ranging over lingual as well as linguistic utterances) can be objectively determined in any comparable way. For one thing, the cultural world is irreducibly subject to one or another form of the hermeneutic circle: meaning by that that one cannot, in interpreting texts, exit from our practice—the practice that first formed us—of imputing cultural significance and signification to the things we encounter and produce: Intentional structure is ineluctably *sui generis,* coextensive with the lives and interests of a society of apt selves. To have "emerged" as selves is to implicate a world in which, alone, we function as selves; but that *is* the theme of the hermeneutic circle formulated "by other (ontic) means."

I mean by the "Intentional," as I have said earlier, no more than the culturally significant—the linguistically and lingually meaningful, the representational, the expressive, the institutionally purposive or rulelike, the intentional and intensional as manifestations of cultural formation, the symbolic, the semiotic, the rhetorical, the stylistic, the traditional, the historical, the narrative.

Secondly, in the cultural world (also in nature at large, to the extent that cognitive resources are, paradigmatically, linguistic and reflexive), objectivity is never more than consensual—in a sense akin to what Wittgenstein favors, in the *Investigations,* as the *lebensformlich,* without ever being criterial (except derivatively), being (rather) tacitly permitted by ongoing social practices that yield to gradual and divergent change without epistemic dislocation. This is not to deny the possibility of testing the aptness of would-be objective categories; only that such testing is itself ultimately grounded, not in self-evident propositions or assured cognitive sources, but in the entrenched practices of an enabling society.[2]

When Derrida notoriously declared: "*Il n'y a pas de hors-texte,*"[3] he did not say (or intend) that there was nothing outside any particular text or outside *the* single inclusive text that is the entire intelligible world, but only that whatever is locally judged to be "outside" a specified text is itself a text or texted: that is, the "*hors-texte*" of any particular text is itself a text—alternatively, a context, the texted conceptual space within which texts, or even the various parts of physical nature, are (may be) relevantly texted. For, surely, "contexts" are human contrivances, perspectived and selective frames of reference uttered to enhance or make legible the pertinently interpreted structure of some particular part of the world. That is, Derrida need not be read as an idealist here, only as a beneficiary of post-Kantian discoveries. (Correspondingly, you may treat the thesis that selves are self-interpreting texts as a heuristic convenience by which to feature the Intentional life of human societies: hence, not as idealist in any familiar sense.)

If (with me) you construe the universe as the "context of all contexts," you may agree that it is conceptually impossible (except on the presumption of a form of cognitive privilege equal to God's competence) to pronounce any textual order as the unique and total system of the intelligible world. I take that to be part of Derrida's meaning—to be, in fact, the master theme of deconstruction. But if that is conceded, then there cannot be an outer limit (an "*hors-texte*") by which valid or objective interpretation can be determinatebly confined: the limits of objective interpretation are themselves interpretively constructed (critically, let us concede); but also and always contingently, endogenously, serially, divergently, by way of "prejudice"—the preformation of our power of judgment—if (as seems obviously true) the universe is never, as such, a *datum* for description or analysis. It is, I would say, the import of the leanest lesson drawn from the

2. See Ludwig Wittgenstein, *Philosophical Investigations,* trans. G. E. M. Anscombe (Oxford: Basil Blackwell, 1953); and *On Certainty,* ed. G. E. M. Anscombe and G. H. von Wright, trans. Denis Paul and G. E. M. Anscombe (Oxford: Basil Blackwell, 1969), for instance §§ 110, 204–5.

3. Jacques Derrida, *Of Grammatology,* trans. Gayatri Chakravorty Spivak (Baltimore: Johns Hopkins University Press, 1974), 158–59. See also Geoffrey Bennington, *Derrida* (Chicago: University of Chicago Press, 1993), under the entry "context."

constructivism that, since the post-Kantian analysis of early modern philosophy (particularly Hegel's), shows us how to avoid the paradoxes of classical realism, without abandoning realism itself.

So seen, the admission of the world's textuality is tantamount to the denial of First Principles or First Philosophy.[4] For textualizing the world is tantamount to admitting the (epistemically) inseparable unity of cognizing subjects and cognized objects, the defeat of objectivisms of every sort, the impossibility of exiting from the hermeneutic circle, the insuperable dependence of meanings or Intentional structures on the historicity of selves, and the endless and endlessly divergent reinterpretability of given texts and their interpretations.

You see at once, therefore, that a generous theory of texts of the sort I suggest brings in its wake strenuous puzzles regarding the "number" and "nature" of denumerable texts—of the familiar sorts considered in professional criticism in the arts, in legal and scriptural disputes, and the like. I intend to address the most important of these puzzles, but in a way congruent with certain contested "axioms" (as I've called them) bearing on knowledge and reality in the largest sense. Frankly, I am convinced that canonical objections to such a theory are almost always ill-founded: both because they insist on forms of privilege they cannot convincingly secure (*de re* necessities, for instance, or the noetic grasp of universals and essences) and because they insist that extreme departures from such constraints inevitably produce paradox and self-contradiction "somewhere." I have in mind such deviant options as the defense of the objective standing of incompatible interpretations (as valid, even if not jointly true) or the admission that the "natures" of interpreted texts actually change under interpretation (though without generating self-defeating paradoxes of any kind).

In any case, what discussants on all sides of the question wish to know is whether there are principled limits on what to regard as a text and what to regard as admissible in the objective interpretation of a text. Clearly, no one wishes to favor interpretive chaos. Nevertheless, it is quite surprising to discover that there are no compelling objections against unrestricted interpretation, except in conformity with the limits of brute memory, fluency, tolerance within habitual practices, pertinence regarding contin-

---

4. Contrast this with Aristotle, *Metaphysics*, Book Gamma, in *The Complete Works of Aristotle*, 2 vols., ed. Jonathan Barnes (Princeton: Princeton University Press, 1984).

gent interests or purposes, and what may be shown to be internally coherent and supportable in evidentiary ways. These, it turns out, are not particularly arduous constraints.

II

Having offered my preamble, I hasten to emphasize that, at the present time, there is no prospect of reducing language (or the lingual analogues of cultural life) to subcultural (biological or physical) processes, or, *a fortiori*, of eliminating language altogether. Many are sanguine on this last score, of course, notably the partisans of neurocomputational models of the mind.[5] But it would not be unfair to claim that they have not succeeded, and have never explained how (apart from a conceptual wave of the hand) the trick is to be turned. I myself believe that the "natural" (but nonreducible) emergence of language and culture is reflexively posited at just that advanced level of enculturation at which we are able to consider, discursively, looking back at evolution, that a threshold "must have been crossed" at some distant hominid moment close enough to our present competence to make sense of it constructively. I find the conclusion unavoidable if, for instance, reference is, as I have argued, impossible to capture algorithmically.

I see no difference here in the matter of judging when a human infant "first" begins to speak and when we suppose language first "began." Both conjectures are necessarily anthropomorphized, modeled top-down on our own linguistic and lingual competence. But if that is so, then the "proper parts" of texts are themselves never less than texts or texted, even though the cultural world surely depends upon, incorporates, and is inseparable from, physical and biological nature. That is the precise sense in which we cannot exit from the hermeneutic circle: for we cannot function as selves if we cannot function linguistically and lingually; but, of course, functioning thus, we cannot discern anything that is not a text either paradigmatically or by the courtesy of anthropomorphizing. Effectively, the world of human culture is both irreducible and ineliminable; hence, its emergence is *sui*

5. See, for instance, Paul M. Churchland, *A Neurocomputational Perspective: The Nature of Mind and the Structure of Science* (Cambridge: MIT Press, 1989), chap. 1.

generis, functional in *reflexive* (Intentional) terms rather than in terms only of the biological processes in which it is incarnate.

Here, we touch on quarrelsome and neglected matters that may seem remote from the question of the objective interpretation of texts but are really of decisive importance. For, if texts may be said to exist as individuated entities (*denotata*) of some kind, then, in accord with a robust sense of existence (eschewing abstract "entities" like concepts or kinds or universals or numbers) and applying the category ("text") to linguistic utterances, actions, selves, artworks, historical events, texts must be materially embodied in some suitable way, though not reducible to their embodying entities. For example, if Michelangelo's *Pietà* is, as a sculpture, a text (as I would say), then, although it is embodied in a block of cut marble, its representational and expressive "parts" (the interpretable details of the sculpture) must be similarly embodied. *They are not "parts" of the marble, but of the sculpture.* That surely affects the individuation and numerical identity of the sculpture, as well as the objectivity with which we may analyze its Intentional structure or "nature."

Similarly, to remind ourselves of another needlessly tormented issue, the expressiveness of music *is* musically perceptible, *is* incarnate in sound, *is* part of the predicable nature of music itself. Expressiveness belongs to a piece of music, because a piece of music is a musical text. It needs no metaphor (in Goodman's sense[6]) in order to be objectively attributed. It needs no fictive human voice within the sound, no "make-believe," to ensure its conceptual adequacy.[7]

6. See Nelson Goodman, *Languages of Art* (Indianapolis: Bobbs-Merrill, 1968), 86.

7. I allude here to a number of the leading discussions of musical expressiveness collected in Jerrold Levinson, "Musical Expressiveness," in *The Pleasures of Aesthetics: Philosophical Essays* (Ithaca: Cornell University Press, 1996). This is not the occasion for dissecting these theories at close range. They all require "a clause too many." They make a mystery of expressiveness and then resolve the mystery by some jerry-built construction that ignores the plain fact that it is already coherent, conceptually viable, and philosophically reasonable to say that *music and painting are intrinsically expressive!*

Levinson, I'm afraid, makes the same mistake as the others he collects—it is an important mistake—which I shall have to make do for the error of the entire raft of similarly motivated theories. (It hearkens back to my analysis of Danto's and Goodman's theories.) It begins with the first sentence of Levinson's essay: "I will endeavor to say exactly what musical expressiveness is," Levinson says, and promptly moves on to do so. But what he offers is "an analysis of what it means to say that a passage of music P is expressive of an emotion E or other psychological state" (90). (This, of course, is a narrower and very different issue.)

Put more carefully, Levinson proposes that "a passage of music P is expressive of an

In saying that music *is* an interpreted text or utterance, I mean: (1) that music (or painting) *is* created or Intentionally constructed; (2) that it possesses, as a result, Intentional properties (expressiveness among them); and (3) that it is in virtue of conditions (1) and (2) that its Intentional properties (expressiveness again) *can be* directly discerned by an informed percipient as easily as any merely sensorily perceivable property. The gain the theory of texts makes possible is this: to speak of the expressiveness (or similar properties) of a piece of music *does not* presuppose or entail that there is, or must be, some logically prior (real or fictive or otherwise contrived) emotional or psychological state *of which* the imputed property is the expression, or that we can only validate its objective attribution *when it is made to depend* (literally, fictively, metaphorically, by make-believe, or in some alternative relational way) *on* some posited psychological state. There's a clause too many there. Once you give up reductive materialism and admit the reality of culturally emergent phenomena, the entire "mystery" of expressiveness dissolves. (If you see the argument's force, you are bound to see the vacuity as well of treating *habitus* as a subterranean "generative structure"; and if you reject the primacy of the inner generative view, you will be drawn to analyze the epistemic importance of explicit Intentional practices. It is there, in fact, that the effective power and structure of Intentional "utterance" are is to be found.)

I hasten to add as well that, by "embodied," I mean (as I have re-marked earlier) no more than that texts are indissolubly complex entities, emergent under the *sui generis* conditions of enculturation, characterizable jointly in material and Intentional terms, where, conformably, the Intentional is complexly "incarnate" in material properties.[8] To exist, then,

---

emotion or other psychic condition E *iff* P, in context, is readily and aptly heard by an appropriately backgrounded listener as the expression of E, in a *sui generis*, 'musical', manner, by an indefinite agent, the music's persona" (107). Levinson himself remarks that this agrees with the general approach offered in the paper "Hope in *The Hebrides*," *Music, Art, and Metaphysics* (Ithaca: Cornell University Press, 1990). But if words are intrinsically expressive—and surely they are—then why shouldn't music and painting be as well? They are also "uttered" by human beings. There's the crux of the error and the essential clue to the remarkably widespread misunderstanding of the ontology of art. That is precisely what the theory of textuality corrects. (Music is expressive—period; it may also be expressive *of* particular human emotions. Levinson does indeed oppose Hanslick. But he does not quite reach up to the general expressivity of music as such: if he had, he could not have featured the question he does.)

8. See, further, Joseph Margolis, *Historied Thought, Constructed World: A Conceptual*

texts must be embodied; they exist in and only in the same cultural space in which selves exist—and no wonder, for they are deliberately uttered or produced by selves, who are themselves culturally "uttered" by the caretakers of their society.

By "utterance," once again, I mean no more than the effective, Intentional, intrinsically interpretable activity of culturally competent selves. So texts are relatively freestanding individuatable entities (*denotata*). Our paradigms are unavoidably linguistic. But since, as I would argue, the linguistic is itself lingual—language not being autonomous—the category, "text," easily includes lingual entities like sculptures and music and even the most complex of texts: selves or persons.[9]

But, if what is meant by insisting that we cannot exit the hermeneutic circle is that whatever belongs to the cultural world is real, emergent, irreducible, *sui generis,* then, for one thing, texts cannot be individuated or identified by way of individuating or identifying their embodying *materiae;* and, for another, their Intentional attributes cannot be specified in any non-Intentional ways. As already remarked, embodying entities lack and embodied entities possess Intentional properties. That is why, for formal reasons, they cannot be one and the same.[10] *Entities* possess Intentional properties and are ontically *hybrid* for that reason.

These are no more than tautologies, but they are hardly negligible. They affect not only our grasp of the peculiar ontology of texts but also the conditions of objective interpretation. They are animated dynamically by being informed by the processes of mutual understanding.

Here, I must respectfully disagree with the forthright and otherwise attractive definition of texts offered by Jorge Gracia, who has in recent years formulated one of the few sustained analytic accounts of what it is to be a text. "A text," Gracia says, "is a group of entities, used as signs, which are selected, arranged, and intended by an author in a certain context to convey some specific meaning to an audience."[11] As it happens,

---

Primer for the Turn of the Millennium (Berkeley and Los Angeles: University of California Press, 1995).

9. I view these formulations, if I may say so, as trimmed-down versions of Vico's master theme: that humans understand history best, since they "create" the events of history. See Joseph Margolis, *The Flux of History and the Flux of Science* (Berkeley and Los Angeles: University of California Press, 1993), chap. 1.

10. Compare Arthur C. Danto, "The Artworld," *Journal of Philosophy* 40 (1964).

11. Jorge J. E. Gracia, *A Theory of Textuality: The Logic and Epistemology* (Albany:

all of Gracia's carefully worded conditions may be challenged along the lines I've suggested, but two (I think) are of signal importance for objectivity. Gracia clarifies his meaning at once, adding: "A proper understanding of textuality requires that we distinguish texts from the entities used as the signs that compose texts. This is important because, . . . the distinction between texts and the entities that constitute them may account for the seemingly incompatible predicates that are often predicated of texts."[12]

It is easy enough to misread what Gracia intends here. One may be tempted to think that the expression, "entities used as the signs that compose texts," signifies *non*-Intentional material marks of one kind or another that are first denoted *as* material *marks,* in order thereupon to identify "*signs,*" which are themselves nothing but the nominalized *denotata* answering to the "sign-use" of the prior marks—which, in turn, permit us to denote, by compositional means, true texts, distinguished by some further function different in principle from the function flagged by the "sign-use" of the original marks. That would be a double mistake, apart from the fact that it is certainly not what Gracia means: it would signify, first, that texts—artworks, histories, sentences—are identified by material, non-Intentional means (which would require supervenience at least[13]), and, second, it would signify that texts are a distinct compositional union of some sort of the "sign-use" of ulterior non-Intentional or nontextual marks.

Nelson Goodman is instructive here—apart from the exaggerated precision with which he believes scripts and scores may be identified, even characterized, by way of inscriptional marks and, by *their* use, the further properties of musical works (musical texts, as I would say) that (Goodman believes) are similarly perceivable in entirely non-Intentional terms. In fact, Goodman commits the error that Gracia escapes—or seems on the point of escaping. "Characters," or elements in a notational scheme, Goodman

---

SUNY Press, 1995), 4. See also Jorge J. E. Gracia, *Texts: Ontological Status, Identity, Author, Audience* (Albany: SUNY Press, 1996), which is the complement of the first. I should perhaps mention the very different account offered in Jurij Lotman, *The Structure of the Artistic Text,* trans. Gail Lenhoff and Ronald Vroon (Ann Arbor: University of Michigan Press, 1977), particularly chaps. 3–5, interesting in spite of its structuralist commitment.

12. Gracia, *A Theory of Textuality,* 405. The same definition is offered in *Texts,* 3.

13. For a brief sense of supervenience, see Colin McGinn, *The Problem of Consciousness* (Oxford: Basil Blackwell, 1991), 179–81.

says, "are certain classes of utterances or inscriptions or marks . . . [and] an inscription is any mark—visual, auditory, etc.—that belongs to a character."[14] This sounds right, and it may be allowed on a suitable reading. But a closer study of his account confirms that Goodman conflates the material or non-Intentional perceptual element—which, given his own sense of "perceptual," *is* "visual, auditory, etc."—with the culturally "perceivable," Intentional element designated by the (same) inscriptions in a script or score.[15] One simply needs to flag the equivocation on "perceive."

To fix what is essential: consider that the proper "parts" of a piece of music (analogously, the proper parts of a score representing the music) are *not* mere physical sounds (or marks) but musically (Intentionally) significant sound embodied in some admissible range of physical sounds. Goodman loses the distinction, and Gracia does not quite explain the relationship between marks and signs; although it is perfectly clear that Gracia does not confuse the two: "strictly speaking," he says, "only the entities or features of entities that function semantically should be considered constitutive of a text."[16] But he does favor something like a two-story theory of texts. He tends to oppose admitting, as textually significant, what is not strictly semantic in the linguistic sense—what, for instance, may be semiotic in a lingual way (the expressive and representational attributes of a ballet or a symphony).[17] I cannot agree: texts are cultural, not merely linguistic, artifacts. "Marks" and "signs" are relevantly related top-down, not bottom-up.

The quibble is not unimportant, because it draws attention to a puzzle about denoting texts; hence, given Gracia's definition, to a question about the two-story nature of a text. There's the point of my complaint. Gracia, I would say, cannot answer the denotative (or individuative) question (nor can Goodman); furthermore, since Gracia is inclined to treat texts only predicatively, he cannot fail to compound the difficulty.

My own sense is that, since predicative distinctions cannot replace

14. Nelson Goodman, *Languages of Art: An Approach to a Theory of Symbols* (Indianapolis: Bobbs-Merrill, 1968), 131.

15. See Chapter 2 above; see also Diana Raffman, "Goodman, Density, and the Limits of Sense Perception," in *The Interpretation of Music: Philosophical Essays*, ed. Michael Krausz (Oxford: Clarendon, 1997).

16. Gracia, *A Theory of Textuality*, 6.

17. This is the actual point on which Susanne Langer faltered, in her defense of "symbolic forms," against an entirely reasonable attack by Ernest Nagel. But it was not necessary to yield. See Susanne K. Langer, *Problems of Art* (New York: Charles Scribner's, 1957).

genuinely denotative or referential ones, the failure to explain the denotation of texts adversely affects the entire matter of interpretive objectivity. (I shall come back to that.) Also, if "signs" are proper compositional parts of "texts," then, as I say, *they* also are "texts." At any rate, once the denotative issue is resolved, there is no need to insist on a two-story account of the Intentional structure of texts: the reason for doing so can only be for the sake of the erroneous doctrine that texts, all Intentional artifacts, may, and must be able to, be denoted by way of denoting non-Intentional marks; or the equally erroneous doctrine that the identification of "signs" is interpretively reliable or privileged in some prior way in which the interpretation of texts is not. Certainly, Gracia means, by distinguishing (however benignly) between "signs" and "texts," to justify restricting the admissible meaning of a text ("intended by an author in a certain context") in such a way as to disallow incompatible meanings (or interpretations) of the text in question: the distinction between signs and text, he says, "may account for the seemingly incompatible but inadmissible predicates that are often predicated of texts." You see how the complications begin to swarm.[18]

III

I have already remarked that the theory of texts is bound to reflect the bias of prior epistemic convictions about our capacity to understand "meanings" and Intentional structures. I am entirely willing to be frank about my

18. I take special note, here, of the very strong difference between the account being offered and Richard Rorty's "disappointment" in Umberto Eco's analysis of "the universe of semiosis, that is, the universe of human culture." In effect, Rorty resists distinguishing ". . . signs and texts . . . from other objects—objects such as rocks and trees and quarks." He insinuates into his argument the (admittedly) misleading *prior* disjunction between the "semiotic" and the "scientific." (Eco is careless on this count.) But that has nothing to do with the legitimacy of distinguishing between the "science" of semiosis and the "science" of the physical sciences—read as a consequence *of* rightly distinguishing between texts and rocks and trees and the perceived requirements of objective inquiry. Rorty's attack on Eco, whom he would have liked to recruit in the service of his "postphilosophical" (or "postmodernist" or "pragmatist") strategies is a last-ditch effort to support a form of reductionism "by other means." See Richard Rorty, "The Pragmatist's Progress: Umberto Eco on Interpretation," in *Philosophy and Social Hope* (Harmondsworth: Penguin Books, 1999), 139; and Umberto Eco, *Semiotics and the Philosophy of Language* (Bloomington: Indiana University Press, 1984), 83–84.

own persuasion. I am convinced, for instance, that it is quite impossible to fix the conditions of referential (or denotative) success as well as of predicative success (in particular, of interpretive success) criterially, by way of rules or algorithms; and I am equally convinced that there is no algorithmic way to fix the very contexts in which reference and predication succeed in natural-language discourse. Or, of course, speakers' or authors' intentions.

This is as true of non-fictional texts as it is of the fictional kind, a fact that colors in a decisive way the issue of the objectivity of discourse about literary texts; *a fortiori,* about texts in general. There is no gradation of objectivity here, along the lines Jonathan Culler has suggested: that is, that "Some texts are more orphaned [less encumbered, culturally, whether referentially or predicatively] than others."[19] There is also, then, no danger incurred regarding the prospects of objective interpretation, by merely opposing the familiar canon that a "literary work"—rather than a mere "text," in the labile sense the poststructuralists have favored (Barthes, notably) and I, by implication, also favor—has a determinate identity, a determinately bounded nature, and also supports our sense of the definite contexts in which its meaning may be fixed with some precision. The canonical argument has been elegantly voiced by Meyer Abrams and echoed by many others. But I'm afraid it has no legs, simply because the puzzles of reference and predication and context plainly affect the presumption of every theory of objective interpretation.[20] (The distinction between "text" and "literary work of art" cannot be more than a verbal convenience.)

From my point of view, therefore, there is no conceivable gain to be had by supposing that "texts" may (or may have to be) denoted by way of denoting material objects first (along, say, Goodman's or Wollheim's or Danto's lines) or by way of privileged signs (as Gracia sometimes seems to

---

19. Jonathan Culler, *Structuralist Poetics* (Ithaca: Cornell University Press, 1975), 133. I find myself in general agreement here with Stanley Fish, "With the Compliments of the Author: Reflections on Austin and Derrida," *Doing What Comes Naturally: Change, Rhetoric, and the Practice of Theory in Language and Legal Studies* (Durham: Duke University Press, 1989).

20. See M. E. Abrams, "How to Do Things with Texts," *Doing Things with Texts: Essays in Criticism and Critical Theory* (New York: W. W. Norton, 1989); see also Peter Lamarque and Stein Haugom Olsen, *Truth, Fiction, and Literature: A Philosophical Perspective* (Oxford: Clarendon, 1994), 276–81.

insist). Referential and predicative success and the fixity of context are entirely consensual and epistemically inseparable from one another—in the non-criterial sense sketched so tellingly in Wittgenstein's *Investigations* and *Culture and Values.*[21] The referential (or denotative) question obviously requires a much closer look, inasmuch as its resolution cannot fail to influence our conception of the possible variety of viable interpretive strategies.

It is an incontestable fact that the linkage between the denotation of texts and the would-be objective description or interpretation of their "meanings" has been completely ignored (or, "solved") by virtue of assuming that there is no pertinent epistemic difference between the description of *denotata* possessing non-Intentional natures and those possessing Intentional "natures." But to believe *that* blatantly presumes that there are no existent entities that have, or can have, natures that are *not* straightforwardly in accord with the familiar picture of natural things possessing strictly determinate physical properties and conforming equally strictly to a logic confined by the principle of excluded middle or (if initial decidability poses a difficulty) at least the principle of *tertium non datur.*[22]

Yet texts *have* only determinable, not strictly determinate, natures (in possessing Intentional structures); and the "meanings" that may be assigned them, objectively, are surely hostage to the historied nature of interpretive practice and the historied formation of the cognizing competence of the selves who undertake the effort. But that is not to say that texts are simply indeterminate or without structure. I put it to you that there simply is no compelling theory that demonstrates the supposed similarity—ontologically, epistemologically, methodologically, logically—between physical properties predicated of mere physical things and "meanings" predicated of texts. All the evidence goes against the analogy. So that, *if* you admit texts as actual entities within a cultural space, you must concede the possibility that they may be entirely determinate denotatively (in fact, as determinate as physical objects are) *without,* as a result, being predicatively determinate as well (as physical objects are said to be). The history of the interpretation of texts—the history of philosophy, for that

21. See Ludwig Wittgenstein, *Culture and Values,* ed. G. H. von Wright and Heikki Nyman, trans. Peter Winch (Oxford: Basil Blackwell, 1980).

22. See Michael Dummett, *Truth and Other Enigmas* (Cambridge: Harvard University Press, 1975), Preface.

matter—has largely assumed the contrary. I take this thesis to mark the single most radical, most far-reaching feature of the theory of texts that anyone could claim.

Accordingly, I offer the following distinctions in the way of logical and epistemic presuppositions (or postulates) that any reasonable theory of texts must address somewhere. First of all, I reject all substantive necessities *de re* and *de cogitatione,* but I do not hold that that rejection counts as a necessary principle of the same sort. Obviously not. It is, I should say, a philosophical "bet," to the effect that no one can show the unavoidability of such necessities (apart from uninterpreted tautologies and contradictions). Second, I would say that it was entirely possible (and noticeably advantageous, particularly in cultural matters) to concede that individuation, numerical identity, denotation, reference, reidentifiability are all quite viable (without producing paradox) in dealing with entities that lack essences or fixed natures, or that possess "histories" or "careers" instead of natures. In fact, texts lack natural-kind natures and have, or are, only histories; that is, their interpretable "nature," their Intentional structure, is and can only be a genuine function of the history of the cultural utterances, the interpretations and self-interpretations, that obtain in the contingent cultures in which they are actually produced and discerned.

These two distinctions go entirely contrary to Aristotelian presuppositions; but, frankly, I take the modal form of the Aristotelian claims to be patently indefensible.[23]

I have two considerations to offer. The first concerns how, denotatively, we should understand the relationship between "marks" and "meanings."[24] I agree that one cannot be aware of uttered words and sentences without, in some sense, being aware of uttered sounds; but it hardly follows that one understands the meaning of uttered words *by* understanding that they are the meanings assigned the sounds (or "marks") first uttered or "used" to signify some determinate, antecedent, objective, independent, intended meaning. The reason is simply that *meanings* (or, Intentional structures) cannot be "objects" that play "the same role [in understanding] as the object [for instance, the perceptual object] in the process of [perceptual] knowledge."[25] There is an insuperable disanalogy

23. See, further, Margolis, *Historied Thought, Constructed World.*
24. Gracia, *A Theory of Textuality,* 22.
25. Ibid.

that counts against the thesis. The clue already lurks in expressions like "the meaning *conveyed*" by would-be signs, "the meaning *of the marks*"—or the meaning of the signs *constituted by* "the *use of* the marks" or by the "*intended use*" *of* the marks. There is no lexical order between marks and signs or between signs and texts.

If you grant that understanding language, texts, artworks, and the like are forms of reflexive understanding—understanding ourselves and what we utter—then there is no satisfactory sense in which when I understand what a poem means (or, by analogy, what a practice means), there is a separable meaning, independent of any interpretive effort, that belongs to the marks (or to the use of the marks printed on a page, or, analogously, to the movements of the body) that I discern and understand, in the same way in which when I see (and come to know by perceiving) that there is a horse on the hill, *there is,* apart from my perceiving the horse, a horse on the hill! Meanings are not objects in any such sense; they are "objects" only by way of nominalization: for what we discern (if we may be said to discern meanings at all) are the Intentional attributes of our own "natures" or histories or utterings—the reflexively assignable meanings of the interpretable texts of a common culture.

In genuine sensory cases, cases confined to the activation of our sense organs, we require a workable disjunction between cognizing subjects and cognized objects. But in understanding texts, there is no such antecedent disjunction: which is not to deny that understanding meanings may be judged to be objectively valid or invalid—or "perceived." It's just that the ontology and epistemology can't be the same in the two cases. Both New Critical theorists (for instance, Monroe Beardsley[26]) and Romantic hermeneuts (for instance, E. D. Hirsch[27]) treat meanings very much like independent properties, though very differently from one another. (Gracia appears to hold a related view.) I take these variant views to commit the same mistake.

There is no way to ensure the standing of "meanings" as analogous to that of the properties of independent "objects" (Beardsley) or to assign "authorial intent" or stylistic genres a determinate criterial role (Hirsch).

26. See Monroe C. Beardsley, *The Possibility of Criticism* (Detroit: Wayne State University Press, 1970).
27. See E. D. Hirsch, Jr., *Validity in Interpretation* (New Haven: Yale University Press, 1967).

There is no way to fix the "intention" or "intended use" or "meaning" of any current text except in terms of the contingent linguistic (and lingual) fluency of apt speakers within a historical culture, who, from the vantage of such fluency, continually reconstitute (as they see matters) the intended meanings of texts produced in past phases of that same history. Objectivity cannot fail to be consensual (in the *lebensformlich* sense already suggested); and if it must be that, interpretive objectivity cannot be the analogue of sensory and allied forms of objectivity. The objectivity of texts is productive, not disclosive; interpretive, not sensory or sensory-like. But, of course, if that is so, the objectivity of sociology or practical politics will be affected as well. Bear that in mind.

Furthermore if, as I have argued, texts may be determinately denoted and reidentified, even though their "nature" or "history" or "meaning" need not be antecedently determinate (but only determinable), then interpretive objectivity cannot convincingly require that a text should possess a single or unique or fixed or independent "meaning." If, also, our interpretive powers are continually reconstituted historically, or are horizonally perspectived as far as self-understanding is concerned, then the analogy between Intentionally structured and non-Intentional *denotata* will be put at mortal risk.

In short, to admit the *sui generis* realism of the cultural world is, effectively, to reject the analogy between texts that we *understand* and mere material or natural objects that we *perceive* in the sensory way. But we cannot deny the existence of texts if we admit the existence of selves; and uttered texts cannot be more determinate than the reflexively determinable nature of self-interpreting selves. Ultimately, the theory of texts *is* a theory of selves and of their utterances.

The second consideration is one that should be credited to the logical empiricist, Herbert Feigl (already mentioned), who, well before the current fashion favoring supervenience with regard to the mind/body problem,[28] realized that there was no known basis for insisting on an invariant relationship between changes or differences in mental (or cultural or intentional) attributes (or meanings) and matched changes or differences in physical (or material) attributes. What Feigl maintained—let me say again—was this: (i) that a meaningful action (or thought) could be per-

---

28. See Jaegwon Kim, *Supervenience and Mind: Selected Philosophical Essays* (Cambridge: Cambridge University Press, 1993).

formed (or conveyed) by indefinitely many different bodily movements (or neurophysiological processes); (ii) that a particular bodily movement (or neurophysiological process) could "convey" (or embody, as I would say) indefinitely many different Intentionally distinct actions (or thoughts); and (iii) that there was no known algorithm or rule by which changes in the one were necessarily matched with changes in the other. (This alone defeats supervenience, of course, which claims a strict necessary correlation between the two.) But if so, then the individuation and denotation of texts are doubly Intentional and cannot be captured by our denotative strategies or, computationally, fitted to non-Intentional entities ("marks," in Goodman's and possibly in Gracia's sense).

Our finding is a double one: first, that of the sheer coherence of admitting the denotative determinacy of texts (comparing favorably with the numerical determinacy of physical objects) together with their interpretively determinable but not determinate nature (as opposed to the nature of physical objects); and, second, following on the first and admitting as well the historicized nature of the interpretive powers of self-interpreting selves, the impossibility of ensuring, evidentiarily, that the objective interpretation of texts (the utterances of self-interpreting selves) can ever yield a uniquely correct or fixed or singular or independent "meaning."

Here, the ontology of texts reflects the essential cognitive difference between knowledge by mere sensory perception and knowledge by understanding (or, as we may say, interpretively informed "perception"). I take this to be very closely linked to the familiar Diltheyan distinction between *verstehen* and *erklären:*[29] except that the cognitive powers in question cannot possibly operate independently of one another; sensory perception has its interpretive (or hermeneutic) side, and self-understanding entails sensory perception. What *does* follow, however, is that it is hardly necessary to subscribe exclusively to a bivalent logic and that it is decidedly unpromising to do so in the context of interpreting texts. The second finding seems a very natural one and neatly outflanks the usual heavy-handed insistence on the "logic of science." Both are, in fact, rather powerful findings for such a modest effort.

In short, what I am claiming is this: once admit (*a*) that texts may be denotatively determinate but predicatively never more than determinable,

29. See Wilhelm Dilthey, *Introduction to the Human Sciences, Selected Works*, vol. 1, ed. Rudolf Makkreel and Frijthof Rodi (Princeton: Princeton University Press, 1989).

(b) that all texts or culturally emergent *denotata* have Intentional "natures" that are inherently interpretable, and (c) that in the cultural world cognizers and cognized are one and the same and culturally constituted, it becomes well-nigh impossible to deny that the objectivity of interpreting Intentional structures cannot disallow the full pertinence of historicism and relativism regarding the reasoned assignment of truth-values. There you have the single most contested thesis in the theory of texts made as plausible as a commonplace.

IV

The lesson I've been pressing about reference and denotation is simply this: that even the denoting of a particular physical object apt for reidentification is, apart from any general theory of language, a decidedly Intentional act; hence, it cannot be convincingly claimed that merely to admit specifically Intentional entities is, effectively, to jeopardize more disciplined discursive resources restricted to physical objects. There is no such rigor to be had. The very idea bespeaks a false optimism that rests on the mistaken notion that predicative resources may, in principle, be counted on to retire our would-be referential and denotative devices, or that the predicative resources of the physical sciences may be segregated from those of the cultural world. I say that that's impossible. I have already taken note of a strong proposal favoring the failed conjecture (about reference and denotation, in Quine's *Word and Object*) that appeals to the limited resources of the first-order predicate calculus.[30] But there is absolutely no known argument to show that numerical identity can actually be captured, in real-world terms, by a mix of quantification and predication.[31] (The insight goes back, as I have also remarked, to Leibniz.[32]) And the indissolubility (or symbiosis) of the "subjective" and the "objective" in referential and predicative discourse completely obviates (unless constructively) the epistemic disjunction of inquiries into the natural and cultural worlds.

What this shows is that the *admission* of a material world lacking

30. See W. V. Quine, *Word and Object* (Cambridge: MIT Press, 1960), §§37–38.
31. See Max Black, "The Identity of Indiscernibles," *Problems of Analysis* (Ithaca: Cornell University Press, 1954).
32. See H. G. Alexander, ed., *The Leibniz-Clarke Correspondence* (Manchester: Manchester University Press, 1956), Leibniz's fifth paper.

Intentional properties presupposes (for epistemic reasons) a world of Intentionally (cognitionally) qualified entities. (That is the supreme lesson of the post-Kantian ethos.) Otherwise, it would make no sense to speak of denoting, individuating, reidentifying, referring to one and the same entity. I mark this a considerable gain in behalf of a realism regarding texts. (Realism, I remind you, cannot, on the gathering argument, fail to take a constructivist turn.)

For somewhat different reasons, the same presupposition makes an appearance in predicative contexts. The two are bound to be connected, for, if (*per impossibile*) denotation could be retired by the joint use of quantificational and predicative devices, we should be driven to decide whether properties may be determinately fixed or epistemically managed in strictly extensional ways. The answer is No, absent Platonism.[33] But, of course, there is no known way to access Universals by any form of human cognition. Furthermore, if that's not possible, then it follows at once that the very idea of an objective property belongs to the indissoluble space of cognizing subjects and cognized objects—certainly not to any merely "objective" (or objectivist) space; hence, it leads, once again, to the presupposition of Intentionally qualified selves.

Again, if texts are, as I suggest, the utterances of reflecting selves, reasonably nominalized or detached as separable artifacts apt for interpretation, then their "meanings," predicatively construed, cannot possibly be managed extensionally, since general attributes (non-Intentional attributes in particular) cannot be. This confirms very trimly the coherence of admitting that texts may be determinately denoted though they lack determinate natures.

Both parts of the thesis are concessive with regard to the would-be determinacy of physical objects. I have no wish to press that issue here: I wish only to secure grounds needed for a cultural realism hospitable to texts. We have only to acknowledge that the "similarities" on which any predicates are justifiably extended to new instances depend (noncriterially)

---

33. Fodor is the most dogged American Platonist that I know of, but even he attempts to defend Platonism in non-cognitivist terms. It is, I venture to suggest, the master theme of his entire *oeuvre*. A recent manifestation appears in Jerry A. Fodor, *Concepts: Where Cognitive Science Went Wrong* (Oxford: Clarendon, 1998), chaps. 6–7, both with respect to nativism and the "atomism" of concepts. But see also Jerrold J. Katz, *The Metaphysics of Meaning* (Cambridge: MIT Press, 1990), for a related Platonism of a very different sort. I shall return briefly to the Platonist issue.

on some *lebensformlich* tolerance, in servicing one societal interest or another (predictive precision, for instance).[34]

If we wished to challenge the objectivist reading of physical nature, then what has thus far been said would be sufficient to carry the argument.[35] I may just add, however, that recent work in the history of the new technology of high-level physics—Peter Galison's study, for instance, of the rather local, somewhat fragmented, heterogeneous "cultures" of professional physicists variously centered on measurement, experiment, technology, explanatory theory, often differing in incommensurable and even incompatible ways—does plausibly show that such "societies" do (or could) in fact manage, despite such discrepancies (which are never quite overcome and never need to be), to cooperate, piecemeal, within established behavioral patterns, without at all understanding one another in terms of a single overarching idiom or theory. I take this to be no more than a corollary of Kuhn's original claim against perceptual and scientific "neutrality."

Galison sees an effective "trading zone" here, both in physics and the market-place, between very different cultures that are neither incapacitated by such divergence nor obliged to overcome it by appeal to a "neutral" idiom in order to function effectively at all. He speaks of a "trading zone" in both settings: in effect, a congeries of *ad hoc*, temporary, behavioral accommodations good enough to coordinate "this" with "that" for the work at hand; so that, "*despite* . . . differences in [practices of] classification, [assignments of] significance, and [commitment to] standards of demonstration, [different] groups can collaborate. They can come to a consensus about the procedure of exchange, about the mechanisms to determine when [they succeed]. They can even both understand that the continuation of exchange is a prerequisite to the survival of the larger culture of which they are part."[36]

I read this as an obvious analogue of my proposal about texts, extended to the work of the most advanced physical sciences. That is, practical

34. See, further, Joseph Margolis, "The Politics of Predication," *Philosophical Forum* 27 (1996).

35. For a sense of the philosophical background, see Richard J. Bernstein, *Beyond Objectivism and Relativism: Semantics, Hermeneutics, and Praxis* (Philadelphia: University of Pennsylvania Press, 1983).

36. Peter Galison, *Image and Logic: A Material Culture of Microphysics* (Chicago: University of Chicago Press, 1997), 803–4.

judgment, logically informal though it must be (for example, regarding reference and predication and context and interpreted meaning), is able to work well enough, in terms of consensual practices, relative to any "given" undertaking, even though what counts as understanding and co-operation and success may never be able to be fixed in any unique, neutral, principled way. Such judgment is able to confirm a measure of "constructed" objectivity, but it can no longer claim to have simply "dis-covered" in a contextless way what the neutral truth finally is. That fiction may well be gone forever. By parity of reason, *in* learning a social practice, *there is* (normally) no fixed or algorithmically defined practice that we learn. Our fluencies, here, are offered in the form of abstracted rules, but the rules are hardly ever more than heuristically advanced and continually recast—even though they may be helpful (for unspecified intervals) in informing spontaneous behavior "in accord with" the practices assumed. (The inertial life of a viable society changes, at different rates, through the different parts of its habituated practices. Needless to say, I offer Galison's view as friendly testimony regarding the advanced sciences—not as confir-mation of my thesis.) But to admit the point is to confirm the need to understand just what is mastered in understanding a "practice."

If, now, distinguishing between Intentional and non-Intentional predi-cates, you add (i) that sensory perception and the understanding of "meanings" are fundamentally different, and (ii) that the objectivity of "meanings" is inextricably bound up with the historical drift of our inter-pretive practices (in a way that is not pertinently matched by any form of mere sensory objectivity, though perceptual objectivity drifts as well), then the following doctrine, already elicited, cannot possibly be legitimated: I mean the doctrine that holds that if we grasp, by interpretive means, the objective "meaning" of a text, then that text must determinately possess that meaning independently of our actually interpreting it.

Ironically, that *is* the canonical view. Only a Platonism could possibly save it. Otherwise, objectivity regarding texts is, first of all, thoroughly *lebensformlich* and (beyond Wittgenstein) historicized; and, secondly, ob-jectivity cannot, as a result, disallow *a priori* the interpretive validity of divergent, even incompatible or historically evolving meanings, or mean-ings that depend on the prior history of interpretation (and *its* interpreta-tion).

Here, the primary question is not one of coherence or mere possibility but of societal memory, tolerance, interest, perspective, prejudice—and the capacity to juggle reasonable attributions (in the way of sorting plural strands of each). That is an unexpected gain. For what it means is simply that relativism, for example—which I espouse but have no wish to defend just here—is grounded in the very same *lebensformlich* sources that we would need to enlist if we had simply insisted on there being no more than a uniquely correct meaning assignable to each particular text.[37] Once you admit the fundamental disanalogy between sensory properties and meanings, you cannot escape the slippery slope of historicizing meanings, in admitting the artifactual and historicized nature of selves. But then, once you admit the *lebensformlich* character of reference and predication, you cannot escape historicizing the conditions of objectivity for discourse about physical nature either.

There is nothing in these adjustments that risks the regularities of cognitive practice. On the contrary, if the argument holds, then the perceptual and theorizing resources of our best sciences will be seen to be grounded in the same fluxive condition; for, here, flux means nothing more than the denial of necessities and fixities *de re* and *de cogitatione*. There is no reason to regard that as paradoxical.

You must turn to someone like David Hume to find a theory of the meaning of terms that actually defeats intelligibility. For Hume accelerates, in the *Treatise,* the effect of flux beyond manageable limits: Hume holds that the least change in a perceived quality signifies an utter change of quality—hence, an utter change of predicate.[38] The theory requires (in principle) an instantaneous, continual replacement of one entire vocabulary by another—which, of course, is impossible. Neither historicism nor relativism requires anything of the kind. The concept of a general predicate concerns no more than the notion of what may be judged to remain qualitatively the "same" *through* perceived "differences" or changes. Consensual practices are enough. If Hume were favored here, we would destroy the very possibility of linguistic communication, or deliberate cooperation for that matter. In fact, many critics of historicism and relativism fall back to similar (pointless) worries about rendering texts unintelligible, once it turns out that they cannot disallow either doctrine

37. See Chapter 5 above; and Joseph Margolis, *What, After All, Is a Work of Art? Lectures in the Philosophy of Art* (University Park: The Pennsylvania State University Press, 1999), chap. 2.

38. See David Hume, *A Treatise of Human Nature,* ed. L. A. Selby-Bigge (Oxford: Clarendon, 1958), Bk. I. Pt. iv, §vi.

on grounds of internal incoherence. (But they do not understand the threat Hume poses.)

The main lines of the argument are now quite clear: texts are artifacts existing in cultural space, possessing real Intentional structures ("meanings," if you wish) apt for continual interpretation. But if Platonism is indemonstrable, if reference and predication are historicized and *lebensformlich,* if selves and their cognizing aptitudes are similarly formed, then the conditions for understanding individuated texts are inseparable from the conditions by which we understand ourselves. But if so, then understanding the meaning of texts cannot fail to be objective (that is, cannot fail to provide for objectivity) since there is no viable notion of what it is to be a competent self deprived of such fluency. To interpret "correctly" the artifacts of human life (texts, if you please)—thoughts, actions, speech, artworks, histories, institutions—*is* simply to function as an exemplary self.

There remains, however, a double hermeneutic drift to be acknowledged, which Hans-Georg Gadamer has pinpointed most effectively: namely, that, as they change historically, enabling cultures change the cognizing horizon of functioning selves and, coordinately, change the potentiating range of meanings apt for subsequent interpretation (or cooperation).[39] (That, of course, is historicism pure and simple.)

If you bear in mind that selves cannot fail to be aware that they interpret themselves and the other "texts" of their world from the vantage of a transient horizon that must have replaced other such horizons in the past, you see that they cannot disallow similar further horizonal alterations, amplifications, revisions, even replacements, diverging and competing streams of interpretation—within the consensual limits of societal memory and interest and tolerance—within which they function.

Admitting all that entails two extraordinary complications that theorists of art and history generally avoid—but cannot justify avoiding.[40] One collects the fact that the meaning of the historical past belongs to the interlocking horizon of an evolving history (itself constructed) in which it is continually relocated; hence, that the meaning of the historical past (*not*

---

39. See Hans-Georg Gadamer, *Truth and Method,* trans. Garrett Barden and John Cumming (New York: Seabury Press, 1975).

40. A very clear recent specimen of such avoidance is, as I say, afforded by Robert Stecker in "The Constructivist's Dilemma," *Journal of Aesthetics and Art Criticism* 60 (1997).

the physical past) must be a changing artifact of changing interpretations. The other complication is at least as strenuous: namely, that texts of every sort acquire ambient trails of interpretive history, always subject to further interpretive weighting, that tend (if undisputed) to define, inertially, the proper context of understanding the particular texts to which they attach. Such fixities can never be more than reportorial conveniences or local hegemonies, as Roland Barthes's interpretation of Balzac's *Sarrasine*[41] and George Thomson's interpretation of the *Oresteia*[42] very nicely confirm.

I must enter a warning here. I am quite aware that, regarding "intentional discourse," certain logical puzzles arise when circumstances affect the *truth* of what is believed, which may be wrongly believed to affect *what is* actually *believed*. This is what Peter Geach had in mind in speaking of mere "Cambridge changes." I grant the point. When, for instance, I believe that De Gaulle is the tallest Frenchman and it happens, as time goes by, that someone else comes to occupy the status of "tallest Frenchman," then the truth of what I believe may be altered but not my belief (which was true at a time but is no longer, or now, true.) I do not, however, admit that changes in the meaning of texts as a result of continual interpretation and historical development *are* mere Cambridge changes! Not at all. You may oppose my view because you oppose my picture of the reality of the cultural world. But that's an entirely different affair.

V

It is in the sense intended that texts are assigned unitary careers. We grasp the meaning of a human life by understanding the sequence of its biological phases within the context of a culturally significant career. By analogy, literary texts, artworks, more amorphous histories—hardly lives, but utterances all—are cast as sustaining unitary careers, chiefly as a result of their interpretive histories. They have no closed form of their own, of course. Think of the "career" of the endlessly reinterpreted American Civil War (or Velázquez's *Las Meninas*, for that matter). There is no way, now, to interpret the War (or *Las Meninas*) responsibly, except through the

41. See Roland Barthes, *S/Z*, trans. Richard Miller (New York: Hill and Wang, 1974).
42. See George Thomson, *Aeschylus and Athens* (London: Lawrence and Wishart, 1971).

scruple of preserving the history of its accumulating interpretations—without yet supposing that *any* interpreted part of it need ever be finally fixed or fixed within its encompassing career. The most interesting texts appear to be both protean and inexhaustible: the Bible, the Vedas, the American Constitution, the *Odyssey*.

Thus construed, the chief constraints on interpretation rest with a society's capacity to remember and bring to bear on new interpretations of a given text some part of that society's present sense of the text's entire history. Generally, much of this will be forgotten or interpretively rearranged or selectively discounted; and the unity of the text's predicated *nature* will be diversely imputed, always preserving *number* in the denotative sense. Just recently, in fact, the practice has been confirmed in a telling but circumscribed way by its deliberate restriction in the reading of a exemplary text, from a vantage that can hardly be called careless or uninformed—in Helen Vendler's important rereading of Shakespeare's *Sonnets*.[43]

An adequate theory of interpretive practice is bound to be far more generous (and more strenuous) than the rationale for any particular reader's practice. But, then, the *society* of the practice of all readers is bound to be more diverse and more tolerant than any individual theory of texts might ever proclaim. That is what I find so neatly illustrated by the absence of any justificatory rationale in what Vendler offers in explaining her own "commentary" as a modest "supplement" to certain important readings that she happens to favor.[44] It is surely worth an additional moment's attention. (The amplitude of a society's tolerance for different sources of interpretation is a soft analogue of a species' need for a diverse gene pool.)

I mean to draw from Vendler's example two strategic gains for the theory of texts: one concerns how naturally even a deliberately restricted commentary like Vendler's may be reclaimed by a more generous theory of reading (the sort, frankly, that I am recommending), which Vendler explicitly opposes; the other, how straightforwardly we may ensure the coherence and plausibility of the more accommodating radical theories of interpretation spawned from the first gain. The point is to soften the

---

43. See Helen Vendler, *The Art of Shakespeare's Sonnets* (Cambridge: Harvard University Press, 1997).
44. Ibid., 4.

charge of arbitrariness and the fear of interpretive chaos that are so often brought against theories that deny that "meanings" are fixed in historical time, as by authorial intent or by essential genres or by whatever else may be thought to govern a determinate set of words; also, to assure us that the theory being championed is not likely (as a result) to be confronted by any intractable paradox or logical difficulty that only a more canonical ("objectivist") view of interpretation could possibly save us from. I claim no more than the coherence and viability of the upstart theory and the incapacity of the familiar canons to guarantee more.

Turn, then, to Vendler's readings. I acknowledge the spare scruple of Vendler's commentary on the *Sonnets*. But she never ventures beyond the sense of the words that earlier authoritative commentaries have already entrenched; she also does not venture beyond certain very limited (antecedently "approved") lines of interpretation that rely heavily on fitting just such established meanings. In this way, Vendler conveys an almost impregnable impression of the sheer objectivity of the entire exercise, of moving with precision toward a uniquely adequate, very nearly ordained reading of each poem. But she barely touches on the possible validity of entirely different strategies of interpretation or the threatening import of their potential validity on the right assessment of restricting interpretation in the way she favors; and she nowhere addresses the question of fixed meanings.

Speaking of her own effort, Vendler offers the following defense:

> I intend this work for those who already know the *Sonnets,* or who have beside them the sort of lexical annotation found in the current editions (for example, those of [Stephen] Booth, [John] Kerrigan, or [G. B.] Evans. . . . And why should I add another book to those already available? I want to do so because I admire the *Sonnets,* and wish to defend the high value I put on them. . . . Contemporary emphasis on the participation of literature in a social matrix balks at acknowledging how lyric, though it may *refer* to the social, remains the genre that directs its *mimesis* toward the performance of the mind in *solitary* speech. . . . A social reading is better directed at a novel or a play: the abstraction desired by the writer of, and the willing reader of, normative lyric frustrates the mind that wants social fictions or biographical revelations.[45]

45. Ibid., 1–2.

This seems to supply a fair reason for Vendler's deliberately restricted undertaking. But, if you think about it, there can't be any reason to suppose that conceding the lyric to be a genre committed to "the performance of the mind in *solitary* speech" adversely affects the propriety of interpreting *such* speech in terms of its supposed "social matrix." I'm afraid Vendler's argument—for it is now no longer an autobiographical admission—is a transparent *petitio*. By its own rationale, Vendler's forthright practice actually strengthens the reasonableness of opposing her essentialized division between appropriate and inappropriate readings of the *Sonnets*. For, in defending her own restrictions, she ineluctably betrays the arbitrariness of insisting on adhering to them!

Vendler offers two specific considerations, both of which backfire badly. For one thing, she says: "The true 'actors' in the lyric are words, not 'dramatic persons'; and the drama of any lyric is constituted by the successive entrances of new sets of words, or new stylistic arrangements (grammatic, syntactical, phonetic) which are visibly in conflict with previous arrangements used with reference to the 'same' situation."[46] Taken literally, this goes contrary to Vendler's insistence on "the performance of the mind in *solitary* speech." For one thing, it is a voiced performance; for another, it is, in Shakespeare's case, often cast in the form of an imagined address to one's beloved; and, for a third, its appreciation is expressly cast (by Vendler) in terms of a proper grasp of the novel language Shakespeare introduces in fashioning the lyric voice he offers. So it is not implausible to view the *Sonnets* as "dramatic" even if solitary (like the soliloquies); and, in any case, "words" cannot be "actors" by themselves: they must be uttered in a "performance of the mind." There *is* a theory (of sorts) implicated in Vendler's practice; but it cannot justify the restriction she intends, and it cannot validate any ideal norm of exclusive interpretation. (It is, I may say, not altogether dissimilar to the views of Beardsley and Scalia, already examined.)

The second consideration is at least as telling: it actually undercuts Vendler's treatment of the first. Here she relies on some plain talk from W. H. Auden (which she cites favorably). Auden offers the following: "The questions which interest me most when reading a poem are two. The first is technical. 'Here is a verbal contraption. How does it work?' The second is, in the broadest sense, moral. 'What kind of a guy inhabits the poem?

46. Ibid., 3.

What is his notion of the good life or the good place? His notion of the Evil One? What does he conceal from the reader? What does he conceal even from himself?'" Vendler glosses these remarks thus: "Like any poet, Auden knows that the second question cannot be responded to correctly until the first has been answered. It is the workings of the verbal construct that give evidence of the moral stance of the poet."[47] Yes, perhaps. But that has nothing to do with what may be called the "lexical" order of the two questions.

In fact, if you reread Auden's remark, you see how reasonable it would be to suppose that the "voice" or "guy" that "inhabits" the poem is quite inseparable from the "verbal contraption" itself: whether read as (as in lyric) the "dramatic" voice of the poem viewed as an imagined utterance *or* as the actual poet's creative utterance creating the "voice" of the other (which, of course, are not the same). The interpretation of Shakespeare's "moral stance" is itself constructed (at least in part) *by* the very reading of the "verbal construct" that is Shakespeare's utterance of the original poem (thereafter read as an imagined lyric utterance). There is no principled disjunction between the two. But, if not, then Vendler's gloss on Auden is simply untenable. (There is, indeed, something of a structuralist predilection in Vendler's method of reading).

You may glimpse the intent of her practice, in reading Sonnet 9 ("Is it for fear to wet a widow's eye"), which is admittedly restricted and occupied with a great deal of word play, where Vendler herself remarks: "Whatever the charms of mirror-image letters [in the spelling of 'widdow' in the Quarto edition] and symmetrical words, the poem has to mean something too, and has to have a general shape."[48] Vendler supplies its meaning, finding in the octave and sestet the "theological contrast" between a sin of omission and a sin of commission.[49] But she confines the commentary (true to her own intent) to the formal structure of the sonnet. The question remains whether, even here, some more adventurous reading of the "theological contrast" (itself already adventurous enough) may be rightly pursued. The operative image is captured in the first two lines, assessed in the final couplet:

47. Ibid., 10–11. The passage from Auden is from W. H. Auden, *"The Dyer's Hand" and Other Essays* (New York: Viking, 1968).
48. Vendler, *The Art of Shakespeare's Sonnets*, 85.
49. Ibid.

> Is it for fear to wet a widow's eye
> That thou consum'st thyself in single life?
> . . . .
> No love toward others in that bosom sits
> That on himself such murd'rous shame commits.

The verdict is too forceful to disallow conjecture.

For example—though I claim no expertise—could the poem be an in-sinuation of the waste of the celibate life of religious orders (analogous to the absurd waste of the young man's demurrer of marriage, alluded to in the sonnet)? That would show at least the impossibility of disjoining the questions Vendler claims to disjoin, as well as the impossibility of getting the first question right without locating would-be "stylistic arrangements (grammatic, syntactical, phonetic)" within the richer conceptual space of the moral and cultural world of human speech and agency. The second possibility shows how arbitrary it would be (and is) to restrict the reading of the *Sonnets* in Vendler's way. I cannot see how that can be denied. There are no easy outer limits to interpretation here.

I seize the occasion, therefore, to remind you of a more adventurous theory and practice among professional readers of Shakespeare (perhaps more usually focused on the plays than the sonnets). Here are some re-marks of Stephen Greenblatt's that convey the intended rigor of the kind of criticism Greenblatt and his associates practice (what has been called "new historicism"), which supports a conception of the open-ended nature of denotatively determinate texts: "works of art, [Greenblatt announces at the start of *Shakespearean Negotiations,*] however intensely marked by the creative intelligence and private obsessions of individuals, are the products of collective negotiation and exchange. Why should works of criticism be any different?"[50] (Commentators like Vendler have no answer.) Greenblatt glosses the announcement as follows:

> If there is no expressive essence that can be located in an aesthetic object complete unto itself, uncontaminated by interpretation, be-yond translation or substitution—if there is no mimesis without exchange—then we need to analyze the collective dynamic circula-

50. Stephen Greenblatt, *Shakespearean Negotiations* (Berkeley and Los Angeles: University of California Press, 1988), vii.

tion of pleasures, anxieties, and interests. . . . art does not simply exist in all cultures; it is made up along with other products, practices, discourses of a given culture. (In practice, "made up" means inherited, transmitted, altered, modified, reproduced far more than it means invented: as a rule, there is very little pure invention in culture.)[51]

Obviously, interpretive practice and cultural ontology go hand in hand.

I shall close my remarks with a final claim that you may find entirely too extravagant. It is, however, the one I prize the most. I have characterized a *text* as any interpretable *denotatum,* either intrinsically such, as being Intentionally qualified (selves or sentences or artworks or histories), or suitably anthropomorphized or modeled on the human paradigm (the utterances of languageless infants, animals, machines, and the like, even physical nature viewed under one or another explanatory theory). In this sense, texts are relatively independent *denotata* apt for interpretation, but their interpretation is inseparable from the reflexive interpretation selves practice on themselves: for texts are, after all, the utterances of selves, whether linguistic or lingual (in the sense already supplied).

Now, if we give up the forms of privilege and modal necessity, we see that all questions of referential, predicative, contextual, and interpretive fixity and objectivity depend, finally, on the consensual tolerance of the fluxive practices of the fluxive society in which our discursive powers were first formed and are sustained. I have already insisted that there are no criterial or algorithmic rules by which any of the cognizing competences associated with interpretive objectivity can be vouchsafed. But if you grant all that, you must see that the peculiar nature of Intentional attributes cannot be counted on to justify any principled constraints (Vendler's, for instance) said to override our local and variable interests, the construction of our capacity to recover past phases of our admitted history, and our spontaneous willingness to enlarge and alter the interpretive resources of our culture.

Already in Schleiermacher, the hermeneutic tradition was forced to admit that authorial intent could not be confined psychologically; further-

---

51. Ibid., 12–13. I find this close in spirit to the view expressed by Michael Baxandall, *Patterns of Intention: On the Historical Explanation of Pictures* (New Haven: Yale University Press, 1985), in spite of the fact that Baxandall professes a more conservative approach.

more, Romantic hermeneutics discovered that, once the historicity of cultural life was admitted, there was no way to assign Intentional fixities to historical "horizons" or genres in any criterial sense suited to fixing interpretive objectivity.[52] Given that Intentionality is *sui generis*, utterly unlike physical properties, emergent only in the sense in which human selves are themselves emergently "second-natured," there simply is no neutral or assuredly unique way in which linguistic and lingual meaning can be fixed objectively. There *is* objectivity to be found—in the sense in which the apt members of a society *are* tacitly prepared to treat, as a continuation of their usual practices, some *further* modification of what can be consensually sustained as still within the objective recovery of the meaning of particular Intentional *denotata*.

If you grant all this, you cannot fail to grant as well two further, distinctly heterodox proposals: one, to the effect that every particular text owes its determinability in part to the shifting family of related texts whose meanings its own changing interpretation affects but which (in turn) affect its own interpretable potentialities; the other, to the effect that there are no clear boundaries to the "nature" of a particular text or to the horizon of a self-interpreting culture, and that even Intentional structures imputed to the historical past or historical origin of a particular text are subject to being continually altered in accord with the present and future saliencies of its evolving ethos.[53]

These are simply corollaries of a realist reading of cultural entities—under historicity; for meaning or Intentional structure has no locus apart from the ongoing consensual life of a viable society and, there, there are no fixities *de re* or *de cogitatione*. There is no interpretive objectivity apart from the collective tolerance of a society's grasp of its own historical saliencies through change, and there are no such saliencies that do not automatically provide a ground for a constructed objectivity. There is no unique *telos* toward which responsible interpretations tend, and the ongoing contest between different interpretive currents simply confirms the *sui generis* nature of objectivity in cultural matters.

52. See Gadamer, *Truth and Method*, 269ff.
53. See, further, Joseph Margolis, *Interpretation Radical But Not Unruly: The New Puzzle of the Arts and History* (Berkeley and Los Angeles: University of California Press, 1995); also, Anthony Giddens, *Central Problems in Social Theory: Action, Structure and Contradiction in Social Analysis* (Berkeley and Los Angeles: University of California Press, 1979).

SELVES AND OTHER TEXTS

Roughly speaking, the diversity of interpretation tends to mirror the diversity of cultural life. Seen that way, it is very likely an elementary blunder to insist that the strong convergence among the natural sciences must be canonically matched among the interpretive disciplines. There is no compelling rationale for insisting on such norms. In fact, recalling the puzzles of reference and predication and context, we may suppose that the model of objectivity in the natural sciences (possibly even plural models) is itself confirmed through the same cultural sources by which we are prepared to test the outer limits of interpretive objectivity. Inquiries of these two sorts answer to different interests. But they are interests of the same inquiring agents and they are sustained in one and the same culture.

EPILOGUE:
UTTERED SPEECH, UTTERED WORLD

I

Consider, finally, some splendid lines from John Donne's *A Valediction: Forbidding Mourning:*

> Moving of th'earth brings harms and fears,
>   Men reckon what it did and meant,
> But trepidation of the spheres,
>   Though greater far, is innocent.
>
> Dull sublunary lovers' love
>   (Whose soul is sense) cannot admit
> Absence, because it doth remove
>   Those things which elemented it.[1]

I offer them in order to introduce a small sample of a familiar counterargument to the theory I have fashioned. It's worth a last reflection.

William Dowling, a teacher of English poetry, whom I don't know except through his book, *The Senses of the Text,* which offers a glimpse of Dowling's "method" for explicating poems, provides, by way of a "close" reading of Donne's lines, the most explicit and

1. John Carey, ed., *John Donne* (Oxford: Oxford University Press, 1990), 120.

most provocative recent challenge I can recall against deviating from the doctrine that "meaning exists 'in the text', and that interpretation always involves something [here Dowling borrows a formulation from Stanley Fish, whose view he unconditionally opposes] that is irreducibly there independently of and prior to interpretive activities."[2]

By this pronouncement Dowling joins the ranks of those he himself names as champions of "close reading," Beardsley and Hirsch and (among others whom he names) Cleanth Brooks, Northrop Frye, and Umberto Eco. (I add Scalia and Vendler to Dowling's list.) But Dowling is more extreme on "close reading" than any of these (even Hirsch and Scalia), both in avoiding cause for doubt about his own position and how he means to proceed step by step:

> In particular, [he says,] this [the method he advocates] will involve the claim that "meaning" as it exists for literary theory does not depend on interpretive communities [Fish's notion], or social conventions, or language games, or ideological systems, or anything else that is, as one could say in a more innocent age, outside the text. In the last analysis, the argument would be that meanings create interpretive communities rather than the other way around.[3]

Dowling tells us that close reading proceeds by isolating "meaning as governed by syntactic and semantic rules," by avoiding "extra-linguistic considerations" such as (Fish's alleged habit of) shifting "questions into a pragmatic or speech-act context," by avoiding "conflicting second-order interpretations" and staying with our "tacit knowledge" of first-order meanings, and in general by avoiding theories (or at least certain kinds of theories) about meaning.[4]

Dowling actually says: "Indeed, I want quite seriously to defend the position that the words and sentences and syntactic rules of a language—and therefore every potentially meaningful utterance in that language, and therefore the meaning of those utterances—could in an intelligible sense be said to exist even if there existed not a single human being who spoke or

---

2. William C. Dowling, *The Senses of the Text: Intentional Semantics and Literary Theory* (Lincoln: University of Nebraska Press, 1994), 1.
3. Ibid.
4. Ibid., 11, 14–15.

understood it. For [J. J.] Katz [whom he professes to follow], whose unabashed linguistic Platonism has room even for languages that no one on earth will ever speak and no earthling will ever imagine—those languages, as he might say, exist in the same 'place' that, for instance, French existed in 2000 B.C.—this presents no particular problem."[5]

I find the claim preposterous. I can imagine Karl Marx musing: well, that's certainly well beyond anything I would have counted as a "Robinsonade." But, whatever else may be said—and I wouldn't for a moment deny the charm of Dowling's extraordinary claim (ultimately Katz's) in favor of what may be called "linguistic Platonism"[6]—there are at least two undeniable, two probably insuperable, difficulties with such an account: one, possibly a quibble but not a negligible one if it is, namely, that Dowling's notion hardly meets his own objections against drawing on theories "outside the text" (for instance, objecting to speech-act theory); the other, that even if we suppose Katz is right (Dowling, derivatively), there is no known way to show convincingly (*pace* Katz, Chomsky, Fodor) that, *in reading literary texts,* we can actually proceed by any method epistemically *separable* (as Katz might insist, for Katz does distinguish between failed Platonisms that fatally rely on sensory experience and those that go full bore for "reason" uncontaminated by experience) from the way we normally make sense of a text we are actually reading; as by checking the meanings of words in an ordinary dictionary.

As far as I can see, Dowling's reading of Donne's lines compromises (cannot but compromise) the "method" he claims to draw from Katz. I have touched (elsewhere) on something close to this matter more obliquely, in reviewing Nicholas Wolterstorff's Platonism and Richard Wollheim's incoherent treatment of types and tokens.[7] But, in general, it's hopeless (witness Husserl, whom Katz considers briefly) to disjoin "natural" experience and "higher" reason; it's also pointless to promote Platonist conditions without providing a confirmable way of accessing the Forms.

Katz is impressive in tracking the principal disputes and confusions

---

5. Ibid., 16.

6. For a sense of Katz's thesis, see Jerrold J. Katz, *Realistic Rationalism* (Cambridge: MIT Press, 1998), chaps. 1–2; see also *The Metaphysics of Meaning* (Cambridge: MIT Press, 1990).

7. See Joseph Margolis, *Art and Philosophy: Conceptual Issues in Aesthetics* (Atlantic Highlands, N.J.: Humanities Press, 1980), chap. 4.

regarding the "realist" treatment of mathematics, logic, and language—and even, in a footnote, music.[8] The trouble is, he nowhere shows us how to invoke the higher Platonist sources. In any case, I cannot see the sense in which "*French* existed in 2000 B.C."; or the sense in which any argument could possibly justify denying that natural languages are historically formed, historically changeable, "systems" of some sort; and I certainly cannot see how poems can be read by "reason alone," or how we could ever proceed from "acquaintance" with a historical text *to* discerning "by reason alone" the meaning of that text. I am not at all persuaded by mathematical Platonism, but I see no satisfactory basis for claiming that a natural language is some kind of "abstract entity" in the same "realist" sense that is said to apply to mathematics.

II

One last delay before turning to Donne's poem. Dowling's actual readings have absolutely nothing to do with Katz's Platonism, except (by way of epithet) wherever the appeal to Platonism is made to disqualify competing readings. There is absolutely no known point at which linguistic resources *separated* from our ordinary familiarity with historical languages plays any criterial role at all. Dowling champions "the idea of determinate meaning," which an imagined opponent, "the colleague across the hall," perhaps (as Dowling supposes) someone sympathetic to Fish's notion of interpretive communities, might take to be no more than "a form of collective free association regimented by the *OED*" rather than (say) by some other would-be norm. Dowling claims that the evidence overwhelmingly supports "the *method*" of close reading that he recommends—"a certain way of reasoning from a tacit knowledge of syntactic and semantic rules to hypotheses about meaning": it's the *method*, he says, "that is doing the convincing."[9]

What's "tacit" is the Platonist knowledge of syntax and semantics—*not*

8. The entire text of *Realistic Rationalism* collects all the principal examples in mathematics, logic, and linguistics. Katz manages, in fact, to add a footnote on a parallel dispute between Peter Kivy, "Orchestrating Platonism," in *Aesthetic Distinction*, ed. Thomas Anderberg, Tore Nilstun, and Ingmar Persson (Lund: Lund University Press, 1988), and Jerrold Levinson, *Music, Art, and Metaphysics* (Ithaca: Cornell University Press, 1990).

9. Dowling, *The Senses of the Text*, 10–11.

our fluency in natural-language discourse (our separable "competence," apparently, not our "performance" or competence idealized from performance). But surely we cannot possibly invoke any Platonist rules until we know the correct way to read the actual lines; and then the question will always nag: Aren't the "rules" projected or idealized from a reading of the lines? And must "empirical" texts have "determinate meaning" in the Platonist's sense?

III

I'll now try to defend the specific interpretation of Donne's lines that Dowling knocks down: not to fix the actual (the true) "determinate meaning" of the first of the two stanzas cited, but to show rather that "determinate meaning" need not preclude what I've earlier called "incongruent" interpretations (interpretations incompatible with one another but validly assigned such lines as Donne's). I mean to show, first, that Dowling is himself in the grip of a theory about poetic texts every bit as partisan as those he believes play fast and loose with their interpretive games;[10] and, second, that there *is,* and can be, no *a priori* way of fixing any changeless constraints on the right reading of actual texts—certainly not from the Platonist vantage.

How to read a poem ineluctably depends on what kind of poem (or text) we take it to be: that, you remember, was very much Scalia's difficulty in reading the American Constitution. Also, the right classification of poems can hardly be derived from the formal syntax and semantics of the Platonist world; for, of course, Platonism cannot decide the question of relevance, even the relevance of how to apply its own would-be "method" to these or those lines. I doubt there is any way to defend a Katzian Platonism about reading actual poems.

10. In fact, one might almost say Dowling's notion of the quarrel about "determinate meaning" echoes the quarrel that Fish pursues regarding God's Word and the human interpretation of God's Word, as by interpreting Milton's *Paradise Lost,* which is itself an attempt to interpret the same. Fish's finding shows the ineluctability of admitting the reader's *role* even in the reading of *Paradise Lost,* which may be thought to test the idea at the most extreme limit possible. I would say Fish has made a very good case. See Stanley Fish, *Surprised by Sin: The Reader in "Paradise Lost,"* 2d ed. (Cambridge: Harvard University Press, 1997), particularly the preface to the second edition.

The knockdown argument against Dowling (really, against Katz and all Platonists regarding language and all the arts) is that there is no way to treat *utterance* (the "utterance" of . . . words, deeds, musical sound, sculptures) in terms of a "system" *separated* from and prior to our "empirical" or historical acquaintanceship with any socially entrenched practices. There is no language apart from utterance; and utterance, the utterance-of-language, is an artifact of historical life. There is no *langue* disjoint from *parole*.[11] There is no linguistic "competence" that can be assessed apart from "performance."[12] There are no "sentences" or "complete [sentential] thoughts" entirely separable from their associated "uses," as in making a judgment or putting a question.[13] These are the results of nominalizing what may be abstracted from actual linguistic practices—as the *denotata* of a timeless world of separate Platonic entities.

Furthermore, even if there were a Platonist system to invoke, *its* relevance for particular lines of poetry would depend on the correctness with which we determined (i) what kind of poem or lines we were dealing with, and therefore (ii) what relationship actually held between the meaning of any uttered lines and the "pure" syntax and semantics of certain ideal sentences the utterances were said to implicate. Nothing bearing on (i) and (ii) could possibly be decided "by reason alone." Furthermore, there is no compelling argument to show that utterance, Donne's uttering his *Valediction,* or the poem's voice uttering its lines, must be determinate in anything like the way Dowling claims it must be (by way of "tacit knowledge"). Tacit knowledge might easily support determinable rather than determinate meanings. Why not? We simply have no basis for not allowing a very generous range of possibilities consistent with the practice of understanding language.

In a nutshell: if Dowling is reading Donne, then he is not reading (mere) sentences but the utterances of a human voice; and if he is doing that, he cannot appeal to any ideal syntax or semantics of sentences to vouchsafe the reading of those utterances. And if that is so, then whatever "determi-

---

11. See Ferdinand de Saussure, *Course in General Linguistics,* ed. Charles Bally et al., trans. Roy Harris (La Salle, Ill.: Open Court, 1986), particularly chap. 3.

12. See Noam Chomsky, *The Minimalist Program* (Cambridge: MIT Press, 1995), chap. 1, particularly 14–18.

13. See Gottlob Frege, *Logical Investigations,* ed. T. Geach and R. W. Storthoff (New Haven: Yale University Press, 1977).

nate meaning" the sentences of the Platonist heaven may claim, there is no assurance that poetic lines are similarly determinate. It's open to us of course to bring our grammar and dictionary (generated by a running review of actual usage) to bear on what we should (now) regard as the sense of the text before us. We read equilibratively, so to say, not algorithmically, judging what to make of this or that line of poetry within the history of reading, and we duly adjust the history as we proceed.

IV

I need only one illustration of Dowling's application of his "method" to gain my point. I'm not happy to be nit-picking in Dowling's classroom lessons. But he is so candid about the incontestability of his elucidations that it would be foolish to refuse the gift. It bears directly on my argument. In any case, I shall feature only the finding Dowling features in explicating the sense of the first of the two stanzas cited.

The first is really the third in a poem of nine stanzas, the first two of which introduce the theme of the parting of a man and a woman. The editor of an Oxford edition of Donne, John Carey, reports (without conviction) the opinion of a friend of Donne's that the lines are motivated by the poet's "leaving his wife to travel abroad in 1611." This is the same Carey whom Dowling treats contemptuously for the latter's analysis of Donne's famous *Elegy: To His Mistress Going to Bed;* here, Dowling relies on William Kerrigan's indictment of Carey's "silly generalizations about the enjoyment of pornography."[14] Fine.

Dowling and Carey agree about the sense of the opening phrase of the third stanza, *Moving of th'earth brings harms and fears*: that is, earthquakes bring harms and fears. Except that Carey offers as no more than a handy note, "earthquakes, taken as portents," whereas Dowling offers the same reading as part of a "knockdown argument" in the context of reporting the effect his classroom handout had on students in English 219,

---

14. Dowling, *The Senses of the Text,* 13. For the remark about the sense of the first two stanzas, see Carey, ed., *John Donne,* 443. For the context of Kerrigan's remark, see William Kerrigan, "Seventeenth-Century Studies," in *Redrawing the Boundaries: The Transformation of English and American Literary Studies,* ed. Stephen Greenblatt and Giles Gunn (New York: Modern Language Association of America, 1991), 69–70.

who, though trained enough to avoid certain mistakes, predictably *mis-read* the phrase in question. Here is what Dowling says:

> The misreading, as most people who have taught the poem will have guessed, concerns *moving of th'earth,* which more than half the class had taken to refer to planetary motion (with two sub-groups, one opting for the earth's motion around the sun, the other for its rotation on its own axis). This was the handout:
>
> HOW WAS I SUPPOSED TO KNOW THAT WAS AN EARTHQUAKE?
> —A PROBLEM IN CLOSE READING.

The handout goes on to report the students' handling of the phrase and summarizes the mistake sympathetically: "Since the whole stanza is obvi-ously about planets and planetary motion, and since the earth is a planet, why couldn't an intelligent reader take *moving of th'earth* to refer, say, to the earth's motion around the sun? (There even is an *OED* definition that refers specifically to the motion of the planets: how were we supposed to know it didn't refer to the motion of the earth as a planet?)"[15]

Dowling supplies information that is at once syntactic, semantic, and factual (regarding seventeenth-century views of astronomy), all perfectly reasonable and perfectly relevant. And then he has the following to say:

> Now [bearing in mind that the phrase, *trepidation of the spheres,* in the third stanza, is best read in the sense in which "*spheres* here must be Ptolemaic spheres"[16]] you have a knockdown argument in your favor: (1) "earthquake" makes perfect sense in this context because it fits the controlling contrast or comparison implied by *but* and *greater* while (2) "movement of the earth as a planet around the sun" doesn't make sense *because in the Ptolemaic system the earth does not move around the sun; it is the fixed or motionless center of the universe.* So the only plausible candidate for the mean-ing of *moving of th'earth* is the more local phenomenon of an

---

15. Dowling, *The Senses of the Text,* 4–5.

16. Carey explains in the notes: "*trepidation.* Astronomer's term for oscillation of the ninth (crystalline) 'sphere,' imperceptible on earth ('innocent') but supposedly affecting the other concentric 'spheres' composing the Ptolemaic universe."

"earthquake," and when you've seen that, everything else in the stanza fits.[17]

Well, not quite and not exactly.

The first point, part a larger objection to Dowling's reading, simply notes that Copernicus simplified the use of "Ptolemaic spheres," making the sun the center of the universe and the earth to revolve around the sun. So the fact (correct enough) that *spheres* "must be Ptolemaic spheres" has nothing to do with reading Donne's lines as being committed to Ptolemy's geostatic theory. That's simply a *non sequitur.* Of course, we *may* read the lines as Dowling insists we should; let me grant the possibility. But Dowling is *not* relying on any rule of "close reading" as a basis for rejecting (*as* a misreading) the students' taking *moving of th'earth* to signify the planetary motion of the earth. He simply prefers his own reading!

Furthermore, there's no evidence at all that Donne's awareness of sixteenth- and early seventeenth-century astronomy restricted him to Ptolemy's specific system. On the contrary, there's good evidence that Donne was aware of and concerned (not always consistently, from one time to the next) about the implications of Copernicus's and Kepler's work (if not more ancient and earlier views about the earth's planetary motion, possibly the views of Aristarchus and Oresme).[18]

Another point deserves to be considered. In *An Anatomy of the World. The First Anniversary* (Carey gives its "probable date" as July–October 1611, which is very close to the date of *A Valediction*), Donne actually offers in the opening lines, which speculate about the import of changes in recent astronomical views about the heavens (probably changes thought to be required in Ptolemy's conception), the telling line *As though heaven suffered earthquakes, peace or war.* This *might* have been a line of thought required by a well-known sixteenth-century comet, which made it impossible to deny that changes (usually confined to the "sublunary" world: earthquakes in the literal sense) might very well affect the crystalline spheres themselves. Hence, if you keep Donne's verbal decisions in mind, it's not in the least difficult to read *moving of th'earth* to mean either

17. Dowling, *The Senses of the Text*, 10.
18. See, for instance, John Carey, *John Donne: Life, Mind, and Art* (New York: Oxford University Press, 1981), chap. 8.

ordinary earthquakes or the planetary motion of the earth (which may be likened to an earthquake) *or* something equivocating between the two.

As soon as you concede all this, you are bound to take note of the entire fourth stanza (the second cited above), which begins with *Dull sublunary lovers' love/(Whose soul is sense)*. I see two very interesting possibilities here: one, which Dowling implicitly prefers; the other, which I'll risk (as a rank amateur). On Dowling's reading, if I understand it aright, the canonical "sublunary" earthquakes deflect those lovers *whose soul is sense* from a higher love (*a love, so much refined,* as the next stanza has it) that it confirms a certain invisible constancy ("our" love for instance, as the poet indicates), which follows the clue of the unperceived *trepidation of the spheres*—so that we *Care less, eyes, lips, and hands to miss* (than those *whose soul is sense*).

The alternative reading seems to me to deepen the matter of relying on the unseen but constant order of the world, by conceding that the earth moves (in the sense opposed to the Ptolemaic), *and* that (perhaps) the heavens move as well (if, say, the lesson of the comet be admitted). There would then be no localized "sublunary" world; the would-be crystalline spheres would have joined the inconstant sublunary world. And then, *sublunary lovers' love* would signify an uninspired love, a love not informed in a way that could *admit/Absence,* could ever know the unseen (*innocent*), now more difficult, constancy that lies even deeper than the unseen *trepidation of the spheres.* That is, our lovers must part, but, in parting, remain constant in a way that cannot be fathomed by "sublunary" lovers *or* even (so to say) in accord with Ptolemaic astronomy.

Here, all the key terms have somewhat different meanings on Dowling's and my own interpretations. But there is no "close reading" or appeal to "primary meaning" that could possibly decide the issue. There is no way to prioritize "primary meaning" and the determinate interpretation of what a given text "means." That is the price of admitting that there is no way to prioritize the analysis of sentences (or a reliance on dictionaries) over the analysis of utterances. To admit the point is to admit the complexity of Intentional life—hence, the unavoidability of interpretation *in* the process of explicating meaning.

More important still, the argument shows that Dowling's students cannot be faulted for simply "misreading" the lines. If they haven't got it *right,* it's because there is no single right reading to insist on. Even clearer: *there is no "method"* of Dowling's kind, there's none that could possibly benefit from Katz's Platonism; there's no such thing as "meaning [that] exists 'in the text'" in the sense in which it "is irreducibly there independently of and prior to interpretative activities."

Let me soften the blow a little: I don't actually claim to know that there's no "meaning in the text"; I argue only that no one is likely to show that there must be textual meaning in Dowling's sense. My own strategy applies *faute de mieux,* but (of course) I claim that every earth-bound argument holds only *faute de mieux.* Yet it has its rigor and its own sense of objectivity.

In *this* sense, the problem of understanding poetry is nothing less than the problem of understanding ourselves; and the problem of understanding ourselves is inseparable from the problem of understanding our world. But if you see all that, then you may see that the puzzles of what I've been calling cultural realism cannot fail to infect the entire prospect of canonical views of objectivity. They are all challenged to yield in the direction of logical informality, the *lebensformlich* (more or less in Wittgenstein's sense), the rejection of the disjunction between realism and idealism, and the legitimation of relativism and historicism. Here, however, I confine my argument to specifically cultural studies. It would require a fresh start to make a fair case for the whole of human inquiry. Though I confess: I begin to find it close at hand.

INDEX

WITHDRAWN